Digital Overwhelm

Digital Overwhelm

A Mid-Career Guide to Coping at Work

Craig E. Mattson

CASCADE *Books* • Eugene, Oregon

DIGITAL OVERWHELM
A Mid-Career Guide to Coping at Work

Copyright © 2024 Craig E. Mattson. All rights reserved. Except for brief quotations in critical publications or reviews, no part of this book may be reproduced in any manner without prior written permission from the publisher. Write: Permissions, Wipf and Stock Publishers, 199 W. 8th Ave., Suite 3, Eugene, OR 97401.

Cascade Books
An Imprint of Wipf and Stock Publishers
199 W. 8th Ave., Suite 3
Eugene, OR 97401

www.wipfandstock.com

PAPERBACK ISBN: 978-1-6667-7221-0
HARDCOVER ISBN: 978-1-6667-7222-7
EBOOK ISBN: 978-1-6667-7223-4

Cataloguing-in-Publication data:

Names: Mattson, Craig E., author.

Title: Digital overwhelm : a mid-career guide to coping at work / by Craig E. Mattson.

Description: Eugene, OR: Cascade Books, 2024 | Includes bibliographical references.

Identifiers: ISBN 978-1-6667-7221-0 (paperback) | ISBN 978-1-6667-7222-7 (hardcover) | ISBN 978-1-6667-7223-4 (ebook)

Subjects: LCSH: Digital media—social aspects. | Young adults—United States—Social and economic conditions—21st century. | Wisdom literature—Criticism, interpretation, etc. God (Christianity).

Classification: HM851 M3835 2024 (paperback) | HM851 (ebook)

VERSION NUMBER 07/25/24

Scripture quotations are from Revised Standard Version of the Bible, copyright © 1946, 1952, and 1971 National Council of the Churches of Christ in the United States of America. Used by permission. All rights reserved worldwide.

For Emma, Annee, Allie, and Winston

Contents

Preface | ix
Digiwhelm, an Introduction | xvii

CHAPTER 1   Switching Things | 1
CHAPTER 1.5   How to Tell Your Digiwhelm Story | 10
CHAPTER 2   Emailing Things | 14
CHAPTER 2.5   How to Write an Email Like You Talk | 33
CHAPTER 3   Saying Things | 45
CHAPTER 3.5   How to Make a Podcast | 66
CHAPTER 4   Meaning Things | 76
CHAPTER 4.5   How to Work Like You Mean It | 97
CHAPTER 5   Fixing Things | 106
CHAPTER 5.5   How to Get Unstuck from Technical Difficulties | 123
CHAPTER 6   Signaling Things | 134
CHAPTER 6.5   How to Survive Video Chat | 152
CHAPTER 7   Advocating Things | 158
CHAPTER 7.5   How to Get People to Do Things | 176

Afterword | 187
Acknowledgments | 193
Bibliography | 195
Index | 203

Preface

OVER THE PAST DECADE, a goodly number of books have come out, aiming to help you become the kind of person who can address digital overload and addiction. I admire these books enormously for the way they toggle between individual and structural moves: *here are some practices for you; here are some changes for communities.*[1] But this is a different sort of book. I am not *un*interested in how to cultivate a character capable of withstanding digital overwhelm or how to pursue institutional and societal change. But my primary concern is to change how you share with your coworkers those virtual zones that settle over organizational structures and personal actions like a vapor.

This book is for organizational communicators who are (and who work with) quarterlife workist deconverts. That's a mouthful, but it might fit you all the same.

- *Quarterlife* used to describe twenty-somethings but has recently expanded to include people from ages eighteen to forty. These days, early adulthood seems to be a condition that happens repeatedly over the course of a single life.[2]

1. Two of the most influential such books for me have been Crouch, *Life We're Looking For*, and Song, *Restless Devices*. But you will also see my indebtedness to Newport's *Digital Minimalism*, Illing and Gershberg's *Paradox of Democracy*, as well as the Substack newsletter by L. M. Sacasas, *Convivial Society*. And as the Pisa of books next to my bed will attest, this list of authors I'm indebted to could go on and on.

2. Wilner, *Quarterlife Crisis*; Byock, *Quarterlife*. If you are a divorcee at age fifty-two who then starts a PhD program, you may be a quarterlifer, working through a bewildering mismatch of age and lifestage. Byock notes, "Currently, many millennials are squarely in Quarterlife while others have entered midlife. More Gen Zers are entering Quarterlife every day, while many more are still in adolescence and childhood. The generation and the stage of life are not equivalent" (*Quarterlife*, 12).

- *Workism* is "the belief that work is . . . the centerpiece of one's identity and life's purpose; and the belief that any policy to promote human welfare must always encourage more work."[3]
- *Deconverts* among Gen Z and millennial professionals disavow corporate infusions of spiritual meaning in everyday work. They also doubt the charismatic assurances of digital capitalist priests like Seth Godin, Simon Sinek, and Donald Miller.[4] Is knowledge work in the attention economy capable of transcendent meaning? Quarterlifers have their doubts.[5]

But no one, whatever their life stage or vocational beliefs, can sidestep the demands of organizational communication. Whether or not you love your job matters less than the fact that, when it comes to communication, there's a lot of job to do. You have humans reporting to you, humans overseeing you, humans collaborating with you, humans waiting for your deliverables.

And then, there are the machines. These tools aren't just devices that you jiggle to convince your manager you're still working; they are your environment. Most organizational communication happens in spaces made chaotic and claustrophobic by digital technology.

I know this about work life, because, as an organizational researcher, I have talked to dozens of millennial and Gen Z professionals. I've sat in coffee shops and taken long walks and opened video chats with people like you who doubt the viability of their work, who feel digitally overwhelmed, and who wonder what those two conditions have to do with each other.

---

3. Thompson, "Workism Is Making Americans Miserable."

4. As Tara Isabella Burton writes, "Concepts like 'mindfulness'—a secularized version of principles associated with Zen Buddhism—have become ubiquitous in our workplaces." Burton, *Strange Rites*, 24. Carolyn Chen has shown how massive shifts in digital technology across the information economy have encouraged managers to cultivate "something that resembled a faith community: members who *belong* to a shared community and *believe* in a higher and transcendent goal." Chen, *Work Pray Code*, 9.

5. In the chapters to come, I will refer to the "information economy," the "knowledge economy," and the "attention economy" to indicate the economic conditions that have pervaded and, in some cases, wholly replaced agricultural and industrial economics. I mean the massive competition for ever-diminishing consumer attention in conditions of information surplus. Richard Lanham has discussed this shift in *Economics of Attention* as the shifting from industrial worlds of "stuff" to informational worlds of "fluff." In his reading, this shift is not linear but recursive. What we think of as "just fluff" in today's economy actually has material and substantial consequence. Fluff behaves like and actually becomes stuff, while stuff turns around and becomes as seemingly light as air. For sources of my uneasiness about the attention economy, see Williams, *Stand Out of Our Light*, and Hwang, *Subprime Attention Crisis*.

If that's you, you are the digiwhelmed deconvert this book is talking to.

What This Book Does

This book isn't a manual for imbuing your job with significance by decluttering your digital life. It's not a meditation guide for rising above tech excess. It's not a scolding listicle for why you should deactivate your Instagram. It probably won't help you become righteous enough to stop scrolling reels.

Here's what this book will do. It will help you learn to see six modes of communication and what they are doing to your everyday organizational life. Modes, as you will learn in this book, are small but shareable zones of action where you have important choices to make. These choices won't overhaul late capitalism or make artificial intelligence comprehensible or save your soul. But, as you will hear in the stories of early-to-mid-career professionals, these modes can help you deal with digiwhelm at the intersection of the human and the technological.

Who This Book Is For

People overqualified and overworked.

Andrew Holmes is a lean, ball cap-wearing cyclist, given to citations from neuropsychology books he's just read. A decade-plus back, he was an art major studying sculpture at a small, faith-based liberal arts college, and today he describes himself as "artsy in a slow, contemplative, pattern-seeking kind of way." After college, he put his skills to work as a carpenter, first in downtown Chicago and then in the suburbs. Industrial carpentry, he quickly found, required working at a forbiddingly massive scale, navigating depersonalized workspaces, erecting thirty-foot walls. "We were very nearly iron workers," he explained. After several years, he quit and took a job with a niche residential carpentry company in a prosperous suburb. This time, Andrew found the work challenging not in scale, but in rigorous detail. He lasted a year, before a candid conversation with his boss suggested it was time to move on. After these two experiences of what felt to him like personal failure, Andrew had a mental health crisis that kept him out of work for half a year. He now works at a UPS distribution center in Willow Springs, Illinois, which, in many ways, puts him at a logistical node of a globalized network. He's a knowledge worker and a blue-collar worker at the same time, moving fast, watching his head, loading the boxes, minding the system. When I asked him if the job was good for him, he responded, "I have no illusions about showing up to UPS and finding some sort of cosmic fulfillment."[6]

I hope Andrew will have a go at grad school. He's a person of remarkable theoretical and therapeutic insight. But when you talk to him, you're also struck by how much is going on communicationally in a fast-paced and tensioned UPS environment, with bosses yelling to be safe and to hurry the f— up. This book aims to help people like Andrew slo-mo his attention sufficiently to adapt the modes of communication he is thrust into.

People with jobs they love but that are wearing them out.

Rachel Alvarado, like so many of us during the COVID-19 pandemic, found herself thrust into workspaces at once familiar and strange, layered with digital and physical interaction. She gave me an unusually vivid sense of this complexity during our interview at a podcast studio at the Chicago incubator 1871. She brought her kids with her—a first for me, having little humans in a studio—and she made it fun by her cheerily flexible attention. Rachel had clearly achieved this proficiency at significant personal cost—like being willing to do calls with international colleagues at three in the morning while her kids were sleeping. She told me about setting up a staging area for remote calls at home, so that her work looked professional in the webcam's frustum—even if her children, just offscreen, were pulling on her knees. She told me about watching for the anxiety of others onscreen: she's learned the ways that digital interaction requires a measure of kind directness—"Is there something you need right now?"

Rachel manages to be an amazing person. But her work requires an adroitness that feels almost unfair. Should anyone have to be so deft with so many things at once? But this book aims to look closely at the in-between spaces of human and technological work where switching up the modes of communication can help make organizational action more sustainable.

People with jobs whose organizational communities are exhausting.

Jill Hammerstein has worked in numerous jobs in her quarterlife professional experience—everything from corporate to nonprofit to social enterprise to startup. She likes to say that, by the time she'd gotten to her third or fourth job, she knew that, no matter how impressive they look, everybody's

---

6. Andrew Holmes, interview by Craig Mattson, March 31, 2022.

actually a mess. She tells a story about when her then company (a social enterprise) was trying to redesign their mission statement. It should have been easy to achieve: they were a group of communication professionals, all bringing good things to the discussion. But as they sorted through the options, tried out fresh phrasings, and named the company's capabilities, Jill kept wondering how they were going to synopsize it all in a "phrase that can be put onto a website [so that] no matter where people are looking at this object, they are seeing the same thing. Which is never true. It's a pipe dream, Craig. It will never get there."[7] Some time after our interview Jill sent me a text in which she described another committee meeting in which she called out, "Communication Overwhelm!" and ended the discussion. Jill's a funny person, but her wryly pained cries highlight the sometime-inadequacies of labored conversations among even the most talented collaborators.

I recently reconnected with Jill to ask some follow-up questions. She's working in a software startup, and I was struck by the overlay of fatigue to her normally buoyant manner. She still made me laugh like usual. But as I was working through a transcription of our conversation later, the bluntness of her words about sexism in startup spaces (without the gentling effect of her humorous tones) pulled me up short. How are organizational communities warping modes of communication that have, in the past, been places of organizational effectiveness and personal flourishing?

People who do their jobs well and suffer intense loneliness all the same.

In a later chapter, we'll talk about a woman professional, let's call her Samantha, who was accused of harassment by someone harassing *her*. This experience so soured her on a field she'd achieved undergraduate and graduate degrees in that she finally decided to pursue less rewarding, less meaningful jobs in corporate America. Samantha says that in each of her jobs, she's suffered loneliness—across organizations as disparate as small business management to community theater to nonprofit engagement to assisting a vice president at Walgreens' executive suite. But she has given up on finding soul connection at work. Her experience of workplace harassment, as well her observation of other workplace dynamics, have taught her how easy it is to love her work, and her coworkers, not wisely but too well.

---

7. Jill Hammerstein, interview by Craig Mattson, January 19, 2022 (name changed to ensure anonymity).

> As much as I want to make personal connections with people at work—and it sucks to feel lonely—at the end of the day, everyone is trying to do their job. You can feel a personal connection with somebody—and you would have been best friends within another context. But I can't let the personal side of things take away my ability to make a living and exist.[8]

Today, Samantha enjoys her corporate job, and she's good at it. But she finds her meaningful relationships—and her sense of purpose—before nine and after five.

Despite criticisms that quarterlife professionals tend to be flaky or finicky, the professionals I spoke with seemed like the reasonable and generous people I'd be happy to collaborate with. They did confess, though, that chronic disease had altered their work experience. They did tell stories of sobbing in a bathroom stall after making a conspicuous mistake on a racially segregated jobsite. They did look at me through their webcam with kind and tired eyes.

These are the people this book seeks to assist. The stories you'll read and the analysis I'll share recommends a peculiar way of looking at invisible but palpable spaces in work and life. Paying attention to these modes of communication won't transform your workplace. But it may change how you find equilibrium with others. The analogy that works for me is learning how to stand up on a giant inner tube on a choppy lake. At first, you can't stay standing for more than a few seconds at a time, but eventually you and your inner tube partners can help each other stay standing whatever the wind and the waves are doing. Those are the sea legs that this book seeks to cultivate.

What Wisdom This Book Can Offer

This is not a book that urges a particular religious framework on you. Mostly I'm trying to help you pay attention in a fresh way to the communicative work you do every day in your organization. Trying to help you achieve more stability and equipoise is a goal that I take to be vital for people of every faith and of no faith at all.[9] But you will notice that

---

8. Anonymous, in Mattson, "Solution to Loneliness at Work." This quote was edited for brevity and clarity.

9. "Wisdom is now regularly mentioned in discussions of poverty, the environment, economics, governance, management, leadership, political priorities, and policies, education at all levels, family life, the health of our culture, the desire for physical, emotional and mental health, and the resurgence of religion and 'the spiritual.'" Ford,

I often connect contemporary questions to biblical texts. Part of why I do this is that technological theorists today are doing so as well, perhaps because digital media's presence in our lives is so profound and pervasive that we can hardly talk about it without appealing to a deeper horizon of meaning.[10] But another reason that I draw on those ancient texts is that they situate the practical questions we're dealing with in this book in larger conversations than this book can discuss fully. As you find your balance on the choppy seas of work and life in digital spaces, you'll take a look around. The horizons you see will be easier to navigate towards with the help of Job and the Psalms, Ecclesiastes and the Proverbs. Or so I have found.

Gen Z and millennial deconstruction from so many things can be startling to Gen Xers and Boomers. But the wisdom books I'll cite make it clear that the story of workist deconversion that today's professionals tell is both new and ancient. One millennial I spoke with described how his Gen Xer father "has had this sense that his work very much is his calling, and he derives basically an infinite amount of energy from the ability to—" Here, I broke good form and laughed at his wry reference to infinite energy. But the interviewee cut back in, "I'm serious. It's like the man has worked almost seven days a week for decades now. I mean, it's absolutely insane." But at the same time, vocational depression is as old as the sages of the Old Testament mulling over the enigma and brevity of toil.

Still, I suspect that for some of you this use of Christian and Jewish Scripture could be a triggering move, especially if those very texts have been wielded against you in cruelly prescriptive fashion. But I hope you

---

Christian Wisdom, 1.

10. Gladstone, "Fraught Promise of Salvation Through Technology." Norbert Wiener, one of the forefathers of the information society, wrote *God and Golem, Inc.* to explore Joban dimensions of technologized society. More recently, Stipe Odak has discussed what he calls "The Technical Book of Job" by "Reading Job from a Transhumanist Perspective." Writers like Meghan O'Gieblyn note ways that sacred books help explain the uncanny dynamics of technologized life and work today. She has noted, for example, that algorithms today have taken the place of providence: they steer the course of our lives in invisible and seemingly sovereign ways. Where we used to say *let God be God*, we today say, *let the algorithms do their work*. "As these technologies become increasingly integrated into the spheres of public life, many people now find themselves in a position much like Job's, denied the right to know why they were refused a loan or fired from a job or given a likelihood of developing cancer." See O'Gieblyn, *God Human Animal Machine*, 207. Other discussions that come close to absolutizing the digital in a way that used to be reserved for the divine include Todd Gitlin, who in *Media Unlimited* suggests that nothing short of a nuclear apocalypse could halt the force of digital media today—in other words, a catastrophe out of the book of Revelation. In *Mediated*, Thomas de Zengotita describes the media "blob" as an ultimately encompassing field of energy within which we can do little but try to practice brief moments of existential awareness.

will give another hearing to these wisdom voices. After all, these ancient texts themselves not infrequently repudiate the abusive Scripture-quoting you may have been yourself forced to endure.

For me, connecting digital overwhelm to wisdom literatures generates a productive skepticism about the vocational commonsense of our own time. The complacent fools that the wisdom literature decries sound like financial advisors in 2008, assuring everybody that the financial system is sound, the economy resilient. But ours are subprime economies, rife with speculative investments, bundled with dubious loans and deceptive tranches. Few of the early career professionals I spoke with gave vent to frustration with the fierceness of Job. But like the sages in wisdom books, early-to-mid-careerists have learned to distrust commonsense linkages between meritocratic capitalism and religious faith. The promise that if you *grind hard, you'll get there* feels just as suspicious to them as the claim *do good, and God will reward you* did to Job.

I won't deny that I have found the wisdom literatures constantly challenging in the writing of this book. They nudge me—sometimes shove me—out of my familiar frames of reference. But even when the work of reading them is long and feels unrewarding, I think I can still hear their voices, like someone calling my name from a crowd. So I suppose my encouragement to all who pick up this book echoes another sage: if anyone has ears to hear, let them hear.

Digiwhelm, an Introduction

We Are All Underwater

I DOUBT THERE'S BEEN more than a summer or two when my family hasn't gone to the Frankfurt Pier on Lake Michigan. My parents often took us kids around sunset when the water was at its deepest blue. In shorts and flip-flops, we'd stroll down the long walk to the lighthouse, wending our way through the other beachgoers, the hand-holding couples, the young parents with toddlers in arms, the senior citizens listening to mood music on a boom box, their feet dangling over the edge of the pier. But for me the main event happened as a wave rose over the edge of the pier like something surfacing from unimaginable depths. It felt like looking into a grave. I rather liked the feeling, but only with my back to the lighthouse, well out of reach of the lake. I remember feeling awed at the dripping swimmers who leapt backwards off the pier, tucking their bodies before slicing the dark blue of the sunset waters.

My wife and I continued the family custom of taking children out on the Frankfurt Pier, though she has always been more casual about the leviathan swells rising at the edge of the pier. One late afternoon when our kids were young, she told them that she would buy an ice cream cone for anybody who leapt off into the water. At the time, none of our kids had yet shown a daredevil streak. We all stood as close to the edge as we could bear, eyeing the swells, staring down at the massive boulders now barely visible some fifteen feet below the surface. But even as I was gathering the tatters of my pluck together, I heard a splash. It was our ten-year-old daughter Allie, now dog-paddling back to the ladder rungs dug into the concrete pier. The promise of an ice cream cone had proven too powerful to resist.

Allie's jump into the lake is a parable for how so many of us jump into digital media for likes and shares and retweets and other yummy rewards. Cautionaries like Jaron Lanier warn their readers that this leap results not just in digital ice cream treats, but in a "baptism," an identification with a quasi-religious outlook. Social media users have, he says, "implicitly accepted a new spiritual framework.... You have agreed to change something intimate about your soul.... You have probably, to some degree... effectively renounced what you might think is your religion, even if that religion is atheism."[1] But the good news is that, if you would just "delete your social media accounts right now," you can dog-paddle back to the pier.[2]

Lanier's religious metaphor feels, at least at first, awakening and empowering. He's warning us all that social media make bad masters and then urging us each to choose you this day whom you will serve. But many rising professionals may reasonably respond that they don't have as much choice as he might imply. Granted, professional life today doesn't require watching TikTok videos or Instagram reels all day. But most organizational communication does require an immersive engagement in digital spaces that you can't eliminate simply by deleting social media accounts. The confusing mix of physical and digital spaces raises questions.

- Is some form of digital fasting or sabbath the only alternative to endless email interaction?
- What would improve remote work, which most days feels convenient and deflating at the same time, better tools or better talk?
- Does digital work mean *dispensable* work? Does my work itself mean anything? If it doesn't, should I quit my job, change my career, or just shrug and find my meaning in something else after hours?
- How do I relate to my tools when they fail to me? What sort of Zen is essential for technological breakdown?
- How do I signal that I need mentoring—without also broadcasting that I'm naïve or clueless or woefully inexperienced?

---

1. Lanier, *Ten Arguments for Deleting Your Social Media Right Now*. The cottage industry of books scolding us about social media has grown nearly as distracting as social media themselves.

2. I am thoroughly indebted to communication scholar John Durham Peters for the observation that people tend to use water imagery to describe digital media's presence in human life, speaking of the floods, torrents, tsunamis, riptides in technologized society. This field of metaphor has been enormously important to all my work in this book. See Peters, *Marvelous Clouds*.

- How do I get cooperation both from those I report to and those who report to me? For that matter, how do I persuade *myself* to cooperate?

I wrote this book after listening to stories from millennial managers and Gen Z team members. But these questions press in on professionals of any generation, often with an exhausting all-at-once-ness, sometimes inviting radical acts of personal and organizational overhaul. I once heard a company president tell how, when she and her team felt lost, they shut down for a few days and started writing on the walls. Multicolored sticky notes blossomed everywhere. People walked around staring up at chalked words and arrows and boxes. Gradually, the team rediscovered their organizational soul, relocated their mission, and were off and running again. But today, the disruptive accelerations of digital technology make it feel like shutting an organization down for a few days isn't enough. The best plans are no sooner implemented than they feel outmoded by the disruptive developments of energy-drinking coders in Silicon Valley.

The last stages of revision for this book, in the spring of 2023, were inundated with news of unnerving developments in artificial intelligence. Some of the announcements sounded fun, as if some dude named ChatGPT had shown up at a party and done a cannonball in the swimming pool, getting a big laugh from all the chaise loungers. But much of the news sounded frightening for professional life. Kevin Roose told *The Daily*'s Michael Barbaro, "I have never seen a moment like this where it felt like something so fundamental to the way the Internet works, the way that society works, really is being upended so rapidly."[3] The book I was writing, I quickly realized, couldn't offer an adequate response to superintelligence scenarios in which machines take over the world.[4] But how do we posture ourselves in relation to the digital intelligences that already infuse our workplaces? "We do not understand these systems," writes Ezra Klein, "and it's not clear we even can."[5] There seems to be no pier for us to retreat

---

3. Barbaro, "Online Search Wars Got Scary."

4. Paul Christiano's imagined scenario was relentlessly dire: "Powerful AI systems have a good chance of deliberately and irreversibly disempowering humanity. This is a much easier failure mode than killing everyone with destructive physical technologies," Christiano writes in "Where I Agree and Disagree with Eliezer." *The Atlantic*'s Derek Thompson fumbled for a reasonable response to superintelligence scenarios where machines take over the world: "Sometimes I think, Sorry, this is too crazy; it just won't happen, which has the benefit of allowing me to get on with my day without thinking about it again. But that's really more of a coping mechanism. If I stand on the side of curious skepticism, which feels natural, I ought to be fairly terrified by this nonzero chance of humanity inventing itself into extinction." (See Thompson, "AI Disaster Scenario.")

5. Klein, "This Changes Everything."

to. Nor is it clear that we could build one high enough or fast enough for the approaching AI tsunami.[6] For early-to-mid-career professionals and the leaders who mentor them, technological disruptions like these create conditions that this book will call digital overwhelm.

What Is Digital Overwhelm Exactly?

Whenever I've mentioned the subject matter of this book to people, I've been encouraged by the *aha* it evoked. (Sometimes, that *aha* threatened to expand into a sobbing *bwahahahahahaha*.) But although everybody seemed to recognize digital overwhelm immediately, the phenomenon often felt indefinite. Based on my research conversations with millennial and Gen Z managers and employees—who, in my experience, are often on the vulnerable leading edge of workplace experience today—I've come to define the phenomenon this way: *digital overwhelm is the affective pressure of technological development that makes organizational communication strange*. Let's take each phrase in turn:

- *affective pressure*: Scholars of emotion distinguish between *emotions* and *affect*. *Emotions* are feelings we can identify. *Affect* entails feelings we can't name yet.[7] Affective pressures can feel like the intensities of sinus headaches or restlessness at bedtime or a caffeine rush. When it comes to our reactions to technology, we may feel energized, restless, deflated, and afraid all at once.

- *technological development*: The unimaginably fast rate of technological innovation today makes digital disruption pervasive, diffuse, and opaque.[8] Every industry is dealing with the arrival of large language networks, faster processing, new Gs of connectivity, and burgeoning virtual spaces. On a more mundane level, each of us suffers through updates for operating systems and platforms, clicks a hurried "Agree"

---

6. See Klein, "This Changes Everything," for example: "Humanity needs to accelerate its adaptation to these technologies or a collective, enforceable decision must be made to slow the development of these technologies."

7. Massumi, *Parables for the Virtual*, 26–27.

8. Sherry Turkle refers to the "opacity" of digital technology today, by which she means interfaces that rely on processes the users do not understand. Designed by specialists, these interfaces allow a remarkable facility but do not offer understanding for how tools function. She writes of "professionals in all of these fields who move easily within their computational systems and yet feel constrained by them, trapped by their systems' unseen limitations and unknown assumptions" (14). Turkle, *Second Self*, 7–15.

to privacy statements, and avoids clicking through advertisements to buy new digital devices.

- *strange organizational communication*: The increasing use of the word "unprecedented" over the past few years serves as one marker of just how uncanny being a human is today. The blurring boundaries of external and internal audiences, the fusing of physical and virtual spaces, the transformation of tools into ecologies—all this makes good old-fashioned goal-oriented organizational communication feel ongoingly weird.

Throughout this book, I'll refer to digital overwhelm as *digiwhelm*, because although the technological always flows through our lives, sometimes it's overwhelming and sometimes underwhelming. But it's always some sort of whelm.

This book pictures digiwhelm in terms of two kinds of currents common along the shores of Lake Michigan or, really, any other body of water across the planet today. The first are *surface currents*. Think of these as the rapidly developing tools that professionals use every day. These technologies—both the platforms and the devices—have vectors to them that make us all feel like it's somehow urgently necessary to fire off emails, launch podcasts, shoot out texts, scatter posts on social media. These surface currents hold promise to take us somewhere fast, even if our experience with past currents suggests the "somewhere" we end up going isn't where we had intended when we started out.

Some of our technologies are long-shore currents, the sort of waves that feel consistent with the work people have always done in organizational life: businesspeople have always corresponded with clients, whether through couriers, letters, telegrams, phone calls, or emails. Some communication technologies function in our work lives more like riptides: they burst upon us as sudden and surprising digital vectors that catch us up, yank us out, and compel us to spend a great deal of panicky effort extricating ourselves from their flow. To give a silly example: think of those times when you receive a notification from Apple or Google that your cloud is filling up and you decide to see if you can "manage" the data better. An hour later, you wish you had just bought more storage for ninety-nine cents a month. The fact that we rarely deal with riptides one at a time recalls the Michigander maxim: "The lake is not your friend."

Digital Overwhelm

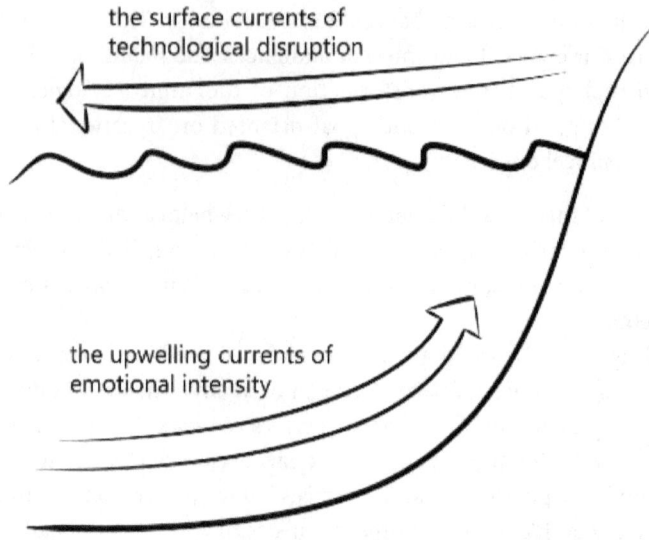

Besides surface currents, there are also *upwelling currents*. These are individual and collective affective reactions to technologized life. I'm thinking of the fear one of my interviewees felt during a marketing event to publicize his book when trolls took over his Instagram feed and created havoc, demanding that he take down all photos from the promotional event. This was a hard decision: the event would thus lose coverage among his nearly thirty-thousand followers. But he submitted to the haters out of a helpless and frightened sense that there was nothing else he could do. Not all emotional responses to digital overwhelm are negative, of course. Just as depth currents bring nutrient rich waters upwards, so people's emotional responses to technology can bring wisdom to the confusing currents of their everyday work and life. This book will be paying especially close attention to the upwellings that happen in the work of relatively disempowered people—i.e., early-to-mid-career professionals—who do so much of the labor in today's attention economy.

But Is It a New Thing under the Sun?

The excessiveness of communication technology cuts deep in history. Think of Job in the Old Testament and Plato in ancient Greece. In Job's quasi-mythical land of Uz, the most important kind of communication happened through spoken proverbs, maxims, and riddles. But after Job's catastrophe, as his friends keep quoting one dubious saying after another, he worries he won't outlast his suffering, much less his friends' speeches, to make his case to God. One solution he reaches for is writing: "Oh that my words were written down! O that they were inscribed in a book! O that with an iron pen and with lead they were engraved on a rock forever!"[9]

But if for Job writing suggested a way to outlast his troubles, for Plato the pen was a way into more trouble. Near the end of the dialogue *The Phaedrus*, he has Socrates discuss a story about an inventor who visited an Egyptian city to announce the new features that writing will bring to human society. In my imagination, he's a Steve Jobs-like character, touting the magical benefits of a bright, shiny new technology. But the king is unimpressed. "You have not discovered a potion for remembering, but for reminding; you provide your students the appearance of wisdom, not with its reality."[10] Plato gives the sense that the pen will make it possible to broadcast words so far that communities will be endlessly disrupted. Our anxiety for what technology will do to human life is ancient.

But technological disruption cuts deep in our personal histories as well. I felt my first tremors of digital disruption in my home on Comstock Street in the 1980s. My earliest household memories center on the spoken word so privileged in the conservative Protestantism of my upbringing. But even as we went to church thrice a week and memorized long passages from the King James Version of the Bible, we kids also loved our one permissible hour of television on Saturday nights, which was painfully interrupted by having to take turns taking a bath. (To this day, tubs give me FOMO.) My mom was a dramatic reader-aloud of the adventures of Lucy Pevensie, Laura Ingalls, Jo March, and (save us all) Little Lord Fauntleroy. She was also an author herself, spending years of our childhood writing a novel of manners longhand on a lapboard, stopping every now and then to daub her Bic pen in a wadded-up tissue. She never submitted the manuscript to any publisher. To this day, remembered vignettes from her novel interleave with scenes from *The Muppet Show* and *C.H.I.P.S.*

---

9. Job, 19:23–24, NRSV.
10. Plato, *Phaedrus*, 80.

But our family's first leap off the analog pier happened when my dad brought home a Commodore 64 to his bill-strewn desk. As a math and physics teacher, Dad could tell stories about his days in college, feeding punch cards into a mainframe as big as our dining room. And now—could you *believe* it!—we had a computer that fit onto a single desk. What we couldn't see, as we kids walked by Dad's complacent Commodore, was how computerized our society had already become. My linear narrative of household media—starting with the oral, moving to the literate, and progressing to the electronic—obscures the simultaneousness of the digital within everything else happening not just in our little house on Comstock Street, but across the workplaces of an increasingly globalized society. That frumpy little 64 was, after all, an incarnation of the information systems that had been spreading everywhere since the 1940s, thanks to the conceptual developments of Norbert Weiner, Claude Shannon, and Harold Lasswell.[11] More than a decade before my dad set up the Commodore on his desk—making it possible for us to play a thrilling lawn-mowing game called Hovver Bover—computer scientists had been stretching the delta of ARPANET across the country, sending each other a new kind of message called email.

You might say that the technological developments that so disrupt our communities are not all that different from what Job and Plato knew. That's true, although the claim elides difficulties peculiar to our moment. To make such bland historical observations, as Plato would say, is not *remembering*; it is reminding. Remembering is a situated practice. This book will repeat the move I just made—connecting historical patterns to personal experience—in order to re-member ourselves, to put ourselves together in our times and places.

Our givens, in a time of digital overwhelm, make certain organizational resources urgently necessary. Some are easy-to-admire goods like attention, mutuality, and cooperation. Others are less obvious gifts like coordination, indirectness, and inducement. My goal in this book is to help you pursue those goods with your team by learning to navigate organizational communication across surface currents and upwellings more stably and dexterously.

---

11. For a smart and accessible recounting of these developments, I commend Meghan O'Gieblyn, who was my own source for noticing how the information society has pervaded our lives. She helped me see that information has come to be "the ultimate metaphor, an umbrella wide enough to extend across forests and cities, insect colonies and highway systems, computers and human minds, all the organic and man-made systems that are now regarded as 'networks.'" *God Human Animal Machine*, 136.

Digiwhelm across Professional Life

My academic profession inclines me to stay on the pier and out of the waves. But I have spent a few years now listening to the testimonials of early-to-mid-career professionals who have hurled themselves into the crosscurrents of the attention economy today. Without their personal narratives of technological disruption and emotional fatigue, I would probably have missed some of the tempestuous realities of digital life today. I came into their stories through an institutional-review-board–approved research project, conducting forty-seven semi-structured, open-ended interviews with early-to-mid-career professionals from ages twenty-two to forty. Most of these professionals were managing some sort of information through political action, marketing, video game design, teaching, social entrepreneurship, coding, public relations, etc. Some professionals I interviewed worked in corporate firms; some worked in start-ups; still others in small companies and nonprofits. At first, I selected interviewees based on alumni from the communication program at Trinity Christian College, but expanded the pool to include interviewees from similar age groups but different backgrounds. My eventual pool included participants 36 percent male, 55 percent female, with a small percentage of nonbinary practitioners as well. A downside of my sampling was that only 28 percent of my participants were nonwhite. I have sought to compensate through more diverse interviewees through the Mode/Switch newsletter, which I started as a parallel journalistic project. Although this book's analysis, argument, and conclusions are grounded in qualitative research, you will hear some stories featured in the newsletter as well. That weave of academic scholarship and trade journalism provides a fuller picture of millennial and Gen Z professional experience today.

The fundamental question in all these interviews has been how workers in today's attention economy respond to overwhelm. Although my interviewees tended to focus either on organizational structures or on personal factors that made them feel overwhelmed, I gradually learned to watch for middle spaces between the structural and the personal, which I will describe in the next chapter as modes of communication.

A Spirituality of Overwhelm

This past winter, my wife and I revisited Frankfurt Pier on a day so cold that it took thought right out of us. Standing on the snowy beach, we could look across the ice-covered harbor to waves swelling as tall as the far-off lighthouse where I used to stand as a kid. Fearsome as they were, we could barely hear them as they swept off the pier and then under the icy shelf of the harbor. But then, as we stared, my wife pointed to a weird thing. Those waves made their way beneath the ice so that the frozen surface of the port undulated like a blanket slowly shaken out all the way to the shore where we stood.

I began this book as scholars and researchers often do, to get control of the material, to point to what others have neglected, to find some solid footing above the whelm. What I could understand through theoretical and historical perspectives, perhaps I could also cope with personally and organizationally. Maybe you cope in other ways. You pursue goals, use tools, practice tactics, deploy metrics—all the reassuringly secular devices of organizational life. *Nothing to see here, folks, let's just keep moving.* But if you're like me, you sense that the organizational communication you do and the digital overwhelm you feel are suspiciously—*extra*. The shootings, the heating up of everything, the threatening changes brought on by AI—does human experience really have to be this destabilizing?

My own account of this weird excessiveness—which may well be different from yours—has been profoundly shaped by the spiritual theology of the British writer David Ford. What rings true for me emerges in his account of how essentially unmanageable life always already is in God's company.[12] As Ford has argued, dealing with flooded human conditions does not mean eliminating overwhelm, digital or otherwise. It means being *differently* overwhelmed—not by the powerful and monied forces of our times, but by the unengineerable words of God.[13]

My recommendation is to do that by listening closely to the wisdom literatures of the Bible. Most people, I've found, keep an ear out for some wisdom behind them, calling out instructions and encouragements. For you that might mean Brene Brown or Adam Grant or Malcolm Gladwell. For me, the voices I strain to hear belong to Job and his friends, to Woman Wisdom in the Proverbs, to Qoheleth the skeptical teacher in Ecclesiastes, to the poets of the Psalter, and even, listening beyond Scripture, to Socrates. I don't flatter myself that I can persuade you of the divine realities these wisdom figures took for granted. Judging by the rage of Job, the weary skepticism of Ecclesiastes, the irony of Socrates, and the astonished

---

12. Think of Noah in his ark, Jonah hurled many fathoms down, the disciples waking Jesus on the waves, the shipwrecked Paul, and even, in the last book of the Bible, the exiled John writing what would become the book of Revelation at the water's edge on island of Patmos. Ford, *Shape of Living*, xx–xxii. I'm also grateful to John Durham Peters for his reminders of biblical references to people enduring flooding.

13. "This can take many forms: intellectual amazement at a God 'than which none greater can be conceived'; imaginative and emotional response to abundant glory, goodness or love; practical dedication to a whole way of life with others." Ford, *Shape of Living*, xxvii.

outcries of the Psalms and Proverbs, the divine life is no pontoon ride anyway. Perhaps this book's treatment will awaken you to a tidal movement that flows below and across the surfaces of late modern life. Perhaps it won't. In any case, my goal is to help you and your organizational members find a way to keep equilibrium together in all the digiwhelm.

CHAPTER 1

Switching Things

I FOLLOW KALEB NYQUIST on Twitter because he's good at managing information overload—without creating overload for other people. He consistently looks for smart ways to digest complex ideas, first by reading articles—not just their headlines—and then by sending out brief leads that help others do the same. But I wanted to talk with him, not just about information management but about digital overwhelm. At first, he felt a little surprised at the direction my questions were taking. "I thought we were going to have a conversation about email, and all the texts that come in and how we deal with that in our professional life. And I was like, 'Oh, I'm so ready to talk about this! I have so many tips and tricks . . .'"[1] That sort of electronic excess and digital disruption is a part of digital overwhelm, of course. The other part has more to do with the affective upwelling—the emotional upheavals—that Kaleb experiences in the midst of all the digital things.

So, he told me about cognitive dissonance in his job as an activist and organizational spokesperson, especially in cases where he hasn't found it easy to *be* the position he's paid to represent. Losing a sure sense of self while communicating with organizational audiences requires, he told me, intimate conversation with friends who consider his experiences carefully and keep him from submerging himself into an organizational persona.

Kaleb doesn't deal with digiwhelm simply by rejecting digital communication in favor of face-to-face interaction. He doesn't tell himself, "Get off

---

1. Kaleb Nyquist, interview by Craig Mattson, July 20, 2022.

Twitter and find a *real* conversation partner." Instead, he shifts his approach among media and approaches as his communicative goals require.

> I don't have that one job, that one title that encompasses every part of my professional identity. I have a lot of projects and volunteer roles. . . . Twitter becomes a place where I can almost make up that professional identity, where I say things that synthesize to different thoughts from different parts of my professional world. . . . In the same stream I can jump from saying something about how people communicate and interpret and understand each other to a really wonky data thing . . .[2]

His tweets are disseminations to people that, for the most part, he'll never talk to in person. But he remains open to unexpected friendship as well.

> You know . . . some of my favorite meetups have been with people that I met on Twitter . . . There's a guy who's been kind of a mentor for me here in DC . . . We only started hanging out because I followed him on Twitter and he realized that we have four points of common interest. We didn't know another person with the same four points of common interest, right?[3]

Kaleb exemplifies numerous ways that millennial and Gen Z professionals cope with digiwhelm. But notice specifically that he is moving in and out of different zones of interaction, evaluating potential approaches, changing his style, and adapting his posture. Kaleb practices what this book will call *mode-switching*.

Aboard the Modes

This book offers reasons that managers and their teams should cultivate mindfulness about modes. Although I can appreciate why some critics propose that we lobby Big Tech to redesign digital platforms for better alignment with human goals, no one will finish this book knowing how to hack the algorithms of the major platforms to realign them for more humane goals than engrossment and profitability. Instead, a mode takes shape in the messy, murky, turbulent *between* of individual choices and institutional structures, like a yellow life raft that someone has pulled the cord to inflate. The stories from millennial and Gen Z professionals you'll

---

2. Kaleb Nyquist, interview by Craig Mattson, July 20, 2022.
3. Kaleb Nyquist, interview by Craig Mattson, July 20, 2022.

read in the following chapters suggest that life and work today can feel like treading water around big ships at various levels of sinking. Here are three samples to show you what I mean:

- Liv Winkowitsch is a manager in a Los Angeles-based key art company, where she is watching massive changes to her guild. Once upon a time in Hollywood, she told me in one of our interviews, her firm designed movie posters—and that was about it. Now, streaming entertainment platforms require an extravagant number of key images for every movie, every show, every short, with the result that the whole industry feels chaotic.

- Rachel Hennessy is a Chicago-based communications coordinator who, when she started out, felt she could manage PR and marketing by following a set of simple rules. *Do these things, and you'll be effective.* Now, even keeping those rules seems kind of pointless. Her industry has been disrupted too many times for those principles to make much sense. Rachel may be one of the funniest interviewees I have ever talked to. But she's very serious when she says that these days she feels perpetually behind.

- Sarah Hao, a user-experience designer from China, told me about the endless numbers of new and quickly discarded social media accounts her information is scattered across in her work. Although she was excruciatingly careful to protect her identity—reading the small print on platforms' privacy documentation—she told me a disturbing story of some guy who messaged her with a photo of her home saying, "Is this your apartment? I'm here now."[4]

As raft after raft goes by, early-to-mid-career professionals look for the right one to board. But heads up! As the stories in subsequent chapters will show, modes are also prone to overcrowding, puncturing, and deflation. Modes require switching, in other words.

I first learned about *mode-switching* from Eric Jenkins, a communication scholar at the University of Cincinnati, who has described the human as "*homo modus,* the mode-switching animal."[5] The word *modes* is a slippery one, although your instinct might be to think of them simply as styles or approaches. Two other conceptions of modes are helpful as well. Jenkins defines them *as ways of coping.*[6] Even on a tough day, a mode

---

4. Hao, quoted in Mattson, "You Can Always Google It, Right?"
5. Jenkins, *Surfing the Anthropocene,* 13.
6. Jenkins, *Surfing the Anthropocene,* 3, 12.

can make you feel briefly stabilized, even energized—*I'm firing off so many emails today!* Most modes come with a feel-good reward structure attached like the Outlook message, "Enjoy your empty inbox." In that sense, modes also function like games that we play when work feels excessively difficult. Just like Ticket to Ride or Sorry, they come with emotional prizes that make us feel good (or bad), and those feelings keep us coming back to engage them again and again.[7]

In *Surfing the Anthropocene*, Jenkins takes a macro-perspective on modes across late-modern society.[8] But interviewing millennials and Gen Z employees gave me a micro-perspective on modes within organizational life. You'll notice that the following chapters describe these modes in theoretical terms such as dialogue, dissemination, semiotics, tacitness, performativity, and rhetoric. These terms help make clear where these modes come from and where they're headed. As the following chapters explore the histories and tendencies of modes, you'll learn their origins in the work of historic cultural theorists and their subsequent amplification by thought leaders, TED Talk gurus, popular writers, and journalists.

But working professionals are more likely to describe them in terms like the following:

---

7. It's helpful to understanding my book's argument if you familiarize yourself with Jenkins's discussion of modes: "Modes orient us towards the world, guiding what we perceive and how we perceive, what we do and how we do it, what we feel and how we feel" (446–47). Jenkins might point out a problem with my life-boat analogy: it underplays the way that modes are virtual. By "virtual," he doesn't mean "not real" but something more like "potential." To engage a mode of communication is to involve yourself in something in which new things can happen, good or bad, predictable or not. In a way, modes are like Pokémon Go, creating a virtual overlay to physical spaces. You know what it's like to be jogging through a park or pushing your niece on a swing, and then suddenly you catch sight of a cluster of Pokémon players moving through the same spaces with their phones at the ready. The digital game adds an energizing layer of potential to the park. *Oh yeah, that's another thing I could do here!* In organizational life, too, communication modes function like games that we all find ourselves playing, a little addictively, sometimes effectively, often desperately. See Jenkins, "Modes of Visual Rhetoric," 446–47. Jenkins has also discussed modes in *Special Affects*, 13–23. Modes are like what sociologists call structures of feeling or affective spaces. Raymond Williams is the theorist known for originating the phrase "structures of feeling." See, for example, Williams, *Culture and Society 1780–1950*. Berlant, *Cruel Optimism*; and Rice, *Distant Publics*, which have been influential in my reflection on affective spaces.

8. He calls these "meditative and immediative, attentional and tending." Jenkins, *Surfing the Anthropocene*, 13.

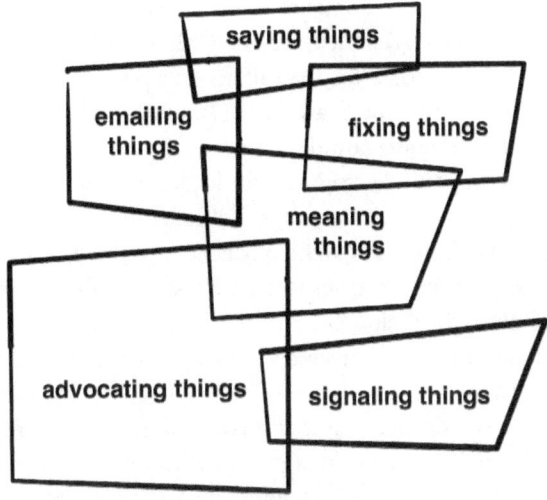

It's hard to attend to zones of communication. They are so vaporous and so elusive that the constant temptation is to get some clarity about a mode by treating it as a tool or task rather than a space you share with others. But modes aren't just things you have to do at work. They are virtual domains you inhabit. That may sound weird to you at first, but my hope is that the conversations of this book pull modes into the foreground for you, giving you a chance to turn them around and around, probing their limits and their affordances. Recognizing these modes as zones helps you see their social character and to keep in mind that switching from one mode to another has to be a collaborative action. That's why in each discussion of a mode, I'll follow things up with a workshop on making a mode switch with art and skill—or what this book will call *mode craft*. Engaging modes can feel like trying to stand up in a canoe or keep a kayak from going in circles. But skill and stability within the modes is learnable. My hope is that by the book's end, you'll have practiced enough mode craft that, even if the boat you're riding in still feels like a life raft some days, your increased skill and equilibrium makes it move more like an outboard.

How Recent Neuroscience Supports Mode-Switching

Modes of communication can be blurry. I spent the first couple of years of this research like a beachcomber with a metal detector, searching for an electromagnetic field in the cubicles and under the kitchen tables of millennial and Gen Z professionals. Sometimes, my research equipment would beep like I'd found something; sometimes everything was frustratingly quiet. Are modes real, I wondered, or are they all just in a person's head? Are they like WiFi domains? Or can you draw a hard boundary around their spaces? If you're stuck in one mode, how do you make the move to another one?

Fortunately, I found equipment for locating communication modes in recent neuropsychology developed by Keith Stanovich.

If you've read popular psychology books, you've probably noticed that many theories of mind work in two-part systems. You may have read, for example, about right-brain/left-brain thinking or been impressed by Daniel Kahneman's "thinking fast" and "thinking slow." Look down Stanovich's list of twenty-seven—count them!—different two-part theories of cognitive process, and I wouldn't be surprised if you find one or two of them that you recognize simply because you're a person who watches TED Talks. I'm the same way. Even the book you're holding uses Michael Polanyi's tacit knowing/explicit knowing in a later chapter to explain a mode of communication.[9]

But these two-system models have problems, especially when it comes to mode-switching.

Stanovich's big reveal is a three-system model for cognition. Here's how it works. Everybody agrees that there's a set of automatic processes that the brain carries out at incredible speeds and without much effort.[10] Stanovich calls this Type 1 thinking.[11] The problem with automatic processes is that they're uninterested in precision. They shoot from the hip. *Let's see here, I need to borrow this girl's car and I want to move in with her—why not ask her for both in the same text?* As a practical matter of navigating social worlds, we often need what Stanovich calls Type 2 thinking, which overrides automatic processes. *Maybe I should think about that text a bit longer.* But Type 2 thinking breaks down further into two kinds of processes.

- The first part Stanovich calls "the reflective mind."[12] That's the chief executive who orders the override and the slowdown.

- But the other set of processes at work in Type 2 processing is "the algorithmic mind"—algorithmic, because it's rule-guided by goals and available resources.[13]

9. Kahneman, *Thinking Fast and Slow*, 20–24; Polanyi, *Personal Knowledge*, 70–139.
10. Stanovich, "Rationality and Intelligence," 350.
11. Stanovich, "Rationality and Intelligence," 350.
12. Stanovich, "Rationality and Intelligence," 351.
13. Stanovich, "Rationality and Intelligence," 351, 355. Per Stanovich, "The algorithmic mind accesses microstrategies for cognitive operations and production system rules for sequencing behaviors and thoughts" (355).

Why two kinds of processing? Stanovich notes that it's not enough for our reflective mind to tell our automatic brain, "Stop it now!" We also need our algorithmic brain to say, "And here's a better thing to do!" In other words, we don't just need to override our reactions; we need to simulate (or game out) other, potentially better responses.[14] Stanovich sees the algorithmic mind as essential for testing ideas to see which best moves us towards our purpose.

Let's say that you need to meet with your one-up to discuss some harsh comments he made on your latest 360 evaluation. You craft a careful email about how you'd appreciate a chance to discuss the evaluation results and conclude with meeting times that work for you. What you receive back from your supervisor is an eight-hundred-word blast that (a) gives you a bunch more things to do and (b) ignores your polite request for a meeting. Your automatic response (if you're like me) is to whip back a two-line email that repeats your request for a meeting (perhaps with the mildly snarky phrase "see below") and maybe cc'ing the vice president for good measure. That would feel good, and it would take no brain power at all. You could justify this choice (dubiously) by saying it would allow you to get all those extra tasks done more quickly.

Fortunately, your reflective mind hits the override on your overeager automatic mind and says, in effect, "Let's think about this a bit."[15] You sit back in your chair, and your algorithmic mind starts to think about your goal, which isn't just to review your 360 evaluation but to convince your boss to revise it before he submits it to the vice president of your division. You also think about how little power you have in this situation, and you remember that one of your few resources at the moment is tact, diligence, and your boss's regard. Your algorithmic mind gets to work, simulating the available modes of communication and evaluating which might work best.

- You could wait for a face-to-face conversation.

- You could advocate to your vice president directly.

---

14. Stanovich refers to this as "the simulation process that computes the alternative response that makes the override worthwhile." See Stanovich, "Rationality and Intelligence," 354.

15. "Type 1 processing encompasses processes of unconscious implicit learning and conditioning. Also, many rules, stimulus discriminations, and decision-making principles that have been practiced to automaticity . . . are processed in a Type 1 manner. This learned information can sometimes be just as much a threat to rational behavior as are evolutionary modules that fire inappropriately in a modern environment. Rules learned to automaticity can be overgeneralized—they can autonomously trigger behavior when the situation is an exception to the class of events they are meant to cover . . ." See Stanovich, "Rationality and Intelligence," 350.

- You could let it ride this time and hope for a better review next year.
- You could do some of the newly assigned tasks, email a status report to your supervisor, and—oh by the way—repeat your request for a meeting.

This shuttling among possible modes is the metacognition that affords your eventual mode-switch a better shot at success. Otherwise, you'd be stuck with your automatic brain's "less than perfectly rational" email whip-back.[16] Perfect rationality is impossible, of course. But perfection isn't the goal of mode-switching. Wisdom is.

The Craft We Need for the Waves We Face

It's a usual thing early in a book to convey the author's qualifications to address the book's subject matter. Here are mine. I'm a communication scholar and instructor. That means you can expect me to work with you to discern what can be communicatively achieved in a project towards a given goal.[17] You've heard me using the word *craft*. In Greek, that word is *techne*, which was for the ancients a word not only for vessel but also for technique.[18] Being an organizational researcher and a communication instructor has constantly reminded me that people don't just need a raft; they need the craft to steer it with. Like so much of communication instruction, mode craft doesn't require that you learn a whole lot more than what you already know. You'll want to notice things like how you breathe when you're in a good space, how you listen to a person you truly admire, how you voice things you care about, how you stand when you've had enough caffeine, how you meet the eye of others when you're feeling good, how you use language when it comes easily—and to do all this in spaces aswirl with the digital.

You get the point. This book brings forward what you know intuitively, bodily, tacitly when you communicate with others and then advises you how to take *that* into digital spaces. It's humbling to realize that you are but one agent in a context made blustery and choppy by coworker choices, administrative policies, client arbitrariness, and technological weirdnesses beyond any one person's management. But if you can learn to pay attention

---

16. Stanovich, "Rationality and Intelligence," 344.

17. This is a gloss on Aristotle's definition of rhetoric. See Aristotle, *On Rhetoric*, Bk. 1, Ch. 2.

18. I'm grateful to John Durham Peters for pointing out this double meaning in *craft* in Peters, *Marvelous Clouds*, 101.

to modes of communication, and find ways to engage them skillfully, you'll find digital seaworthiness in the bargain.

Let me offer two examples, one from your likely experience and one from a UX designer's actual experience.

Think about the last time you stopped texting long enough to look up and squint at passersby, asking, "Now, how would I say this if she were standing right here, just us two, talking?" In that moment, you were weirding the mode a little. Instead of going along with the quickness and pushiness that texting seems to require, you were slowing down, pausing mid-finger tap, trying to remember what good in-person talk entails. By switching back and forth between modes of sending and talking, you were recollecting things your body knows about communication—even as annoyed passersby looked up from their phones just in time to avoid colliding with you. For the merest second, they wonder why you're just standing there on the sidewalk with sunlight falling down your face.

A second example comes from a story that a company president, Jon Berbaum, told me on the podcast *Spiritual Capital*. Jon runs a user-experience company in Chicago called Highland Solutions. During the height of the pandemic in 2020, as his company was bleeding out clients and profits, he sensed how dispirited his thirty-five employees had become. As a former pastor, he felt the impulse to enter into the dialogic mode, offering them conversation-rich care. He wanted to sit down next to them and say empathetically, "Tell me how you're doing today." But Jon didn't do that, at least not directly. He intuited that the kind of dialogue his colleagues needed wasn't therapeutic but collaborative and project driven. They needed good work to do. So, he mode-switched by asking a different sort of question, "How can we give here?" Then, he and his colleagues started building out pro bono digital workshops for other struggling companies who couldn't afford branding strategy at the time. Highlanders were infused with energy. They had good collaborative projects to work on—and they eventually pulled in more clients from these practical and generous initiatives.[19]

These stories illustrate what mode craft can look like at its best—sometimes counterintuitive, sometimes innovative, sometimes risky. In the chapters that follow, we will examine each of these modes in turn. And in each of the corresponding workshop chapters, we'll take a closer look at a particular example of mode craft that will help you steer your raft in the middle of whatever digiwhelm you find yourself in.

---

19. Jon Berbaum, interview with Craig Mattson, *Spiritual Capital*, season 1, episode 40.

CHAPTER 1.5

How To Tell Your Digiwhelm Story

Mode/Switch Workshop

Goal: To sharpen your attention for the intersection of digital disruption and emotional intensity in your own life story.

It's RIDICULOUSLY EASY NOT to notice digiwhelm in your experience. This book's analysis proposes that digiwhelm happens where technological density meets affective intensity. Again, tech density happens wherever the digital develops in a way that's hard to understand. Its functions, in other words, are nontransparent or dense. Affective intensity, on the other hand, is any hard-to-name emotional experience. You might feel something and not know what to call it. After some thinking about it, though, you can usually tag it as exhilaration or deflation or joy or melancholy or—something else. The challenge is to bring that emotion into words.

If you're like most people, you might ignore either one of these factors:

- Some people have a generalized sense that technology is developing quickly, but they don't bother their heads about large language networks or superintelligence scenarios.
- Other people cope with chaotic technology by maintaining as much of a stoic calm as they can. They try not to feel their feelings about digital disruption, in other words.

But coping with the excesses of digital overwhelm requires you to notice the phenomenon itself. That will mean, first, looking closely at how digitality has invaded your life, often in a subtle but decisive way. Then, you'll need to learn to name your feelings about that invasion clearly.

One good way to enrich your attention for digiwhelm is to tell your own story of technological excess. Locate a moment in your experience where you felt pressured or propelled by technology and, at the same time, endured a lot of feelings.

In this workshop, I will encourage you to record or write a digiwhelm story from your life. Here's a template for telling the story:

1. Start by narrating an event that seemed to have nothing to do with technology.
2. Name a problem you faced in that event, which you then decided to solve with the help of digital tools.
3. Describe how the digital technology became excessive and created its own problems. (You might think of how the tool you used became a space you found yourself living in.)
4. Name the emotion(s) this created in you as precisely as you can.
5. Conclude with a wise saying that you find yourself hanging onto after that experience.

Here's a sample from my life to get you started.

My Parable of Digiwhelm

I'm in a hospital bed listening to my wife on my cellphone saying one brutal word: "*Again?*" She has a point. Only a year before, I had collapsed while running the Chicago Half Marathon. At the six-mile marker, I started hearing a blunt declaration from my body that I was done, so I turned to a partner and confessed, "Not feeling 100 percent. Gotta fall back." Minutes later, I blacked out. A race organizer would later say he watched the whole thing on camera, as my swoopy stride turned into a nosedive. My chest hit the ground, and I didn't come to consciousness till I'd been carted off to a med tent. And now, from yet another hospital bed, after yet another race day collapse, I had to concede that my plans to become a competitive runner had once again brought me to a place where "*Again?*" was the only thing to say.

Much of my aspiration to be a runner has been animated by a misguided confidence in digital technology. A careful biographer could probably map my path from high school track to early adult forest preserve to this hospital gurney with a trail of Walkmans, handheld CD players, iPods, and smartphones. Over the years, the digitech became more steadily sophisticated and seductive. A subscription to *Runner's World* magazine opened for me a whole other world of devices to buy: heart monitor, GPS watch, and a new pair of gel-soled shoes every six months. And that was just the stuff I could afford. Even after it was clear I would never be anything like an elite runner, I stayed with the high-tech training regimens, following the latest science on tempo running, trying to maintain athletic aspiration on route-tracking apps like MapMyRun and Strava.

I suppose I could tell you a hundred other stories about the convergence of technological innovation and emotional excess in my biography. But when I try to get a genuine feel for digiwhelm, I have no truer moment to turn to than looking up in a medic's face and hearing him say something like, "Dude, blood pressure this low's as lethal as hell." For me, the overwhelm of the digital feels like hypotension: empty-bodied and lightheaded and bewildered.

Okay, that's my story—or one of them. What's yours?

Take out your phone, turn on your voice recorder app, and capture a story. You may need to record it a couple of times before you're happy with it. (If you want to share it, you'll want to keep it to about two to three minutes.) Or if you're more of a writer type, open a journal or flip open a Google doc or Word document and scribe that story!

Putting the experience of overwhelm into words like this keeps you attentive to the digital density and affective intensity in your particular workplace. And sharing these stories with each other across the community of early career professionals—like the interviewees in this book have done—strengthens our collective wisdom of how to respond to digital overwhelm.

Once you've either recorded your story, taken a picture of your handwritten story, or created a digitally written version, would you consider sharing it with me, using this QR code?

I won't publish it without your permission, but if you're open to sharing, I'd love to include it in an issue of the Mode/Switch newsletter. Even if you'd rather not share, I'll be glad for a chance to hear and learn from you.

CHAPTER 2

Emailing Things

This chapter explores the mode of dialogue, looking for the mutuality that conversation and encounter sometimes make possible.

THERE'S A GEN Z meme that goes something like, *I don't have a job, I just write emails all day.* But given that most organizations today strain to produce, acquire, distribute, and secure information, email has pretty much become the paradigmatic task for everybody's day. Virtually everybody feels an imperative to get better and better at shuffling, archiving, deleting, and sending email. Want to impress the higher-ups? Simple. Be an amazing email-traffic controller.[1] So, let's start our conversation about digital overwhelm with email, a tool used by more than 300 million global citizens, a medium at once intimate and public, as private as a phone notification, as public as your company's next lawsuit.[2] Everybody seems to agree that email is a personal and an organizational cause of scatteredness. But let me ask a potentially naïve question: what exactly is overwhelming about email?

Is it simply addictive? Are the reward structures just too hard to resist? Do we keep hoping, at some preconscious level, that *this time* the inbox will deliver the big message? I suppose we must reach for some psychological explanation for the power of email's overwhelm. But it's strange. Email is the quintessence of rapid information flow between senders and receivers, an ideal tracing back to mid-twentieth-century information systems theorists

---

1. Petersen and Warzel, *Out of Office*.
2. "Email Statistics Report, 2018–2022."

like Norbert Weiner and Claude Shannon, who did their best to remove psychology, or more accurately *subjectivity*, from their model of communication. They insisted that everything, or very nearly everything, could be explained in terms of encoders transmitting messages via channels to decoders who shoot back responses. Think missile technology, meteorology, and computer networks. But think trees, too, and social networks and, well, *you*. Everything is explicable in cybernetic terms, regulating information flows across networks.[3] So, *does* the language of psychological addiction explain this seemingly machinic predicament?

Other people say the problem is not psychological merely, but has more to do with the hyper-efficient media environment we find ourselves in. Scholars like Marshall McLuhan, James Carey, Neil Postman, and Walter Ong have long urged seeing technology and media not just as distributors of information but as shapers of culture.[4] Today's tech gurus like Cal Newport use this media ecology theory to show how the design and dynamics of the medium make the flow of information too fast and too efficient and too easy. Our brains haven't evolved to handle all that ease and all that efficiency any more than our hunter-gatherer bodies can handle lime tortilla chips in giant bowls next to an easy chair. Like the astute engineer that he is, Newport notes that workplace conversation *needs* a certain amount of awkwardness and inconvenience to keep our information systems from working too well.[5] Without friction, we are trapped within the "never-

3. No book has so guided my own theoretical sense-making on this point as Meghan O'Giehlyn's *God Human Animal Machine*, which helped me see the almost unimaginably vast relevance of information theory for human life and communication today. Newport's *World without Email* offered me a model of joining info systems theory with media ecology theory in a popular voice. See also Shannon, *Mathematical Theory of Communication*. For a discussion of the rise of efficiency as a governing maxim for much of modern life, see Princen, *Logic of Sufficiency*, 50.

4. McLuhan, "Media and Cultural Change," 89–96; Carey, *Communication as Culture*; Postman, *Amusing Ourselves to Death*; Ong, *Orality and Literacy*.

5. We have been deceived into thinking that we needed "some way to combine the *speed* of synchronous communication with the *low overhead* of asynchronous communication." Newport, *World without Email*, 65, 59. Walter J. Ong would come to similar conclusions, but from different premises. For him, the problem is the privatization and objectification and de-vocalization of human communication. See Ong, *Ramus, Method, and the Decline of Dialogue*, 9, 12, 291, and Ong, *Orality and Literacy*, 5–16, 170–73. The account of mode-switching I offer in this chapter is closer to Ong than Newport, for what it's worth. Think of it as a signal capable of input and output and only distinguishable in contrast with what information theorists call *noise*. We usually think of noise dismissively. But information theory sees noise as providing the essential background against which the signal leaps forward. The disseminative mode builds on this insight of information theory to say that communication fails to be productive if it becomes too transparent, too easy. "The idea that eliminating friction can cause problems

ending, ad hoc, unstructured flow of messages" via *"the hyperactive hive mind,"* perpetuating workplace conditions of "shallow busyness."[6] Newport asks, "How many of the quick asks for someone else's time and attention that you dash off over email during a normal day would you still make if you had to instead walk down the hallway and interrupt someone's work?"[7] Maybe *that's* why email is overwhelming: the medium is designed to offer a too-perfect satisfaction for our efficiency urges. The medium is, as Kenneth Burke might say, *rotten with perfection*.[8]

I'm dissatisfied, and I'm guessing you are, too, with where the psychological vs. structural argument leaves us in dealing with email's digiwhelm. Of *course*, we are weak creatures, prone to all sorts of bad inbox habits. But to simply tell everybody Stop Doing That seems unlikely to do anything but induce guilt. This is not one of those books telling you to *do you better than you ever have*. On the other hand, the focus on technological environments doesn't give us much room to maneuver either. My guess is, there's no lever on the third floor of your office building that enables you to power down the Death Star of email. I would adore hearing stories from you of throwing your laptop in the dumpster and starting a picket line chant, "Bring back the landlines!"[9] But my hunch is, you won't take up that sort of activism.

I do think there's some help, though, in looking at the uncanny meeting point of the psychological and the technological. Precisely there, we see our instinctive modes of communication taking shape. Precisely there, we notice spaces where we have some choices to make. But modes are hard to name and easy to miss, and what you can't name, you can hardly see. Sometimes, modes of communication feel to me like those body-sized inflatable bubbles you see at picnics and parties. We're all rolling around in our mostly transparent modes, and even if we look silly now and then, we don't mind. The body suits protect us from the pressures of digital life—sort of. And then we bump into someone else's body bubble, someone else's way of coping with overwhelm, and everything gets weird. When it comes to email, for example, you might buffer yourself from

---

might sound unusual, as we're used to thinking more about efficiency producing more effectiveness, but among engineers like me, this concept is commonly understood. Too little friction can lead to feedback loops that spiral out of control, as happens when a microphone gets too close to a speaker and the self-amplification recursively explodes into a deafening screech." Newport, *World without Email*, 59.

6. Newport, *World without Email*, 258.
7. Newport, *World without Email*, 59.
8. For "rotten with perfection," see Burke, *Language as Symbolic Action*, 16–18.
9. I credit this idea to Andrew Holmes who, in a conversation about these things with me, once envisioned Cal Newport kicking a shirt with this slogan.

email's excesses by always responding quickly. You're the kind of person who seems to shoot back an email before the other person has pressed send. People are always saying to you, "Did you get my email?" and you feel this quantum of disappointment because you responded to their email last night at 10 PM. Your response time after their email's arrival was about two minutes and twenty-five seconds. It's intense, but it keeps you from the insanity of an overstuffed inbox. Your manager, on the other hand, might deal with excessive email pressure by waiting five days to respond to any and all messages. That's her inflatable body suit, and it annoys you something fierce. But it's all too easy to think that your mode of communication is *the* mode. I think it's better to have multiple modes to put on, depending on the communication, depending on the community, depending on the day. Changing your way of digital coping helps you deal with the different kinds of pressure email puts on you. Mode-switching also helps you coordinate better across all the boundaries of our weirdness.

Notice, too, that your mode of email engagement assumes a cybernetic mode of communication. For the quick responder like you, workplace communication is all about inbox management—or as information systems theorists might say, it's all about regulating the movement of information across a network. Your inbox is a node on that network, and you don't want it to become blocked and jam the network. You'll probably be drawn to Newport's concept of *digital minimalism*, which tries to regulate the amount of information you have to take in and the number of devices you use to connect to a given network. I tend to respect this decluttered inbox/decluttered mind approach to email engagement, but I don't think it's the best mode of communication for navigating electronic culture in your workplace.

In this chapter, I'm going to suggest another approach to email: the dialogic mode. I know. I'm not likely to sell many books on the familiarity of *that* term. "Dialogic" isn't a word we use a whole lot, at least outside of college courses in existentialism or graduate seminars in clinical therapy.[10]

10. Ron Anderson has gathered the core principles of dialogue into a seven-point list, here paraphrased by Ron Arnett:
- Presence. Dialogue requires a willingness to follow the conversation as it leads in "unrehearsed" directions.
- Unanticipated consequences. Dialogue cannot be predicted to assure an outcome known a priori to an exchange.
- Otherness. The mystery and uniqueness of the other is accepted.
- Vulnerability. Willingness to engage in some risk when knowing the outcome of an exchange is not apparent at the outset of a conversation.
- Mutual implication. We discover in message interpretation something

But you know the approach already: it is communication characterized by usually two-way conversation and shaped by the values of equity and authenticity. What do you say we examine the usefulness of this approach for inbox management? I think you'll find it addresses a kind of digiwhelm that cybernetics too often misses—the madness of other people's inbox management. For me, at least, it's hard not to think, "What are they *doing* with what I sent four days ago?" Alternatively, it's hard not to be hugely irritated by the ways people use quick response times to elongate an online conversation. There are simply uncountable ways for people to be weird selves in email exchange. But I'm feeling hopeful as we open some talk about the dialogic mode. It's been an approach that keeps saving my life.

When Did Email Stop Being Weird?

When I became a professor in the early 2000s, email took up relatively little of my attention, at least in comparison with the dissertation I was trying to complete and the course work I was trying to prepare and the books I was trying to digest. I did not have a laptop at home, and nobody had a smartphone yet. It sounds funny now, but putting one finger on the "on" lever on the back of my chunky desktop PC of a Monday morning gave me a quantum of expectancy each morning. You get a similar feeling today, maybe, when a UPS truck pulls up outside your house.

I remember hearing my more seasoned colleagues tell stories about the free-ranging intellectual conversations of the 1970s. They spoke of computerless and telephoneless offices, full of books, cigarettes, and good talk. Nothing, in fact, had persuaded me more to accept a position at this college than hearing a senior faculty member tell me, "The talk is good here." There was a history to that talk. The story goes that one day, some faculty members and their students hammered together, in a few short hours, a shaky building they christened "The Tab," short for "The Tabernacle." This sanctuary would pass no building codes today, but back then, it

---

about our communicative partner and much about ourselves in the unique way we hear the message.

- Temporal flow. Dialogue presumes some historical continuity of communicative partners and a sensitivity to the time of the address—past, present, and future anticipations enter the conversation.

- Authenticity. A presumption of honesty, until proven otherwise, is offered to the other.

Arnett, *Dialogic Education*, 11. Arnett is digesting a conference paper by Anderson, "Anonymity, Presence, and the Dialogic Self in a Technological Culture."

gave everybody room for discussion, disagreement, deliberation. I suspect my fellow professors exaggerated just how good those good old days were. But there was no mythologizing the monument that, to this day, marks the spot where The Tab once stood. I have on more than one occasion gone out to look at that stone, pondering the face-to-face conversational practices that used to mark our community so conspicuously. And then I've always returned to my office and the waiting inbox.

Twenty years ago, email felt to me like a weird space in a good way. Maybe that sounds like I'm rationalizing an addiction. But I loved email exchanges the way the builders of The Tab loved conversation. Maybe this comes with a guild like academia where people often live by their rhetorical skills. But my colleagues and my students were just so wondrously weird in their emails. There was voice and craft and personhood in the notes. I often found myself quoting things people said, jokes they made, maxims they made up. I even created a filing system to archive all these emails with so many subfolders that the system had in-my-email's-house-are-many-rooms sort of vibe. Of course, caring so much about email meant that sometimes I grieved moments when interchanges went badly. One time, a colleague was struggling to finish a publication on time, and I sent what I thought was a cheery email of commiseration. It was the wrong time and the wrong note. The colleague whipped back a terse response, an email exchange that made it hard for us to talk for months and which still lodges uncomfortably in my molars whenever I talk with this admired friend.

I hope you're getting the sense that when email felt overwhelming back then, it was the overwhelm of encounter. I felt hilarity or grief or anger or even a kind of reverence. A dozen or so years into my career, and that overwhelm had changed in character. Now, I felt a quantitative fatigue of a crowded inbox. It felt less like the scene for exchange and more like trying to hold a snowball fight in a blizzard.

Attempting Minimalism

I eventually decided I needed to do something about this new kind of digiwhelm. About ten years into my career as a professor, I started going back into the office after Wednesday night supper to zero out my inbox. Sometimes one of my daughters came along, reading and sleeping in one of my office chairs, lured with the promise of a Frosty on the way home. Other times, I went in alone and opened my window to the autumn night, playing Patty Griffin songs to get me through several hours of relentless processing. Sometimes, I'd hear undergraduate actors headed over in a merry cluster to the campus black box theater for that night's rehearsal. Then, around the time the performers were headed back to their dorms, I would walk out to my car in the now-empty lot, feeling dazed, as if scattering so much messaging had also scattered *me*.

It wasn't supposed to feel that way, at least not according to my paperback copy of David Allen's book *Getting Things Done* (or *GTD*, as the devotees refer to it), which had promised to give me "a mind like water" as I filed, deleted, scheduled, and delegated tasks in my inbox.[11] As messages and tasks arise in your workday, Allen said, the free-flowing mindset responds "totally appropriately to the force and mass of the input; then it returns to calm. It doesn't overreact or underreact."[12] Allen gave me an imagination for being a peacefully productive professional with an uncluttered mind.[13] Minimize what's on your mind, he said, by (1) sending things to your waste bin, (2) delegating things to your colleagues, and (3) finishing things in two minutes.

I was determined to deal with my professional overwhelm through Allen's suit-and-tie spirituality. So committed was I to this organizational minimalism that once, in a fit of GTD fervor, I spilled everything out of my office cabinets and drawers and off every surface, piling it all up on a giant mound on the floor. Many a mystic has climbed a mountain to draw close to the divine. As an aspiring workplace contemplative, I didn't climb my mountain; I *processed* it piece by piece, treating every strange item like a bit of data to be archived or delegated or destroyed. Halfway through the mountain, I heard a knock at my office door. Prying the door open a few inches, I peered out with the contained irritation of a monk interrupted at prayers. The student started to ask a question, caught sight of what must have looked like a burn pile of manila folders, magazines, receipts, quizzes, binders, and batteries on the floor, and backed away hurriedly. I shut the door and turned again to my mountain, the determination rising in me to turn my office into a solitary tabernacle of efficient yield.

But you know what *wasn't* on that office pile? Email. Allen helped me keep up with receipts and stapled-together articles and student quizzes and stray conference programs with notes scribbled on the back. What he couldn't do was help me keep up with email traffic as it increased across

---

11. Allen, *Getting Things Done*, 10–11.
12. Allen, *Getting Things Done*, 10–11.
13. "Think about the last time you felt highly productive. You probably had a sense of being in control; you were not stressed out; you were highly focused on what you were doing; time tended to disappear (lunchtime already?); and you felt you were making noticeable progress toward a meaningful outcome. Would you like to have more such experiences?" Allen, *Getting Things Done*, 11.

my work life. So, it felt like an absolute rescue to read Cal Newport's book *Deep Work* on a long flight from Milan to New York. That book helped me recognize that, although Allen had told me what to do with *information*, I needed help rationing my *attention*. It did not sound easy, this asceticism. But exerting willpower to focus my attention, Newport explained, would enable me "to quickly master hard things."[14] Such mastery required making a commitment to keeping "deep work" time segregated from "shallow work" time. I found the time-portioning daunting, but I wanted to try it. The rewards seemed worthwhile. "Professional activities performed in a state of distraction-free concentration that push your cognitive capabilities to their limit" will—Newport assured his readers—"create new value" and "improve your skill."[15] Newport's expressed goal was to set his readers up for competitive advantage in the knowledge economy. Most people, he pointed out, are preoccupied with "logistical-style tasks, often performed while distracted."[16] But if you can do deep work, you will find plenty of it to do—and you'll make bank in the bargain. "Deep work is not some nostalgic affectation of writers and early-twentieth-century philosophers. It's instead a skill that has great value today."[17]

Deep work presented me with another minimalist approach to workplace communication. *You know all that work you have to do each day just to be an accountable member of a learning community, teaching, mentoring, scheduling, planning, corresponding? Yeah, just don't let that stuff expand to fill your attention. And for the love of deep work, keep all those logistical matters out of the spaces where you need to do slow, concentrated, important work.* The deepest work I had to do was seeking publication in peer-reviewed journals. Although I couldn't generate the full-on productivity that Newport managed, I thought I could keep out of my inbox long enough to publish a rhetoric essay every other year or so and write a few articles for flagship journals and maybe a book or two.[18] The question was, was I minimalist enough to say things like I heard Newport saying?

> I became ruthless in turning down time-consuming commitments and began to work in isolated locations outside my office.

14. Newport, *Deep Work*, 30.
15. Newport, *Deep Work*, 3.
16. Newport, *Deep Work*, 6.
17. Newport, *Deep Work*, 12.
18. "In the ten-year period following my college graduation, I published four books, earned a PhD, wrote peer-reviewed academic papers at a high rate, and was hired as a tenure-track professor at Georgetown University. I maintained this voluminous production while rarely working past five or six p.m. during the workweek." Newport, *Deep Work*, 16.

> ... As this year progressed, I became a deep work machine—and the result of this transformation caught me off guard. During the same year that I wrote a book and my oldest son entered the terrible twos, I managed to more than double my average productivity, publishing *nine* peer-reviewed papers—all the while maintaining my prohibition on work in the evenings.[19]

Wow, yes, especially to that last bit, a passage which would have looked (especially to my early career self) like the quintessence of academic achievement. But wait, what was that bit about ruthlessness and working in lonely locations? And what is this contempt for logistical work? Isn't what he's calling *logistical* the good labor of mentoring and collaboration and instruction and idea generation? Sure, scheduling meetups is obnoxious, but logistical stuff is human stuff. Isn't all that logistical stuff like hammering together a rickety tabernacle for human encounter and dialogue? I also knew, from having taught theories of symbolic interactionism, that Newport's vision for deep thinking was too solitary.[20] Even when deep workers are alone, staring for hours at a solitary problem, they rely on voices, sources, and texts that inform and enable their problem-solving abilities. If anything, Newport's deep work *works* only because it enables us to hear the indispensable outbursts of voices in our heads so easily drowned out by digital voices outside our heads. Digital minimalism and its cybernetic mode of communication got me only so far. I still needed a way to engage workplace community that wasn't hyper-responsive on the one hand and hyper-individualized on the other. I could not have said this at the time, but I needed a way to remember the fundamental weirdness at the basis of all human communication, online and off.

Finding Dialogue

During finals week on the cusp of one summer break, red-eyed from too little sleep and too many emails, I looked up to see a lanky student named Ethan in my office doorway, eyeing me through a forelock, and asking if I'd be willing to do some reading together that summer. All I wanted to do in that moment was to submit my grades, put the semester to bed, and be done with emails for a while. But Ethan's invitation wasn't the sort which a self-respecting liberal arts professor could say no to. He and I started meeting up

---

19. Newport, *Deep Work*, 16.

20. For an accessible introduction to symbolic interactionism and how it shapes thought and speech, see Griffin, Ledbetter, and Sparks, *First Look at Communication Theory*, 53–64.

at the tail end of his day job, after he'd been painting yellow lines in a parking lot all afternoon. Later, he'd come over for toast and coffee on Sunday mornings, and we'd read some more. Our practice went on for years. During the COVID-19 pandemic, we met online. There was a time or two when we sat, reading, in my garage with the door open to the street.

Reading together meant that suddenly we were playing a different game than we'd played when he was enrolled in my Persuasive Speaking class years before. Now, we had to feel our way forward without a syllabus. So, here's what we did: one of us would read a paragraph or a page, after which we took turns talking and taking notes. Small things mattered: we had to read aloud; he had to call me Craig; and we always had coffee that was a little too strong. But other things mattered, too, like trust and openness. I soon learned that he was a more talented reader of texts than I, and that I could rely on his help in some of the thornier passages we were reading. We learned together that we could trust texts to take us to unpredictably good places. Sometimes we ended up on what the Jewish existentialist Martin Buber would call a wind-whipped ridge, where you can fall into an abyss on either side. But up there, dealing with the risk of dialogue, we remembered what we'd always known about good talk.[21]

One of the windy ridges where we met together was the Old Testament book of Job, a text that more than any other in the Bible exemplifies the difficulties and possibilities of dialogue. It's a book that dramatizes the disjuncture and misunderstanding native to conversation.[22]

Job opens with establishing shots and telling statistics from a righteous and productive life in the land of Uz, but then abruptly leaves earth to capture a dialogue between the Almighty and a lawyerly figure, a satan, who stalks around a heavenly council chamber, accusing Job of a transactional piety. "Does Job fear God for nothing?" the satan asks, bellowing like Al Pacino. The Lord, sounding like Morgan Freeman on a sad day, gives the accuser a chance to test his theory out. The tale whips focus to the ensuing mayhem. Job's property, his children, and his health are brutally taken. As the good man sits on the ground, ash clinging to his bald head, his three friends Eliphaz, Bildad, and Zophar come to sit and grieve with him. They all sit in silence for seven days as Job scrapes at boils on his thigh with a broken piece of pottery.

Then, the silence breaks, as Job gives release to his grief and curses the day of his birth. Like his friends, Job had long accepted the basic economics

---

21. Fall one way, Buber said, and you lose yourself; fall another, and you lose the other. Discussion of the narrow ridge can be found in Buber, *Between Man and Man*. See also Buber, *I and Thou*.

22. Peters, *Speaking into the Air*, 2, 5–6.

of a retributionist worldview in which the good are rewarded and the evil punished. But Job now knows something has gone wrong in that economy. As his pain shakes itself out into words, he declares that, although he's not been a perfect man, he hasn't done anything to deserve *this*. The Almighty has done him wrong; his friends have misunderstood him; even his wife has urged him to give up. All the intimate exchanges of his life have fallen apart.

But unlike most of these intimates, the Almighty now strikes Job as dangerous. The suffering man speaks of "the arrows of the Almighty" and describes how "my spirit drinks their poison." When he speaks of the Almighty, he speaks not of the steadfast love but of "the terrors of God . . . arrayed against me" (6:4). How can you deal with a massive and inhuman intelligence?

> Look, he passes by me, and I do not see him;
>   he moves on, but I do not perceive him.
> He snatches away; who can stop him?
>   Who will say to him, "What are you doing?"[23]

No wonder Job thinks that speaking to this divinity would be ineffectual at best, dangerous at worst. "If I summoned him and he answered me, / I do not believe that he would listen to my voice" (9:16). But as the speeches wear on, Job changes his mind. The one mode of communication that will rectify this catastrophe is dialogue.

> Oh, that I knew where I might find him,
>   That I might come even to his dwelling!
> I would lay my case before him,
>   And fill my mouth with arguments.
> I would learn what he would say to me.[24]

Job's friends have little interest in this sort of mutuality, either in their conversations with Job or in their reflections on the Almighty. With Job, they listen impatiently and offer tiresome explanations for the workings of human life: *Here are the rules. Whatever else fails you, you can count on these principles holding firm.* They seem uneasy about his suffering and speak of it only abstractly. Job asks them at one point if they would please just look at him for once.[25] Similarly, they do not talk to God directly but speak of him as an inaccessible being in a great beyond. Zophar speaks for the others when he says, "Can you find out the deep things of God?" and

---

23. Job 9:11–12, NRSV.
24. Job 23:3–5, NRSV.
25. Job 6:28, NRSV.

then adds, "It is higher than heaven—what can you do?" (11:7–8). All they know is that God observes reciprocal trade: so much good behavior yields so much divine reward. The friends, in short, are attentive to reciprocity, but not to mutuality. Later, the Almighty will say to them: "you have not spoken of me what is right, as my servant Job has done" (42:8). What does the Lord mean by this? Job has said many reckless things. The friends have spoken of God with cautious conservatism. Perhaps by refusing to speak directly to God they have failed to speak truth about God. They have theologized in the third person.

Near the end of the book, after Job and his friends have fallen silent, a wind picks up, steadily increasing until a whirlwind has arrived, obliterating attention for anything else. In the center of that storm, the Almighty speaks to Job. "Who is this that darkens counsel by words without knowledge?" There follows a series of questions that poke at the ineffectualness of Job's power and knowledge and speech: "Have you commanded the morning since your days began, / and caused the dawn to know its place . . . ?"[26] "Can you lift up your voice to the clouds, / so that a flood of waters may cover you?"[27] "Is it at your command that the eagle mounts up / and makes its nest on high?"[28]

This list of questions makes me feel exhausted. If I read the book of Job as an explanation for human suffering, I am disappointed. If I read the book as a defense of the goodness and justice of God, I am again disappointed.[29] If I listen for emotionality in God's speeches, I may hear a rough teasing in the lines, but the lines never achieve a compassionate or even respectful manner. What the reader does find is an unexpected celebration of a fierce and humanly unmasterable world. "God's involvement with the world," writes Ellen Davis, "expresses itself in huge, unapologetic delight in a creation whose outstanding quality is quite simply magnificence: power

26. Job 38:12, NRSV.
27. Job 38:34, NRSV.
28. Job 39:27, NRSV.
29. As Ellen Davis points out, "the question of whether or not God is just . . . .while present in the book, proves to be a red herring, and Job's hapless counselors get lost following the scent." Davis, *Getting Involved with God*, 122. Lindsay Wilson agrees, suggesting that "many readers approach the book hoping to find answers that it never intends to give. For example, the book does not intend to make pronouncements about the problem of suffering (though suffering is a problem), or about whether a righteous person can suffer (obviously one can). If you are looking to the book of Job to give fresh or conclusive answers to these questions, then you will be sorely disappointed." Wilson, *Job*, 8. Wilson identifies one of the purposes of the book to deconstruct a "fossilized misunderstanding of retribution that had misrepresented the mainstream wisdom of tradition of Proverbs" (8).

and freedom on a scale that is bewildering and terrifying."[30] The enormous joy of God in the wildness of creation decenters Job and gives him, so to speak, a new communicative project. It's not a one-on-one conversation, but a multidirectional and multivocal conversation.

God speaks of how the sea bursts forth, the stars sing, the dawn shakes out the earth like a blanket. The east wind scatters, the rivers tear through their channels, and the thunder bolts. Everything from constellations to lightning to dust clods has its say. Even the ostrich, too silly to hide eggs properly, "spreads its plumes aloft" and "laughs at the horse and its rider."[31] The challenge of communication in this sort of world is how to stay with a conversation whose center you cannot find and control.[32]

Job puts his hand on his mouth and changes the angle from which he's addressing God. When he says, "now my eye sees you; therefore I despise myself / and repent in dust and ashes," he sounds if he is saying, "You've gotten the best of me in the argument. I'll shut up." But that interpretation doesn't fit the Hebrew phrasing, which has Job saying that he repents not *in* dust and ashes but *from* them. He is finished, in other words, holding his fixed and lonely position as the aggrieved party in a one-on-one argument with God.[33] His first task, upon returning to town, is to pray for his friends, a surprising sort of speech, given how deeply his friends have misunderstood him. He is newly prepared to admit the incompleteness of what he has to say to God and others in the midst of a joyously cacophonous creation.

Job does not find himself on Buber's windy ridge. Instead of two people facing one another, trying to hold on to their integrity, there's a community of voices and strange collection of variegated creatures whose cries make a larger pattern to join in. Anne Morrow Lindbergh has talked about marriage this way. Although it feels like a dyad, it's always involved in a larger pattern. She describes it as a country dance, like those quadrilles you see in Jane Austen movies where the dancers vary their direct stares with turning and crossing and spinning and queuing up within a larger pattern. Writes Lindbergh: "Now arm in arm, now face to face, now back to back—it does not matter which, because they know they are partners moving to the same

---

30. Davis, *Getting Involved with God*, 139.

31. Job 39:18, NRSV.

32. I'm indebted here to Ellen Davis's question: "The great question that God's speech out of the whirlwind poses for Job and every other person of integrity is this: Can you love what you do not control?" Davis, *Getting Involved with God*, 140.

33. The insight about Job's repenting from dust and ashes comes from Lindsay Wilson. "Job is now ready to resume normal relationships in society," Wilson notes, "the very thing he proceeds to do in the following verses." Wilson, *Job*, 206–7.

rhythm, creating a pattern together, and being invisibly nourished by it."[34] I think we need both these metaphors for the dialogic mode: the windy ridge and the country dance. They show different ways that mutuality can be achieved and enjoyed. But we also need the polyphony Job has learned to hear through conversation with God.

How Conversation Expands

Ethan's and my reading duo eventually broke up. He got married, had a daughter, moved to a faraway suburb. Eventually, he started working at a shipping company, just trying to hold body and soul and family together. But talking with him had given me a taste of something that I wanted to find again. It was strange: our conversations had seemed to have nothing to do with the deep work that I still saw as central to my professional life. No articles or books came out of these conversations, at least not directly. But our dialogues were practices of anamnesis, reminding us how to talk.

So, hardly knowing what I was doing, I started emailing during the pandemic some former students (and then other young professionals they introduced me to) and inviting them to dialogue digitally about their experiences of professional overwhelm. I was a little startled by how eager they were to talk. Our conversations spilled over from email into podcasts, Zoom interviews, a newsletter called *The Mode Switch*, and finally this book. What took shape in these conversations felt *somewhat* like what Ethan and I had enjoyed reading Ecclesiastes in Adirondack chairs under the flowering pear tree in the backyard. But the Gen Z and millennial professionals I was speaking to were increasingly far less like me than Ethan had been (or, at least, than Ethan had let me know). I'm a straight, White, academic Christian. My conversation partners now were LGBTQ+ folk and Black and Brown citizens in industries very different from my own and espousing sometimes no faith at all.

These conversations reintroduced me to a kind of digital overwhelm I'd lost track of. At the intersection of technological disruption (in our case, the sudden rise of Zoom) and affective intensity (the sometimes weepy, sometimes exultant, sometimes bored affect of online dialogues), I encountered the overwhelm of the weird all over again. In our shared digital conditions, I heard story after story that cued me to just how different my dialogue partners were. Usually, my favorite relational move is to achieve identification and to show recognition and empathy. My customary subtext is, *I know what you're feeling.* But I couldn't say that with these people, I was starting to realize. There

---

34. Lindbergh, *Gift from the Sea*, 104.

were moments of identification, of course. But there were also moments of profound disconcertment. Here's a parable of what I mean.[35]

I remember during this time being invited to a book talk with some younger professionals in downtown Chicago. The first person I met at the event was a lesbian dating a trans man—a set of arrangements I hadn't encountered before. They showed up a few minutes later, as the woman hosting the event introduced me to her wife. Just when I thought I might be the only het in the room, a straight guy showed up—and let us know he was divorcing his wife. I'm embarrassed about this now, but I remember feeling lost. I kept asking questions, and, when somebody's joke didn't make sense to me, I'd ask about it. (What *is* a U-Haul lesbian? I wondered.) I tried to laugh as often as I could, but mostly I remember feeling like I had no footing in this conversation.

At one point during the night, the person hosting invited us to tell a story. I can't remember her prompt. It had spiritual overtones, if I'm remembering right, because our book that night was about spirituality in business. But as I listened to the stories and munched the pizza, I didn't have to be a qualitative researcher to figure out that these people had lived radically different lives than I ever had. They had been burned by organized religion. They had arranged their social and sexual lives very differently from mine. My nuclear family in the suburbs was not a vision of goodness for them. And I realized that trying to pretend to identify with them would erase important differences between us—but then, what could I say in response to the storytelling prompt?

My turn came. Remembering that it was Advent and deciding to just own the fact that I was one of those Christians everybody's always hearing about, I told the story of Zechariah in the temple in Luke's Gospel, when the angel appeared to him and told him he was going to have a son in his old age. "You mean when he took cocaine and hallucinated all this," the trans guy across from me said with an enormous laugh. We all laughed, and I said, "Wait, stay with me—" And then I said that I'd always thought it was a punishment for Zechariah was struck mute, but now nine months of silence sounded good, like a sort of sabbath.[36]

As it turns out, telling a Bible story—not the savviest approach to talking with people embittered by organizational religion—somehow didn't shut the conversation down. Everybody seemed to know what I meant

---

35. This story doesn't come out of my research among rising professionals, but it happened during that research project and, like everything else in my life at the time, offered illumination for interviews.

36. I had actually heard that insight in a chapel sermon at my college that week preached by Dr. Kyle Dieleman.

about the gift of silence as rest. Or they nodded like they did. I don't think anybody had any illusions about the sort of insensitivity that people like me are prone to. I was working my usual dialogic tools for all I was worth—identifying with people, exchanging stories, taking turns, saying back what I was hearing—but looking back, I'm pretty sure I was lost for much of the time. All night long, in fact, I kept feeling lost and found and lost in rapid sequence. What that table conversation gave me access to was the sheer strangeness of exchange. And recovering that sense of the amazing weirdness of people also showed me new ways to care for them. Like I said, I usually try to identify with people at work—that is, I respond to their disclosure by disclosing myself as authentically as I could manage. But that wasn't what that table conversation required. The mystery of my strange self and the mystery of their strange selves couldn't be simply laid bare in a searing moment of authentic contact. But we could enter into conversation with the goal of care and service. "To treat others as we would want to be treated," writes John Durham Peters, "means performing for them in such a way not that the self is authentically represented but that the other is caringly served."[37] I'm not sure I managed to do that, but when I said goodbye and said I was off to take the Brown Line, the trans guy said, "Hey, it's a cold night for a walk—let me give you a ride." I didn't feel comprehensively known as a result of that dialogue, but I did feel "caringly served."

I believe those dynamics are translatable into email experience. The rising professionals' stories I will share throughout this book came to me almost exclusively through electronic dialogues—email and text and video call and even the occasional phone conversation. But what that night in north Chicago gave me was an affective experience that cut across later technological experience with a different kind of overwhelm. Call it awe or reverence, or simply call it being weirded out. But across these interviews, I started to feel the sense of utter seriousness in the company of people whose words I didn't know what to make of yet. This was a mode switch, and no mistake—a mode switch from the cybernetic concerns of data management and attentional rationing to the dialogic concerns of radical mutuality.

Strange Gifts

Let's return to Job to wrap up this chapter. At the beginning of the story, Job had been everyone's caregiver, everyone's philanthropist.[38] But now at the end of the story, he has to change roles. He becomes, in short, the beneficiary

---

37. Peters, *Speaking into the Air*, 268.
38. Job 29:12–16, NRSV.

of his community's gifts. His family "ate bread with him in his house; they showed him sympathy and comforted him for all the evil that the Lord had brought upon him; and each of them gave him a piece of money and a gold ring."[39] Job finds himself amazingly in a new world where he is the beneficiary not the benefactor. It's not a safe and manageable world. But as Davis points out, after suffering the trauma of so much loss, Job remarkably has more children. And, what is more, in a culture long accustomed to moving at the measured pace of patriarchal tradition, he gives his daughters playful names and—can this be the straitlaced Job who never breaks with tribal custom?—inheritances along with his boys.[40]

The gifts that close the book of Job have me thinking about how digital communication, too, might move at the cadence of gift. My electronic dialogues with rising professionals, after all, felt constantly like gift. It was gift that we had the digital means to make the conversation happen in the midst of a global pandemic. It was gift that these people bore with my misconceptions. It was gift that they sent follow-up emails and texts to further elucidate our interviews. You can understand why I have so frequently felt an amazed gratitude after we had waved at one another through our webcams. (We'll be discussing the modes of the remote meeting in a chapter soon to come.)

But what does the strange rhythm of gifts have to say about digital communication in general and email communication in particular? Try thinking of it this way. When someone gives you a present, you feel a startlement, a surprise, a moment of affective intensity that you might not be sure how to name in the moment. And then comes the unnerving recognition that you should now offer some kind of response. It's a tricky business. If you gush your thanks, that could spoil things. If you whip around and hand them a present right away—well, that's another way to spoil the gifting moment. So, what do you do but cradle the gift in your lap, your mouth hanging a little open, holding still for a moment. Whatever gives you pause, instinctively, is the fear of turning this gift into something that it's not: a lease, a trade, a purchase. And so you pause, you gather yourself, you swallow hard, and maybe you just meet the eyes of the giver and shake your head slowly. The gift has come, like something tossed over a wall. It's landed in your lap, in your hands. And although everything in you is yearning to respond in kind, you want this gift to *stay* gift as long as possible. You hold back on the quick rejoinder that conversation so often requires and let the present be present.

That, I think, is how we can think of email interaction as well. That might make you snort in derision. Email as gift? As a site for mutuality? *Um,*

---

39. Job 42:11, NRSV.
40. Davis, *Getting Involved with God*.

no. Just no. I can't treat email like dialogue. You haven't seen in my inbox. If I tried to treat those emails like personal conversations, it'd be like waving at everybody on the interstate. I take your point. And I do think Newport isn't entirely wrong to use the cybernetic mode to deal with email overwhelm. Sometimes the only thing that keeps you sane in the midst of digital excessiveness is to return to digital minimalism.

But if that's our only mode of engaging email's digiwhelm, then we end up privileging efficiency over encounter. We need both. It's a marvel how efficiently our email exchanges work most of the time. It's also a mystery that these ordinary emails mediate contact between humans whose hearts are full of madness and eternity.[41] When I recommend that you try out the mode of dialogue in your inbox, I don't mean that you should respond to *every* email with an intimate and searing account of your interior life in the moments after their red-flagged message arrived. But try letting email be gift as often as you can, and see what comes of it. Try letting it be an exchange that you're not entirely sure how to respond to, at least not right now. Instead of treating it as a demand to respond as fast as possible, let it be what the message mysteriously is for a little while.

Can we agree that inboxes are weirder places than they look? I'm guessing that, even if you'll concede the weirdness of email, it still sounds like a dubious proposition to call it gift. *Those flagged messages are not gifts,* you're thinking. *They're demands.* Even when they speak altruistically (*I hope this email finds you well*) and philanthropically (*Please let me know if I can be of assistance*), emails can feel tactically motivated. But does that mean they're incapable of generosity? Don't let the organizational practicality of email deceive you. As Stephen Webb has said of gifting, so we might say of email: it is a communication in which exchange is not less than but always *more than* transaction. Gifting, Webb suggests, always has both a kind of reciprocal practicality to it (*Oh boy, I'm going to have figure out how to give a gift in return now*)—but also an extravagance, an excessiveness, a mystery.[42] Without the reciprocity, it wouldn't hold promise for

---

41. The sage writes that God "has made everything suitable for its time; moreover, he has put a sense of past and future into their minds, yet they cannot find out what God has done from the beginning to the end" (3:11). But the sage *also* writes that "the hearts of humans are full of evil; madness is in their hearts while they live, and after that they go to the dead" (9:3). Peters has helped me see the weird bifocal vision we need for the strangeness and the practicality of human exchange. Recognizing both the hugeness of the human heart and its madness seems to inform Peters's injunction that "the task is to find an account of communication that erases neither the curious fact of otherness at its core nor the possibility of doing things with words." Peters, *Speaking into the Air*, 21.

42. Webb, *Gifting God*, 3.

ongoing relationship. It would just be a vague spray of niceness. Without the mystery, it would just be a payment. Engaging the dialogic mode in your inbox might help you remember the quietly startling information that both you and your coworkers are mortals who work too much and sleep too little and who someday soon will come to death and into an encounter with the Maker whose conversation even the traumatized Job came to see as our final shelter.

Making the Mode Switch, Needing the Mode Craft

Crazy as it sounds to treat digital communications like email as a site for conversational encounter, I am recommending a mode switch from the cybernetic to the dialogic. It's not a shift that will eradicate our overwhelm; it is one that will give us contact with another and better sort of overwhelm. It's a mode switch that enables us to regain our feel for the awe and gratitude we feel in the dignified presence of the human.

But this mode switch brings with it a need for the artfulness that I will call mode craft. What are the skills and practices and dispositions we need to seek the community we yearn for? Let's take a few pages to tease out that mode craft by thinking not about what your email looks like, but what it sounds like. Let's think about how you *voice* your email.

CHAPTER 2.5

How to Write an Email Like You Talk

Mode/Switch Workshop

Goal: To improve your emails by remembering how your communications sound.

I'VE BEEN ENCOURAGING YOU to use email to create mutuality with your supervisor, your coworker, your client. But what does that look like?

Wrong question. A better query would be, what does it *sound* like? I understand that for a while in the early 2020s, it was a thing to send voice notes rather than emails. I'd like to suggest that if you want to craft a relationally intelligent email, you might start by thinking about what happens when you record a voice note.

How it begins.

Not everything starts by tapping "record" on Voice Memo. The recording starts when your diaphragm pushes out from beneath your ribs, and your lungs sink into your abdominal cavity and fill up with air. When your diaphragm returns to its place, it pushes against your lungs, shooting air out of your lungs and up into your windpipe and through your vocal folds. Put your finger alongside your laryngeal prominence—also known as your Adam's apple—and say something. You'll feel a vibration, a hum, a burr, some sort of sound, depending on the speed at which your vocal folds rub against each other. The effect resembles an inflated balloon when you release the air slowly and hear a funny squawk. All that humming CO_2 pushes up into your mouth, where your lips, tongue, and teeth shape—that is, *articulate*—the sound into meaningful noises. That's how the process of recording a voice note starts.

When you press "record."

Somewhere along the line, you'll have to start the voice note. Maybe you'll do that just after you inhale. But as soon as you utter a sound into the tiny condenser mic in your phone—also known as a MEMS, or microelectromechanical system—your voice's sound waves strike a membrane. Think of it as a tiny cookie hovering above a plate: the membrane trembles at the force of the sound waves, but the plate beneath the membrane remains static. The relationship between the two creates an electronic signal, which your phone can work with, capturing it in a voice note.

This process, which turns your spoken word into an electronic word, is called *transduction*. It's a nifty analogy for writing email as well.

When you craft an email, you transduce your speech into electronic form. The email becomes an extension of your body, a translation of your whole-personed way of speaking in the world. Your voice is always converting the *what* of your message into the *how* of your delivery. The same thing happens when you email someone.

So, let's try it out. Remember that sometimes mutuality means listening as much to the sound of your email as to its content. And by *sound*, I mean the force, pitch, quality, and rate of your communication.

Force

The first element of spoken communication is your speech's volume or force. It feels like the least subtle of the aspects of your communication. I mean, people can hear you, or they can't—right? But the force of your spoken communication affects how people stand in relation to you. If you're speaking too loudly, they will back up. If they can't hear you, they'll lean in or just walk away. But if "using the Force" is a critical aspect of oral speech craft, it's no less so when it comes to your email craft as well.

Take a quick look at this email promotional.

> **to:** _____ cc bcc
>
> **subject:** _____
>
> Dear Gail,
> We stand ready to do SO MUCH MORE THAN INVEST YOUR MONEY. We are prepared to make you an offer you CANNOT REFUSE. Consider us as your allies in dangerous times. WE ARE READY TO SAVE YOUR LIFE! Never have things been more RISKY than they are now.
> So let us be the rescuers of your account, your business, and your LIFE. You will be remiss if you miss this unmissable opportunity and let it miss you by!
> Blessings & best regards,
> GF STANSON & ASSOCIATES

Let's start with the physics of this absurd communication—that is, with the email's amplitude, its loudness or softness. This email bellows at Gail in intermittent all-caps and changes in font size and color. The phrasing is loud, too: the word choices shout out unrefusable offers, dangerous times, and saving Gail's life. And then, incongruously, the email sign-off includes the religiously extra phrasing of *Blessings and best regards*. Perhaps these jumbled visual effects and grammatical choices seemed like good ideas to GF Stanson & Associates as they sat, fingers hovering above the keyboard on a Saturday morning. *Everybody's pretty distracted today, right? Better make some moves to capture their attention.* But by turning things up to eleven, this email simply adds to the cacophony of today's attention economy. It becomes something Gail has to filter out.

This is a silly example. But as you craft your emails, you'd be wise to think about how your grammar increases the force of the electronic word. Email dynamics aren't just about physics, after all; they're about psychodynamics, too. They create a relational distance. When a coworker speaks too loudly one cubicle over, the sound invades your head, vibrating in your skull, tingling in your bones. Your emails, too, can get in your coworkers' heads. Or they can mumble and sound detached. How might we improve the email for GF Stanson? Let's start by changing its physics.

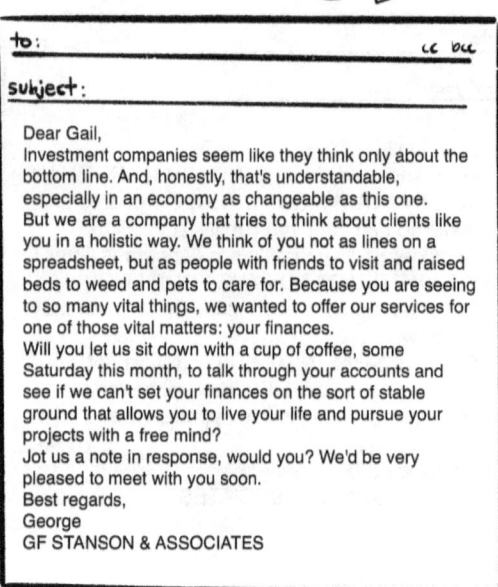

Notice the revisions:

- Got rid of the obnoxious caps
- Gentled the phrasing
- Maintained an appropriate distance, but also . . .
- . . . included a first name in the signature line.

These changes make the email close enough to the reader to open things for mutuality. But they don't speak with such force as to invade Gail's consciousness and force her to hit the little trash can just to filter out all the noise.

Now, let's think about a second element of vocal dynamics, the highness or lowness of your words, and how that could shape your electronic communication.

Pitch

In my experience as a teacher of oral rhetoric, people tend to use a narrow range of inflections. Alternatively, they may vary their pitches a lot but in a too predictable manner. Think of the former as the Tired Telemarketer and the latter as the Tour Guide. You can tell when someone's just reading a script to you over the phone, especially if their inflections are invariant. You can also tell when someone is trying to sound enthusiastic on a museum tour, especially if their pitches go up and down at exactly regular intervals, rising and falling at the beginnings and ends of each sentence.

When someone speaks with a very narrow range of inflections, they may well be doing so out of an abundance of caution. Enthusiasm in a public space can be risky. You might draw more attention than you want. You might be ridiculed. Accordingly, nervous speakers are prone to monotonal deliveries as a kind of personal hedging. But women speakers also hesitate to use upper ranges of their pitch because, at least in contemporary culture, such inflections are coded as weak or vulnerable. (Think of Elizabeth Holmes, the fraudulent entrepreneur at the head of Theranos, who addressed the world with a much remarked-upon bass voice. Or think of the mockery Hillary Clinton endured for her high-pitched laughter.) Think of inflectional range, then, as a sharing of oneself with the other. There are certain pitches I may be hesitant to share with you until I know you. There are certain pitches that public norms consider to be appropriately moderate or leaderly.

How might emails convert inflections well for a reader? Let's take another look at a sample email, this time from a manager to an employee.

Maddie means well. She's taking time out in the hurled pacing of running a store to jot a thank-you note. But the pitch is off. Why does it sound so flat?

- The phrasing moves slowly and ominously. But the wording of "It has come to our attention" also sounds vaguely surveillant. What Joe gets is a communication whose inflections sound both dry and scary.
- The overuse of prepositional phrases (*of* the displays, *at* the storefront *on* alternate Mondays *in* tandem, etc.) lowers the pitch of the email by slowing it down to .25 speed.
- The cliched language choices deaden the email's registers. This does not sound like a manager who wants to be writing a thank-you note, because her language inflections dampen rather than ignite.

When you're crafting an electronic word, listen to your email's frequencies. That doesn't just mean being transparently clear. It also means getting a feel for the vibrations of your prose. Do those vibrations hum along quickly? Or do they burr slowly and deeply? Both might be helpful for converting your spoken words into electronic speech.

Let's rewrite Maddie's email, shall we—and see if we can improve the inflections.

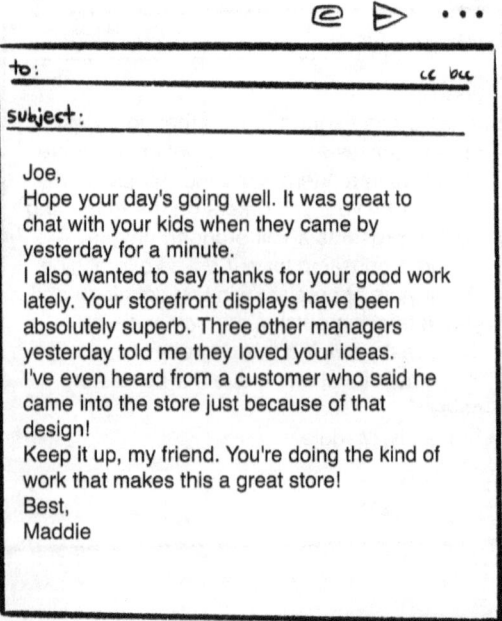

What's changed about this communication? Notice a few things:

- Mutuality happens with the quick reference to Joe's family.
- Thanks arrive quickly. There's no doubt what kind of message this is.
- The phrasing moves snappily, which increases the hertz of the email. It feels energetic, crackling, and alive.

Think about pitch as a way to share yourself with the other. Sometimes broaching the personal like Maddie did in the second email increases the inflectional range of professional communication. More of the self becomes hearable, so to speak. I think of humor as another way to change the pitch of an email. But however you share yourself or notice someone else's self, that sort of inflectional attentiveness can make an email pop.

Quality

I still remember how startling it was in a college Voice and Diction class, when my speech professor helped me notice my reliance on nasal resonance. I was talking through my nose, in other words. Michiganders do that. When I got a radio job, my supervisors told me I had a sibilant delivery, which at the time coded as "feminine."

Quality has to do with the feel of your voice. Breathiness. Nasality. Fry. Moistness. Chestiness. Sorry, those are uncomfortable words—mostly, I think, because they evoke very physical, very bodily conditions. But they also evoke cultural norms. Think of differences between ethnicities and genders and orientations. These all hook into painful rifts in American history. Think of Black NPR announcers who feel like they have to switch vocal qualities from "Black" to "White," in order to comply with "Standard American Dialect."

All that to say, talking about vocal quality is personally and politically tricky. And when it comes to email, it's that vocal quality that transduces cultural norms into the electronic word.

Nothing helps improve the vocal quality of your speech more than writing like you speak. I can't list rules for how to do this, any more than I can tell you how to "improve" your vocal quality. (Back when I was in college in the early 1990s, professors felt like they could say, "Stop doing that—you're doing it wrong." Fortunately, few people are foolish enough to talk that way about their colleagues' work today. Or so I hope.) How do you write like you talk? Try reading your emails aloud as you type. More importantly, read your emails aloud after you've typed them and before you've sent them. That gives you a chance to sound both authentic and professional—always a tricky tension for emailers.

And as for cultural norms—like sounding "Black" or "gay" or "bro-ey" or whatever—I'm afraid I can't give you rules for that sort of code-switching, either. The best I can do is to help you notice how much the aural quality of your prose affects your relationship with your reader. Vocal quality is all about *aliveness*. If you take out all the regional or cultural particularities of your writing, your email will sound dead. That sort of writing tends to sound like corporate-speak, using phrases like *doubling down* and *low-hanging fruit* and *adding on to what you just said*. But if, on the other hand, you speak in a way that only your immediate family could understand, your email will sound strange.

Please note that when I say write like you talk, I'm not saying write "naturally." Emailing is a bit of a performance. You're playing a role. Sometimes that role calls for a measure of formality, even elegance. But there are ways to speak with an appropriate grandeur *in your own way*. Think of how you might write wedding vows, for example, or how you might craft a funeral speech for an admired friend. That's writing in the grand style. Now, consider how you'd hiss instructions to a child in a crowded theater or give quick street directions to a passerby; that's what your plainer style sounds like. There are no explicit and stable rules for what style is right for what situation. But converting your vocal quality to lively emailing requires a good ear for the style you're trying for. Making your email audible in this way is a gift of mutuality.

Rate

Here's another email gem to consider. You can tell from the header what the problem is, but take a close look at the choices the writer makes and see if you can catch the email's sound.

> **to:** _____ **cc bcc**
> **subject:** _____
>
> Sooz Wud U send me yer contact info for Jake? I want to him for tomorrow's thing. lxh.
> Keithl

This email was written in a tearing hurry. The message may still achieve the desired result: Susie can probably figure out that she's supposed to send Jake's email and cellphone contact information. But quite apart from the explicit content of the message, think about what the pacing itself says. Perhaps the message functions like a friendly text for Susie; maybe she's entirely used to that sort of sloppy brevity from Keith. But the hurry of the email could also communicate disregard.

But there are other aspects of pacing that matter in email communication. Think about *chronemics*, or the temporal aspects of a message. If you pace your response quickly, it can communicate eagerness. It can also convey a sense that you just want to be *done* with the other person and their projects. But notice this chronemic element, too: we almost always experience email asynchronously. The promise of asynchrony is that we can respond whenever. The problem with asynchrony is we can be intruded upon—whenever.

Take a look at this marvel of asynchronous tact.

> **to:** ⎯⎯⎯⎯⎯⎯⎯⎯⎯⎯⎯⎯⎯⎯⎯⎯⎯⎯ cc bcc
> **subject:** ⎯⎯⎯⎯⎯⎯⎯⎯⎯⎯⎯⎯⎯⎯⎯⎯⎯⎯
>
> Frank, Sam, Andrew, and Tania -
> Yeah, so, our department's budget report is due by tomorrow 8 AM. I know it's late, but could you take a look at the attached and send me your edits. Tonight, or in the next 6 hrs would be great. I'
> If you have suggestions for next month's budget, too, that's great.
> Plus we have a PPO for our RFT due Thursday. Thoughts?
> In the trenches,
> JM

The email above feels blatantly pushy. But there are ways to make emails *subtly* pushy. Even the time of day I send the note conveys something chronemically. When I send an email at ten o'clock at night, I may feel a little martyr-like: "Here I am, *still* working on a Friday evening." That martyr sensibility may well show up in unobvious (to you) urgencies of style—like the probably unintentionally anxious line, "Looking forward to hearing your feedback on this!"

Let's try to revise JM's email to make it more tactful in its timing.

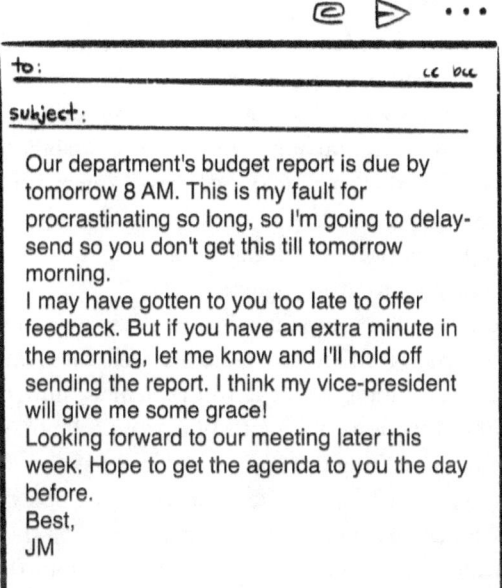

In Sarah Marshall's podcast *You're Wrong About*, the host and guest discuss these sorts of tacit forms of pushiness. They encourage including a phrase like the following, not just in tardy emails like JM's above, but in *all* your professional communications: *I may be sending this message at a time when you're not working. Life is full of other good things besides email, so please don't feel obligated to respond immediately!*[1]

That language raises the potential for generosity in oral communication. When you're talking to someone and you sense that they're not quite ready to answer your question, you pull back and say, "Hey, some other time. No worries." Good talk isn't concerned about efficiency so much as giving space for more good talk. Similarly, you may need to change up the cadence email of communication, making it more open to mutuality.

When I coach public speakers, I tend to say, "Fill the room with your sound." Perhaps that's a good norm for email communication as well: to write so that your voice comes into the room with them. Emailing for mutuality offers the gift of presence.

---

1. Petersen, "How Email Took Over the World w. Anne Helen Petersen."

A Final Word

We have traced the dynamics of speech converted into electronic words. But everything I've said here can be summed in a single maxim: *as often as you can, let email be gift*. The digital word can all too easily become transactional, but if by transaction we mean accountability, fairness, and ongoing relationship—that's a good thing! I have been much helped by Stephen Webb's description of gifting as an exchange that's never less than, but always *more than*, a transaction. Gifting, he suggests, always has about it an extravagance, a surplus, a surprisingness.[2]

There's some wisdom in the maxim, *email the way you talk*. But this chapter's workshop suggests another maxim as well: *email the way you give*. You know what I'm talking about if you remember how your everyday speech sometimes functions like a gift. When you call out, "Morning!" to me, you are doing something that's conventional and yet, at the same time, something that you don't *have* to do. You could just nod or do nothing. But that act of spoken exchange puts another person on the lookout for a way to reciprocate. Maybe not at your enthusiastic volume (because it's before coffee, after all). Or not at that pitch (because of something awkward that happened yesterday). Or not with that quality (because that's just not how other people talk). Or not at that rate (that is, right *now*). But you've opened space for reciprocation *of some kind*, and that's a gift.

Similarly, voice-noting your email generally means crafting it with energy and dynamism, but not with invasive *force*. It means *inflecting* it with the emotional transparency that often accompanies authentic self-disclosure. It means sharing a *quality* that's your own but also open to the other. It means pressing send on the email without anxiety about response, trusting that the other person will, at some point and in some way, get back to you. (Maybe their delay is a gift, in itself.) Keeping these speech dynamics before us as we type may help us to conduct our email sendings with the force and inflection and quality and rate of gift.

2. Webb, *Gifting God*, 3.

CHAPTER 3

Saying Things

This chapter discusses the mode of dissemination, asking what becomes possible when one-way communication proceeds bottom-up as well as top-down in our organizations.

THE ONLY PIECE OF furniture in my family's new living room in Grand Rapids is a red canvas lawn chair. I'm not in the chair; I'm on the floor, kneeling before an Xfinity router whose only signal at the moment is a relentlessly blinking red light.

"Hi, thank you for calling Xfinity," the bot on the tech support line begins. "This call may be monitored or recorded. For more information about our privacy practices, visit us at xfinity.com/privacy." Little does this machinic entity know it, but I am its nemesis. My only goal is scheming *against* its virtual assistance, conniving for a way to mess with its script and to weasel past it to the human help I think I need as quickly as possible. The imperturbable voice says, "I have the number for your street. Is this the account you're calling about?" I am suddenly unsure about my vocal obligations. Should I answer with upwardly inflected tones and chipper friendliness? That feels dumb. On the other hand, what does a dull, flat tone say about me? Am I only cheerful when it's likely to do me good? I finally answer that, yes, that is my house number, and I hear the sound effect of keyboard typing, as if the virtual assistant is sitting at a monitor, squinting down a list of files, pursing its lips, and then smiling before clicking on my name and information.

"If you are calling about your bill, press 1," the voice continues. "If you're calling to check your account, press 2 . . ." As it turns out, none of these options work for me. But if I groan into the phone, the machine replies, "I'm sorry, that was not one of the options. Press 4 and the pound key to hear the menu again." Suddenly, I hear the voice say crisply, "Thank you, and goodbye." This is not the first time in the past few weeks that I have been defeated by a machine. But each time feels dismal.

I punch the tech support phone number in again. And a little astonishingly, by dint of digital hopscotch, I dodge the bot and connect to a flesh-and-blood technician. Heaven comes down, glory fills my soul, and the technician arrives on the line, full-voiced, jovial, and reassuring. It feels like someone has stepped into my empty living room, slinging her own canvas lawn chair to sit down next to mine, knee to knee, laughing at that silly router over there next to the wall.

"Okay, Mr. Mattson, here's what I want you to do . . ." I'm not sure those are her exact words. All that matters is that finally we are *talking*. Sure, her first idea does not work, but there's another. And, yes, her second idea also fails, and now her voice is sounding a little strained, but she has more ideas still. I am struck by the inadequacy of our usual conversational norms. What should the back-and-forth sound like when the person you're talking to starts reading lines from a script designed by a marketing team? What does turn-taking look like when this conversation is being monitored, perhaps to compare this technician's performance to a chatbot now in the wings, ready to take over her job?

The technician breaks silence and asks me what it's like living in Grand Rapids. She tells me that she's been staying with her mom since the pandemic started and that she really likes the NBA. But as the solution to the router continues to elude us, I notice she begins to shuffle, a little confusedly, among different styles of delivery. "Mr. Mattson, thank you for your patience as we resolve this technical difficulty," she says like a radio announcer—and then stops abruptly. Then she sighs and say, "Is the app just sitting there? Okaaaaay, let's try something else." The air feels laden with unease. I reach over and rest my hand on the router like an inept faith healer. The technician offers me thanks for hanging in there so patiently. A few minutes later, she offers these same thanks again, as if she's forgotten where she is in the script. The conversation having begun so cheerfully is deflating rapidly.

I tell this story because it dramatizes the way digital overwhelm pervades remote interactions. The stubbornly resistant router, along with the baffling cabling of my new home—a half-dozen coaxials all a-dangle by the basement power box—disrupts what the tech support person and I are trying to do. Our affective responses are a confusing mix of misplaced optimism, fatigued irritation, and a Midwestern urgency to Be a Nice Person. One thing was clear: this digital overwhelm was not going to be resolved through the dialogic mode. The next day, a service truck pulled into our driveway, resolving our "connectivity issues" in about ten minutes.

Two Models to Explain Digiwhelm

My story is a cutdown of the fuller complexity faced by rising professionals doing remote work of many different kinds. My situation was describable in a linear model of communication: source (me), message (help!), receiver (Xfinity support personnel), feedback (try this, Mr. Mattson). But the digital overwhelm I heard in the tech support agent's voice by the end of our call was more complicated. She's probably fielding more than one customer at a time, dealing with her manager, thinking about her performance on the recording of our call, and worrying whether a chatbot is about to replace her.

What could cure the digiwhelm of rising professionals conducting hybrid and remote communication within and on behalf of their organizations? Here are two attempted prescriptions.[1] The first is technologically focused, suggesting we should improve our tools; the second is therapeutically focused, saying we should improve our techniques. What's striking about these explanations is that although they use very different models of communication (the technologists assume an information systems model and the therapist assumes an interactive or dialogic model), they agree on the underlying *mode* of communication. They both prescribe better back-and-forth communication in a way that will remind you of the dialogic mode. (In contrast with those two prescriptions, I'm going to recommend a mode switch, as you might have guessed.)

We need better tools.

One diagnosis of my digiwhelm would focus on the capabilities of our tools, especially by aligning digital tools with human goals. Peters helps trace this approach back to the Cold War era when the vast explanatory power of information theory was first becoming apparent.[2] Today, there's an ever-expand-

---

1. Following John Durham Peters, I call these two explanations for digiwhelm as technical and therapeutic. See Peters, *Speaking into the Air*, 22–31.

2. "The technicians of communication are a diverse breed," but they all "want to mimic the angels by mechanical or electronic means." Peters, *Speaking into the Air*, 29. Peters cites the AT&T slogan as an exemplar of this mindset: "telecommunity is our goal; telecommunications is our means" (29).

ing field of trade journalism urging companies to adopt artificial intelligence to improve technical support and customer engagement.[3] There are potential risks from AI's tendency to eliminate jobs or to hallucinate information. "But done well, an AI-enabled customer service transformation can unlock significant value for the business—creating a virtuous circle of better service, higher satisfaction, and increasing customer engagement."[4]

My experience of the robot on the Xfinity line was that it did not know much about me, that it had little sense of context, that it could not understand my emotional responses to the situation, and that its decision trees were too limited for what I needed. But the large language networks of recent AI could handle these tasks far better than the bot I spoke with. In fact, AI platforms could probably handle the work just as well or even better than the human technician I spoke with.[5]

This perspective on improving tech-based interactions with clients came clear for me on the last day of 2021—just as the Omicron variant of COVID-19 was appearing in the US—when I interviewed Joe Barrera, who works for Phaidon International's subcompany EPM Scientific. He's not a tech support guy but a recruiter. Still, he makes hundreds of calls a day, seeking out the partners the company needs for health care advertisement production. Like many rising professionals conducting digital interactions with clients, Joe's job requires patience and deftness in keeping people in conversations they don't necessarily want to be in. And Joe seems artful at this. But even someone as technically and interpersonally put-together as Joe can be stressed out by the work of client calls. The phone rings, and fifty questions pop into his head, questions like, *Will I know what to say? Will they be pissed at my interruption of their day? Is what I have to say a huge waste of time?*

Joe told me a story about a time a call came in and, instead of answering, he swiped the hang-up button. He felt so embarrassed about the story that at first he asked me not to share it (and then changed his mind by the end of the interview). But the AI enthusiasts would not be surprised by this moment of overwhelm. Employees like Joe, these pundits would say, need better, savvier collaboration with AI platforms. Tech support enabled by large language network machines would be a net gain for both sides of the service provider/customer experience aisle. Rising professionals would be doing less of the depersonalizing work of placing hundreds of calls daily, and customers would more quickly find the answers they need to run the

3. McCann, "Can ChatGPT-4 Elevate Your Customer Service?"
4. Das et al., "Next frontier of customer engagement."
5. Rafalski, "Instant Assistance."

tools they use.[6] Instead of worrying that machines will replace people doing online technical support, we should recognize the possibilities for improving AI and providing people like Joe a chance to do other, more creative work less vulnerable to digital overwhelm.[7]

We need better talk.

Another explanation for digital breakdown in remote professional work would be therapeutic. The malfunctioning communication with the router that I endured with the Xfinity technician are symptomatic of a larger psychological and sociological problem: overdependence on cyber-communication as opposed to face-to-face conversation. Sure, the pandemic made virtuality a necessity for a while. But humane conversations are best conducted through the vulnerability of in-person talk. This therapeutic account of communication breakdown traces back a long time—at least as far back as Cold War communication theory in the work of Carl Rogers, which, as John Durham Peters notes, offered therapeutic correctives for lonely people in a mass society.[8] Today, psychologists and sociologists like Sherry Turkle (she straddles both disciplines) argue that technological connections have depleted our capacities for genuine conversation. My intuition that I just wanted to talk with a human, she would say, is an instinct worth trusting, as opposed to the naively optimistic promises of digital technologists.[9]

In *Reclaiming Conversation*, Turkle borrows a metaphor from Henry David Thoreau's *Walden*. In his little house in the woods, he had three chairs, which Turkle says we need in our lives and workplaces today. The first chair represents contemplative conversations with oneself. The second

---

6. Trivedi, "10 Ways Artificial Intelligence Can Improve Customer Service."

7. Paul R. Daugherty and H. James Wilson represent this perspective, arguing that companies have been focusing on the linear, mechanistic possibilities of machines, neglecting the adaptive powers of AI. See Daugherty and Wilson, *Human + Machine*.

8. Peters, *Speaking into the Air*, 27.

9. Turkle's attitude towards technology in community has shifted over the decades. She greeted the arrival of the personal computer in the 1980s with critical questions about personality and community but also with optimism for new forms of digital community. She asked, for example, about "where we stand in the world of artifact" and about "a link between who we are and what we have made, between who we are and what we might create, between who we are and what, through our intimacy with our own creations, we might become." Turkle, *Second Self*, 18. For her basic hopefulness for computers in human society, see *Second Self*, 298–99. Her more recent works, however, have taken an urgently prophetic tone. In *Alone Together*, she warns people against enthusiastic reliance on digital innovation, which has made us lonely and less capable of empathy.

includes the twosomes and threesomes of interpersonal interaction of romance, friendship, and collegiality. The third chair entails conversation for civic life, representing the deliberations of democracy.[10] Turkle's appropriation of Thoreau's metaphor situates her work within the dialogic commitments to open-endedness, vulnerability, and difference discussed in this book's first chapter.[11]

Despite some important counter-arguments, there's a lot to be said for Turkle's recommendations for recovering in-person conversation.[12] There's research suggesting that rising professionals need physical presence in order to figure out the subtle cues of workplace culture—and the non-subtle ones, too.[13] I interviewed Kelly Folkertsma, a just-graduated health communication major, now doing intake at a clinic during the COVID-19 pandemic. Although her job put her between digital and physical interactions, as she inputted data for just-arriving patients, quite a lot of her work came down to her ability to keep people talking in distressing circumstances. The patients would stagger into the lobby, balk at wearing a mask, and demand to see a doctor. Kelly told me about one Monday in the pandemic when their department was so jammed with patients that she was telling people it would be five hours before they could see a doctor. A given patient might nod his head, turn to sit down, and then be right back within the hour, convinced his condition had worsened. Kelly felt irritated and empathetic at the same time. She'd go back through the clinic doors and try to advocate for the patient. The nurse in charge would wearily say no. Back out Kelly went, trying to placate the patient. Sometimes, the best thing she could do for the sufferers was to listen to their meandering stories about their families and admire grandbaby pictures on somebody's cracked phone screen.[14]

---

10. As Thoreau noted a little wryly, "When visitors came in larger and unexpected numbers [to his little house in the woods], there was but the third chair for them all, but they generally economized the room by standing up." See *Walden*, 184.

11. Turkle, *Reclaiming Conversation*, 46–50.

12. Other interviewees helped me understand situations where remote work is better for nonconforming persons or for people of color or for women. The research data I'm pointing to includes an interview with Olivia Winkowitsch, who noted the problems that come with proximity to her male boss. Sight lines, odors, and posture can all become intense areas of performative concern in the physical company of a manager. My interview with Em Orendorff also suggested ways that queer folk may find it easier to find companies hospitable to nonconforming identity—and also to signify their queerness easily to others. Turkle seems likely to agree: "Sometimes face-to-face conversation is not the right tool for a particular job." Turkle, *Reclaiming Conversation*, 56.

13. Emanuel, Harrington, and Pallais, "Power of Proximity to Coworkers."

14. Kelly Folkertsma, interview by Craig Mattson, February 4, 2022.

The Mode beneath the Models

A little stocktaking is in order. Although the technological and the therapeutic perspectives we've just discussed use language deriving from their very different communication models, they are saying much the same thing: *we can cure digiwhelm with better reciprocity.* The AI pundits adopt the language of information processes and systems and encourage a kind of cybernetic interaction between humans and machines. Turkle speaks as a clinical psychologist with a background in psychoanalysis, urging attentiveness, empathy, interiority, and authenticity for the sake of deep conversation. But both perspectives are interested in improving communication as a reciprocal process, whether through better-designed technology or therapeutic technique.

If the digital overwhelm were due to interpersonal complexities alone, these two approaches would be just fine. But working professionals face a digital overwhelm that is far more than interpersonal. Doing hybrid and remote work means being embedded in digital environments that shape what we can do with, and who we are to, others. Thomas Rickert describes this as our ambient experience of the technologized world.[15]

This chapter makes the case that organizational culture in general and rising professionals in particular need more than the dialogic mode to work with each other and to deal with our digital ecologies. We also need the mode of dissemination. To *disseminate* is to scatter messaging, like a farmer spreading seed on soil. For the rising professional this sort of scatter requires you to speak up in situations where you worry you won't be heard. But this worry mostly derives from our overdependence on the dialogic mode, which *thrives* on the sense that the other person hears and understand. The disseminative mode works differently. You *speak up*, not in order to express your innermost self to another, but in order to *act with* another. Speak up to sync up, in other words.

In making this argument, I have my work cut out for me. Unilateral communication is not highly regarded in organizational communication—and with good reason! All too often scattered messaging supports the worst

---

15. Not that Rickert thinks of ambience as unique to our time: he locates ambience in ancient Greece and in cave paintings, suggesting that an environmental awareness of the world's enveloping us and, in a sense, collaborating with us, is a recurrent human experience. But of ambience he notes how "the surrounding environment becomes understood as more than a neutral, objective stage on which human drama and activity play out or the objective, at-hand material we source, craft, and use." This ambient perspective contrasts markedly with the technique- or technology-focused approaches that Turkle and the AI folks are so excited about. See Rickert, *Ambient Rhetoric*, 9.

sorts of managerialism.¹⁶ Add to this the dissemination of bullying, racist remarks, sexually harassing comments, and unilateral communication can feel even more threatening. So, let's just concede up front that our intuitive preference for the dialogic mode makes a certain sense! At the same time, if you think back to moments when you felt ostracized for reasons of sexual identity or gender or race, you may be a little startled how often the destructive communication happened conversationally.¹⁷ You may have found yourself walking away from an interaction saying, *Did she just say what I think she said?*—and then adding, *And why did I say what I said?*

My plan in what follows is to examine the role of dissemination in three rising professionals' experiences of digiwhelm. In each of these case studies, you'll notice their uneasiness about unilateral communication and their intuition that organizational communication should be conversational. But you'll also see ways that the dialogic is not entirely sufficient unto the day. Pragmatic and productive workplace culture needs broadcast as well as conversation, especially when it comes to relatively disempowered practitioners doing their work immersed in technologized environments.

Stories of Uneasy Dissemination

Broadcast alongside conversation.

Paige Rogers graduated in December of 2020 and, after a brief, strange stint for Microsoft, which mostly entailed adding keywords to paid advertising accounts, she began work for a California-based social enterprise called Angel Aid. The mission of the company, as the website says, is to offer "mental health and wellness services to rare families through sustainable psychosocial training, transformative retreats, and a connective caregiver-to-caregiver multilingual network."¹⁸ The work focuses on those giving care to caregivers for victims of the some seven thousand rare diseases for which there is no cure. The company is especially alert to the "raregivers" who care for suffering children, some of whom don't make it to the age of five because of these diseases.¹⁹

---

16. Few communication theorists have discussed the importance of speaking and listening carefully within organizations more than Stanley Deetz. See, for example, Deetz, *Transforming Communication, Transforming Business*.

17. For a valuable discussion of the harmful organizational communication, see Lutgen-Sandvik and Davenport Sypher, eds., *Destructive Organizational Communication*.

18. *Angel Aid*, "Passion with a Purpose."

19. *Angel Aid*, "Passion with a Purpose."

At the time Paige was hired, the company was working to address the isolation of "raregivers" during the COVID-19 pandemic. Angel Aid created virtual meetings to provide support, mostly targeting overwhelmed mothers isolated with children in conditions of rare disease. The company's approach hoped to use the dialogic mode to address the needs of these parents. But Paige's part in this work was largely disseminative. As the company's community manager, a position that entailed marketing and partnership-seeking, she spent much of her time informing parents what Angel Aid was in the first place—and then trying to persuade them to join a support group online.

It was a heavy lift at times. *You don't want to say,* Paige explained to me, *hey, your life is terrible, so you should come to an Angel Aid meeting.* But at the same time, as Angel Aid's website notes, "The caregiving burden on rare families is unimaginable, particularly for mothers."[20] Paige's communications featured weekly emails trying to draw people to the meetings. At first, she got very little response at all. She tried changing her email address. She experimented with a more personal voice, connecting her own experience with the mission of the organization. What seemed to help most was when her boss, Cristol Barrett O'Loughlin, went to a conference. People would meet her, hear her speak, watch her TEDx talk, and then want to join a meeting.[21]

Paige also helped the company with the online meetings, although her role was largely as a technician. Sometimes she offered a small talk to a parent just joining the meeting, an especially vital contribution if only one mother showed up. But by the time, Paige was interviewing with me, she had managed to garner five to ten attenders at a time for these meetings. Mostly, she kept her camera off during the meetings, while the mothers spoke with each other or talked with an Angel Aid facilitator. Paige sometimes felt a little uncomfortable with how her job as a disseminator positioned her in relation to these conversations:

> I feel a little weird sometimes. Actually I feel a little bit like a peeping Tom because I do not participate 'cause . . . I actually don't have any affiliation with rare disease. That doesn't . . . run in my family, so I'm really just there . . . helping them get into the Zoom, making sure they don't have any technical questions. . . . I'm just kind of there listening, and I collect quotes from them to use for marketing purposes. I try to take video snippets.[22]

20. *Angel Aid,* "Relief for Raregivers Who Need it Most."
21. O'Loughlin, "Caring for the Caregivers."
22. Paige Rogers, interview by Craig Mattson, January 3, 2022.

Paige felt ambivalent about her work and about the mission of her company. As a Christian, she wondered about the effectiveness of the company's recommendations for what she described as New Age spirituality. As a marketer, she wondered what her role should be in the company's conversations. She soon transitioned out of Angel Aid to another nonprofit.

Broadcast replacing conversation.

Mallory Donaldson was slow to realize she was professionally overwhelmed. But once she figured out the excessive nature of the work, she made a rule for herself: every time she got frustrated at work, she had to apply for another job after work. She called these her frustration applications. "So, if I got really frustrated, I'd be putting in a lot of job applications. And if I wasn't really frustrated, then it was just like a one-off way to blow steam." She filled out quite a few frustration applications because her company malfunctioned a lot. She described those malfunctions as "the right hand didn't know what the left hand is doing," making her feel stuck in the in-between. Once, when a manager came to her with an extra project, Mallory explained that although she couldn't do the project immediately—she was embedded in other work already assigned to her—she would be willing to take it up later. She then got an irritated message from the top saying, "Well, I have way more important things to do than this." Mallory felt a little stunned that her efforts at boundary-setting were met so stiffly, so obliviously.

When a trusted manager left near the end of the year, Mallory and her team again felt anxious. They had built great camaraderie, and the manager had definitely been a part of that. When the company management called a meeting on Zoom to announce the new leader, the administration seemed pleased with their announcement. The normally cheerful group team listened in silence to the information that the person transitioning to the managerial position was the very person Mallory had tussled with about extra work and personal boundaries. Not long after, one of Mallory's frustration applications turned up a new job, and she took the leap.

In our conversation, Mallory seemed leery of the ways that broadcast too often replaced conversation in organizational culture. These broadcasts, she noticed, move downward to early professionals more easily than they moved back up to the management. But they also shaped interactions on the ground. At one point in our interview, she noted the ways that gender complicates organizational communication:

> I do think that especially in certain fields, maybe, there's an expectation for traditionally women to ... be the note taker at that

meeting or they'll be in charge of all of these birthday parties and recognition events that don't contribute to their . . . movement up in the workplace. But it's still kind of the expectation that if we're quiet long enough, the girl in the room will raise their hand.[23]

Again, I was struck that, for Mallory, organizational communication suffers a troubled relationship between conversation and broadcast. Of the three case studies I analyze here, Mallory's may be most leery of dissemination. For her part, reciprocal conversation was almost always the better route.[24]

Broadcast disguised as conversation.

What makes Joycee Black so good at organizational communication is that she is a no-phony-cake kind of person. The phrase "phony cake," she told me, comes from her Ohio roots and refers to the dubious art of pretending somebody you distrust is actually a good friend. Still, even a no-phony-cake person like Joycee can tell a story when she confused a broadcast for a conversation.

Joycee was sobbing, she told me. "Ugly-crying" was one word she used during our interview. "Boo-hooing" was another. She had been watching a diversity, equity, and inclusion video with some colleagues on Zoom. If you've gone through a professional development seminar at work, you know that training videos aren't usually written and directed by the film greats of our time. I don't think Joycee had expected this presentation to move her so much.

The story centered on the experience of a Black man, wearing sweats, who enters a courthouse. Everywhere he turns, he is stared at by White citizens who clearly don't want him near them, especially not on the same elevator. The video follows the White folks as they enter a courtroom and then shows the deputy calling out, "All rise for the Honorable . . ." Then, the camera pulls focus to the very African American who had been, just moments before, wearing informal clothes, but who is now ascending to the bench in judicial robes. The man, formerly judged suspect, is now himself the judge.

The depiction of a Black citizen who'd done everything right but who still faced contempt was abruptly shattering to Joycee. The story came all too close to her own experience as a woman of Haitian descent, an Ohioan

---

23. Anonymous, Interview with Craig Mattson, February 18, 2022.

24. The name of this interviewee has been changed to respect the interviewee's request. Anonymous, interview with Craig Mattson, February 18, 2022.

who had migrated to Chicago. And now, she found herself in a situation intended to cultivate interracial dialogue and mutuality. And she was sobbing instead at how this video had gone from being a workshop to being an unveiling of Black experience in American professional life.

She flipped off her webcam and gave way to some serious feelings all on her lonesome.

From what she told me, it's not clear that her colleagues were *opposed* to workplace dialogue about matters of race. In fact, Joycee seemed to genuinely like her colleagues—maybe not as best friends, but nonetheless as decent people to work with. It was a synchronous meeting, usually a space where people can converse. Why couldn't they talk right then about what was troubling her and how it might matter for their professional comportment? But in that moment, Joycee's teammates were signaling that the meeting was not a time for talk so much as a time for spectatorship. *Let's watch this video, do this training, and get back to work.*

When Joycee could bear to flip her webcam back on, she wore an expression she likes to call the Face. During our interview, she showed me what this expression looks like. She was clowning a little with me, but the look *was* a little fearsome: strong, set, ironclad, giving away nothing. Whatever else the Face signifies, it does not invite the back-and-forth of the dialogic mode.[25]

What These Stories Share in Common

Each of these case studies shows how remotely conducted organizational communication (invitations to support meetings, announcements of personnel changes, DEI training videos) is haunted by the ideal of conversation. Paige's stories showed the most appreciation for the work of getting the word out: being a message-sender was quite simply her job as a marketer, a job that, even at its most technical, supported a company's mission to show care for needy people. But she also confessed an uneasy relationship to the conversations her broadcasted communication was intended to support. Was she a lurker, a peeping tom, when she kept her camera off and surveilled for parts of the meeting that would make effective cut-down videos for later sharing? Mallory's stories suggested that her experience of dissemination was darker than Paige's. For Mallory, one-way communication from the higher-ups didn't allow for the needed feedback. Like Paige, Joycee is good at dissemination. I've witnessed her as a public speaker, and she's eloquent and funny and comfortable with a crowd. But like Mallory, Joycee

25. Joycee Black, interview by Craig Mattson, March 4, 2022.

felt stunned by a dissemination that she had expected to be a dialogue. Her intense affective response came from a surprised grief at the gaps that had opened between her and others in the Zoom room.

Why Organizations Need the Disseminative Mode

The intuitions of these research participants tend to align with the reigning commonsense of our time, that reciprocal communication is always better than unilateral messaging.[26] But there are initial reasons it's worthwhile to at least question this intuition.

1. Organizational mission creates imperatives that are so demanding that hierarchical decision-making is essential. Given the importance of what a company or church or nonprofit is trying to accomplish, it may not be practicable to flatten out the decision-making process through extended dialogue.[27]
2. Organizational communities must make room for people of radically different experiences. Sometimes these experiences are so far removed from other people's lives that even intense conversation does little more than deepen those differences. As Peters notes, "We might like each other less the more we understood about one another."[28] This seems to have been Joycee's experience with her White colleagues and her rationale for putting on the Face rather than trying to explain her disappearance from the Zoom room or any tear smudges on her face.
3. Organizational work often requires cooperation more than intimacy. A pragmatic approach to organizational communication would suggest that members of teams can coordinate what they do even without

---

26. "In certain quarters dialogue has attained something of a holy status," writes Peters. "It is held up as the summit of human encounter, the essence of liberal education, and the medium of participatory democracy. By virtue of its reciprocity and interaction, dialogue is taken as superior to the one-way communiques of mass media and mass culture." Peters, *Speaking into the Air*, 33.

27. This claim finds support in my own organizational research among social enterprises. In one case in particular, Jos Knowles of the organization Beyond the Streets talked about a hiring conflict in her company in which some of her team wanted to hire someone who could provide pastoral care for the employees, while the job description was focused on a set of service requirements in support of the company's mission. This conflict between the interpersonal needs of the staff and the pursuit of the company's mission drives my observation in this chapter about dialogue and mission. Mattson, *Why Spiritual Capital Matters*, 47.

28. Peters, *Speaking into the Air*, 30.

knowing each other's hearts.²⁹ Paige did not share her higher-up's New Age spirituality, but she could understand the worthwhileness of meditation well enough to market Angel Aid's services.

Faced with the uneasiness and occasional digiwhelm evidenced in these case studies, it is all too easy to parrot the commonsense about how we all need to talk more, how what we need is better communication, how differences melt away in face-to-face exchange. These commonplaces can be briefly, sporadically helpful. But as Peters notes, dialogue regularly fails us, especially when people use supposedly reciprocal communication to abuse and to fight rather than to inform and persuade.³⁰

Dialogue can also lock us into a logic of retribution. *You said that to me? Well, okay, fine. Now, I got something to say back to you.* Mallory and Joycee's experience of sexism and racism in the workplace cause them to wish for redress. And they are right to wish for that. Without reciprocity, an organization's community would be unjust. But if there is *only* retribution—if the only logic of communication we can use is the back-and-forth, the tit for tat, then we will lose our hold on other values that matter in our communities as much as justice does. That's why we need dissemination: it encourages other sorts of virtues and practices: Peters lists these as "hospitality, gift giving, forgiveness, and love."³¹ I would add to his list *wisdom*, without which we cannot discern how to make the mode changes our work requires.

Why Wisdom Requires Dissemination

If you want to challenge the commonsense assumptions of your own time, there's no better way to do that than to read really old books—like the

---

29. See Pearce and Cronen, *Making Social Worlds*. Their accounts of the construction and coordination of meaning have been influential in my own thinking for this book.

30. Peters notes that our tremendous respect for one-on-one dialogue can "risks missing the defects in the notion of reciprocity. One-way communication is not necessarily bad. Reciprocity can be violent as well as fair. War and vengeance obey a logic of strict reciprocity as much as do conversation and trade. Justice demands an eye for an eye and a tooth for a tooth. Its underlying logic says, one turn deserves another. This crime, we say, warrants that punishment; this commodity, that price. If nothing but reciprocity governed social relations, life would be a monotonous round of quid pro quo. Social life would be a cycle of payment, rather than of gifts. Without reciprocity life would be grossly unfair. With only reciprocity, it would be desolate." Peters, *Speaking into the Air*, 56.

31. Peters, *Speaking into the Air*, 56.

book of Proverbs. The most counterintuitive element of this collection of wise sayings and speeches is that its personification of wisdom is not as a deep-voiced, middle-aged, male philosopher. Wisdom doesn't get pictured as a Socrates figure, who wants nothing more than to draw you into extended one-on-one conversation. Nor is Wisdom depicted as an romantic intimate.[32] Instead, we see—hear!—a strong woman with a bold voice standing in the middle of the street, belting out what amounts to a stand-up routine. The Woman Wisdom heckles passersby, trying to awaken them to wisdom, or *chokmah* in Hebrew.[33]

> 32. In contrast, the Song of Songs, another wisdom book, uses sexual dialogue between a beloved woman and her lover to pursue its communicative aims. There the conversation opens with a similarly abrupt call—"Let him kiss me with the kisses of his mouth!"—but the woman's cry is an invitation to intimacy, mutuality, and equality, to which the lover responds. "The echo expresses the full reciprocity of their love relationship," writes commentator Ellen Davis. "But their expressions are not quite identical. Each calls the other by a distinctive term of endearment. These are not adequately rendered by the NRSV translation, 'my love' and 'my beloved'—as though they used active and passive forms of the same word. She calls him dôdî, 'my darling, my lover.' He most often calls her 'my comrade/friend' (ra'yatî), a term that implies a relationship of equality . . ." Davis, *Proverbs, Ecclesiastes, The Song of Songs*, 247. It's important that the Proverbs go out of their way to depict Woman Wisdom as the opposite of an intimate figure. She is contrasted with the depiction of the Woman Folly, another disseminator in public spaces but one with a sexualized cast:

> The foolish woman is loud;
>   she is ignorant and knows nothing.
> She sits at the door of her house,
>   on a seat at the high places of the town,
> calling to those who pass by,
>   who are going straight on their way,
> "You who are simple, turn in here!"
>   And to those without sense she says,
> "Stolen water is sweet,
>   and bread eaten in secret is pleasant" (Proverbs 9:13–17, NRSV).

> The word "loud" there can be translated as "seductive," which in conjunction with her posture, gives her invitation an erotic charge (Proverbs 9:13, ESV).
> 33. It's not that Proverbs *never* depicts private, dialogic communication: "Listen, my child" is a common conversation piece throughout the book. But the wisdom personified in this book is Wisdom the Public Speaker. Readers of Peters, *Speaking into the Air*, will recognize my persistent indebtedness to his reading of Jesus' parables, which I use as a guide for my reading of Woman Wisdom's broadcasted speech. Peters helps me to notice in Lady Wisdom what he notices in Jesus' approach to communication: "a radically public, exoteric mode of dispersing meanings—even though the hearers often fail to catch the hint—in which the audience sorts out the significance for itself" (53). Peters helps me to notice, too, Lady Wisdom's "suspension of fair exchange" in her indiscriminate dissemination of a dinner invitation. Why draw on Proverbs at all? Why not use the sermons of Jesus instead? This book makes use of wisdom literature,

> Wisdom cries out in the street;
> > in the squares she raises her voice.
> At the busiest corner she cries out;
> > at the entrance of the city gates she speaks:
> "How long, O simple ones, will you love being simple?"[34]

Chokmah calls to passersby in the busiest and most distracting and overwhelming of contexts. Although wisdom might feel like it invites quiet conversation and low-voiced contemplation, *chokmah* is here represented as a public speaker scattering messages. When we are not talking *about* wisdom, but actually listening *to* Wisdom, what we get is a broadcast, not a dialogue.

> Does not wisdom call
> > and understanding raise her voice?
> On the heights, beside the way,
> > at the crossroads she takes her stand;
> beside the gates in front of the town,
> > at the entrance of the portals she cries out:
> To you, O people, I call,
> > and my cry is to all who live.
> O simple ones, learn prudence;
> > acquire intelligence, you who lack it.
> Hear, for I will speak noble things,
> > and from my lips will come what is right.[35]

Does Lady Wisdom call because no one is willing to converse? Perhaps. Will conversations ensue if people respond to the call? Certainly. But *chokmah*'s cry also discloses the world to us in the busiest intersections of our lives. Why then does Wisdom cry out rather than engage a conversation?

---

because I sense it is more immediately appropriate for a post-secular audience. It is a way into biblical conversations that does not begin with "And the correct answer is Jesus." Of course, I believe that all this literature points to Jesus who himself is a crier in public and the source of all wisdom (Colossians 2:3). But I think there may be one other reason to stick with the Proverbs for now: Peters talks about love and justice, setting them over against each other. The semantic field gets narrow; the oscillation between love and justice can, at times, become bewildering in Peters's gorgeously complex prose. But wisdom, I think, is a term that encompasses both the reciprocity of justice and the indiscriminateness of love.

34. Proverbs 1:20–22a, NRSV.
35. Proverbs 8:1–6, NRSV.

To expand the invitation.

One of the gifts of Wisdom's scattered communication is its nondiscrimination: "my cry is to all who live." That's a grace that the broadcast bears that the conversation often does not. Conversations can be discriminating: we talk to those who will listen and respond, to those who understand enough about us to know how to connect to our thoughts and attitudes through interchange. But *chokmah* addresses anyone willing to listen. The gifts of this dissemination are not for a select few. They are for any who wish to "learn prudence" and "acquire intelligence."

In the book of Job, the dialogue is selective. To be a part of this painful conversation, it is necessary to be friends of Job and to be learned. Late in the book, we learn that others have been listening to the extended conversation; but, unlike Eliphaz, Bildad, and Zophar, these listeners-in do not have the status to speak up.[36] They lack the credentials, so to speak, to be in the conversation.

But in the book of Proverbs, wisdom scatters its prizes recklessly, heedlessly, and in every direction. Job begs his friends to look at him as he talks, asking for the mutuality that preconditions understanding. His effectiveness as a communicator depends on the intensity of his listener's attention. But Woman Wisdom belts out her message, regardless of whether anyone is listening or not. She has no concern for whether a listener might be an appropriate recipient: they simply need to be alive to be worthy of her words. In fact, the credentials for receiving this *chokmah*'s cry are ignorance, simplicity, and folly. You can hear in her invitation an anticipation of the Jesus call for anyone with ears to listen.

To create community.

One painful feature of the contemporary workplace is a pervasive loneliness, which makes some rising professionals yearn for soul connection among coworkers.[37] But in this text, *chokmah*-with-a-megaphone offers a differ-

---

36. Job 32–37, NRSV. When a younger person, Elihu, stands up to speak, he has first to defend his right to speak at all, in a way that Job's friends do not. (And no one replies to Elihu, which deepens our sense that he wasn't a welcome participant.)

37. The 2021 study "Loneliness in America" notes that 61 percent of young adults feel lonely, a desperate statistic when it comes to workplace culture, especially given the number of rising professionals working remotely. See Weissbourd, Batanova, Lovison, and Torres, "Loneliness in America." One Mode/Switch interviewee noted, "Loneliness is something that I've experienced at most every workplace that I've worked." Anonymous interview.

ent social vision. Instead of offering one-on-one conversation and intimate relationship, the Woman Wisdom creates community by inviting everybody to what is essentially a big party. The call of *chokmah* in Proverbs is not an invitation to deep intimacy so much as to open conviviality.

Lady Wisdom takes the role, after all, of a preparer of a feast. She is depicted as running a large household economy and must make plans to represent its concerns in public.

> Wisdom has built her house;
> > she has hewn her seven pillars.
>
> She has slaughtered her animals; she has mixed her wine;
> > she has also set her table.
>
> She has sent out her female servants; she calls
> > from the highest places in the town,
>
> "You who are simple, turn in here!"
> > To those without sense she says,
>
> "Come, eat of my bread
> > and drink of the wine I have mixed.
>
> Lay aside immaturity and live,
> > and walk in the way of insight.[38]

The relationship with listeners sought for here by Woman Wisdom is not an intimately interpersonal conversation, a laying bare of the soul to another in radical mutuality. It is, instead, a form of community consistent with the disseminative mode: it's a feast full of banqueters. But what a strange group! This is not a dinner party organized on the customary rules: invite those who can do you some good in return. Nor is it a feast organized on a principle of choosing those most worthy to attend, like a philosopher looking for a "good" student to hold fellowship with. No, this is a feast for the foolish and the ignorant and the people who can barely manage to be alive.[39] In other words, this is not for people who have anything to offer Woman Wisdom, except to receive her gifts.

In contrast with the spareness of dialogue, where each communication must make room for another, where turn gives way to turn, where

---

38. Proverbs 9:1-6, NRSV.

39. The author who has most helped me to think through the implications of displacing customary kinds of cultural capital is Barclay, *Paul and the Gift*. Of Christian community in the book of Galatians, he writes, "Within this community there arises, of course, an alternative system of worth, a new form of 'symbolic capital.'...But...the hallmark of this alternative system of value is that it is specifically direct against rivalry: the greatest honor is for those who work *against* the competitive spirit of honor itself" (435).

every quid must have its quo, the banquet that *chokmah* prepares is a generous squandering. She prepares her food even before she knows who will attend. Unlike the seductress, who offers a few stolen morsels; the wise woman offers a laden table.

To speak the barely speakable.

Woman Wisdom's dissemination reminds us all of how important the pained cry is in human community. Companies, nonprofits, even churches can be surprisingly rational, deadeningly bureaucratic and buttoned-up places. But wisdom's call here is anything but contained and manageable. The utterance, says David Ford, is "a sign of the limits of speech, a gesture towards the inadequacy of any words to this content, an indication of the superlative, of breaking the bounds of terms and categories, of transcendence."[40]

This dimension of Wisdom's call reminds me of Joycee's facial expression of strength and pain at once. That, too, was a cry. When there are no words for our experiences of working community, there is still need for the broadcasted cry. One-on-one communication can be very talkative, very language-driven. But wisdom's cry takes us to the edges of incommunicability. Charlie Wurzel and Anne Helen Peterson note after the pandemic, "that everyone, up and down the org chart, is a full messy, complex, vulnerable and struggling human in need of support and affirmation, and boundaries."[41] Part of what that means is remaining open to the speaking of what is only barely speakable. In other words, it means making room for people to speak up, even if *chokmah* is so loud that some want to cover their ears.[42]

The word you have to say in any given moment may not feel like a word in season to the people around you. As a non-binary professional, as someone on the spectrum, as a woman, as a differently abled person, you may need to utter a cry for which the company currently has no categories. But take courage that your cry may be the *chokmah* call that enables others to start moving in a new way. That's the recommendation of this chapter,

---

40. Ford, *Christian Wisdom*, 19.
41. Petersen and Warzel, *Out of Office*, 103.

42. I'm also struck that this crying voice is an invitation to a similar cry from the hearers. The point of wisdom's call, in other words, is to teach others to call out as well, which is why the book of Proverbs go on to encourage us to "cry out for insight, / and raise your voice for understanding" (Proverbs 2:3, NRSV). Like so much of communication with pained humans, this is one broadcast to another, a dissemination answering another, even in situations where it seems as if no one might be listening. The Woman Wisdom requires us to call out, which implies a felt absence, but promises a response even if not one that comes immediately.

not just that you find the courage to express yourself, but that you find the cry that will prompt, poke, and push. Dissemination enables you to speak *out* in order to act *with*.

Why the Digitally Overwhelmed Need Dissemination

I have been arguing that organizational culture needs the broadcast as well as it needs the conversation. You noticed that each of my case studies were embedded deeply in digital spaces. That blunt fact points to what Rickert calls our ambient digital conditions. The digital is more than a collection of devices. The digital includes our ambient surroundings, our environment.[43] This baptism, this inundation in the digital makes remote interaction not just about conveying a message between sender and recipient but also about making a world with other senders and recipients.[44] Dissemination does this superbly well.

In contrast, the dialogic mode can make us feel like the only context that matters is Just Us Two. You and your conversation partner *are* the social world, at least for that moment. But an abrupt and urgent and possibly untimely utterance, blasting up and out of the fog of committee discussion, can sometimes make clear, as no patient conversation ever would, just how in over our heads we are in a technologized world.

A Mode Switch Worth Making

The mode switch I have been urging in this chapter from conversation to broadcasting is not a permanent one. We need both modes (and, as subsequent chapters will show, other modes as well), so a flexible shifting between the two seems essential. What we *can't* do is lock into the dialogic mode in the hopes that conversation will deal with whatever problems and overwhelms arise in workplace culture. To a man with a hammer in hand, everything looks like a nail. To a person in a dialogue, everything sounds like a comeback.

The gift of broadcast is that it enables us to respect the gaps between managers and employees and among coworkers. Institutions are

---

43. "Computer and telecommunications technologies are not only converging but also permeating the carpentry of the world, doing so in networks and technological infrastructures, houses and buildings, manufactured products, various sorts of content, and more." Rickert, *Ambient Rhetoric*, 1.

44. Rickert, *Ambient Rhetoric*, 3.

constantly strange; they rarely get all their various projects and divisions to work in concert. Effective use of the disseminative mode enables us to see the gaps, the chasms we are broadcasting across. But individuals are constantly strange as well. To ignore the gaps between people is to subject ourselves to constant frustration. *Why do we keep misunderstanding each other? How come this process is taking so long?* Dissemination allows us to continue communicating towards one another even when we do so across a gulf of difference or even antagonism. In any given moment, someone who cannot understand you feels like an opponent (*Are they just being stubborn or stupid right now?*). Wisdom's cry enables love for people who feel like enemies. *You and I are not alike, we do not understand one another perfectly, but we can broadcast in each other's directions.*

Like wisdom's cry, the mode of dissemination requires courage. Martin Luther used to encourage his parishioners to *sin boldly*, counting on the provisions of grace to cover for our misguided actions. Unilateral communication's call, I think, is similarly transgressive: *send boldly*. This is not perhaps a word for those in power, although presidents and directors and managers also need courage to (as a friend of mine puts it) "carry the water for corporate priorities."[45] But sending boldly may be especially important for the disempowered within our workplaces. For them, dialogue can be harmful, especially if it intensifies the power of those at the organizational center. But to send boldly can enable team members, coworkers, and ordinary employees to put their message in front of the workplace community, whether or not the audience will immediately grasp its significance.

You may have noticed that this challenging mode switch requires mode *craft* as well, so let's turn to practices for sending boldly in the next chapter's discussion of podcasting.

---

45. Ben Hoekstra, personal email to author, May 8, 2023.

CHAPTER 3.5

How to Make a Podcast

Mode/Switch Workshop

Goal: To guide you through four key decision points of podcast development

Job and His Three Friends Walk into a Studio

Go with me for a minute: imagine Job and his friends in headphones, leaning into studio mics to process their grief and anger and bafflement—and maybe hoping that the Almighty would start following them on Spotify. Play engineer for them for awhile, and you'll notice the intensity of their exchange. It's thick in the studio, so claustrophobically thick with emotion, that you want to tear your headphones off and pace the halls for a while.[1] For Job, at least, it's a failed intensity: his friends are sitting next to him, but they are oblivious to his actual experience.

Just down the hall, in another studio, Woman Wisdom is belting out her message. After you adjust the fader levels for how loudly she's talking to you, me, and all the other simpletons, you'll notice that her address sounds completely different from Job's. He's always trying to make eye contact with the friends or with the Almighty. But she's speaking her words to everyone,

---

1. A term Bethany Keeley-Jonker and I tried out to describe such a quality is *immanence*. Theologians used this term to describe God's transcendence to creation. In historic Christian teaching, to say that God is transcendent to creation is also to assert immanence. Because the divine is nowhere containable within creation, God is able to be present to creation at every point. See Keeley-Jonker and Mattson, "Stop Talking That Way."

squinting at no one in particular. She's speaking publicly, trying to cross gaps between herself and her hearers.[2]

What these fantasy scenarios highlight is that producing a podcast engages two modes of communication at the same time: conversation and broadcast. Most people use podcasts for the sake of conversation, seeking to create connection and mutuality between host and guest. But notice that the podcast is also a dissemination, a scattering of communication to far corners of the internet. Over the past few years, I've started several podcasts, usually in collaboration with students or other professionals, and have sometimes enjoyed the intersection of conversation and broadcast that the medium affords. Still, the "public intimacy" of being Job and Woman Wisdom at the same time is constantly tricky.[3]

Once I interviewed a social entrepreneur from New England on an interview podcast called *Spiritual Capital*. Things had started well. She had come fully prepared, having listened to previous episodes of the podcast, and she had plenty of stories and insight to share. She had done her homework more than most of my guests and was ready to *talk*. Not only that, but she was ready to *send:* thanks to a snazzy USB microphone plugged into her laptop, her audio was nearly studio quality. But the interview suffered breakdown when she disagreed with my use of a term. We tried to laugh it off, but we never found our footing, really. Our exchange never stopped being subtly uneasy. And then, when she sent me her audio on a digital sharing platform, I didn't notice that the download had an expiration date. When I got to postproduction, I found that her audio share had expired. I emailed her about it, and she said she no longer had the audio. I could tell she was disgusted. Podcasting's an intimate medium: the other person's voice is in your headphone or your earbud like the closest of intimates. But that very proximity makes disconnection with the other person all the more conspicuous.

What Makes Podcasting Challenging?

When your boss puts up a Trello card that says "Launch Company Podcast," you might feel a burst of excitement. But you will quickly fall into a streaming list of things to decide:

---

2. Although electronic exchange seems to promise proximity, podcasting requires acquaintance with public immanence. Keeley-Jonker and I put this concept together in the article, "Stop Talking That Way."
3. See Berlant, *Queen of America Goes to Washington City*.

- What to talk about, what research to do, what stats to use, what studies to cite, how to frame the issues, what you're *not* talking about, but also . . .

- What equipment to use, why mic two is janky, whether to use the video editing software you already know how to use or to finally figure out ProTools, whether to use SoundCloud or Spotify for Podcasters, but also . . .

- How to handle a guest who talks too much, how to keep from talking too much yourself, how to discern what attitude to perform (the skeptic, the friendly optimist, the blunt cynic, the totally, totally relatable host), how to move from talking to the audience to talking to the guest, whether to use last names, but also . . .

- How to design the logo, whether to use Free Music Archive, what marketer to consult with, whether to use ads, how many episodes you should capture before launch, when to schedule the launch date, but also . . .

These questions give me shih tzu brain: moving from spot to spot, sniffing eagerly, my whole body quivering with curiosity. The sheer number of decisions to make can be fun, but it can also create cognitive overload. Fortunately, you can readily find checklists to organize your podcast-related decision-making. Here's one that works for me:

1. content: questions about discerning and inventing what to say.
2. design: questions for preproduction, production, and postproduction processes.
3. roles: questions related to the parts each person will play.
4. sounds: questions about to how to speak words and make noise.

You've noticed that my heuristic is a collection of buckets for decisions you'll need to make about technical, stylistic, conversational, and relational issues. The buckets make things more manageable, but they don't get rid of the digital overwhelm, which has more to do with the qualitative than the quantitative aspects of podcasting. What makes podcasting overwhelming is not that it presents you with a lot of decisions, but that those decisions require a lot of mode-switching between the dialogic and the disseminative modes of communication.

To get at why this can be confusing, we might compare it to talking to people in different time zones. Each mode—conversation or broadcast, dialogue or dissemination—has its own time zone, so to speak. Think of the dialogic mode as being in mountain standard time. From the perspective of people out east, this mode is *behind*. It's moving slower, because conversation is often probing, exploring, palpating what's more or less immediately present, although as soon as something is discussed the conversationalists move on, leaving the last topic in the Pacific standard time of the past. In contrast, the disseminative or broadcast mode might be thought of as being in central standard time. It's *ahead* of the conversation, oriented towards the future. Instead of palpating the present, the person thinking about producing the podcast is projecting towards the possibilities of the future (where people in the eastern standard time zone somehow already reside).

In the last two chapters, I've been encouraging you to be open to switching your modes from dialogic to disseminative, from disseminative to dialogic. But in making a podcast, that switcheroo is constantly going on, whether you want it to or not. So in this half-chapter, I'd like to think with you about how to handle the mode-switching with mode craft. This discussion won't be exhaustive. It's mostly intended as a set of conversation starters that teach you a light, flexible, collaborative way of acting that I take to be essential for good podcasting.

Discerning Content.

The conversation doesn't start when you turn on the On-Air light and press Record. It starts when you and your team sit down to chat about the conversation in advance. This discussion about what could be said and maybe what should not be said is what ancient rhetoricians called *invention*. Aristotle described it as a process of discovery. For him, as for most other theorists of speech, invention pretty much *was* what rhetoric did. But for you, as your team tries to figure out what's talk-about-able in the zone of your podcast, you're dealing with audiences who will experience your messaging from many angles. A lot of inventive labor is just finding a starting point for the conversation.

Don't worry about finding the One Right Starting Point, at least not in your planning sessions. Just jump in and get to it. In the banter, you will discern something sayable. When you hear it, note it. "I think that might be the story we could launch with!" But what you're feeling around for in this pre-conversation is resonance, some moment when the energy intensifies, the pace quickens, the pitches rise, the laughter happens. Those affective cues signpost a pathway for the talk. Sometimes you guess wrong, of course. Sometimes you treat the conversation too schematically, too literally, too logically, too linearly. When that happens, hop up and change seats or go for a walk around the building.

Even when you do eventually press Record, you're still inventing. You're still figuring out what's sayable. You're palpating the moment, listening for resonance, feeling around for the gift that's hidden in the conversation somewhere. But as the conversation unfolds, you'll also want to be mindful that discerning the endpoint is just as tricky as finding the start. Some of the best podcast comments I've heard have happened after I've turned off the Record button. What feels like a terminus can be a transition.

Doing Design.

It's likely that somebody, somewhere along the line, is going to choke or cough or simply run out of words. The beautiful thing about podcasting is that you can always cut dead air out later. When somebody gets stuck making little verbal clutter sounds—uh, uh, umm, uh—and then peters off into silence, you all feel a mild panic. *This isn't supposed to be happening!* And then, you all grin and laugh with the realization that everything about this conversation is editable. Notice the way the modes of communication are stacked in that moment. You're conversationalists working things out one sentence at a time, yes. But you're also broadcasters, projecting the conversation forward to the form it will eventually take after the editor's done with it.

But if you're the editor, the doubleness of the modes can make you anxious. I used to podcast with a couple of guys on Saturday mornings, a little show called *Two Cities, Three Rubes*, discussing Augustine's writings. The nerdiness of it was terribly fun. But sometimes when the other two rubes were talking away about St. Gus, I'd be sitting there grinning vacuously into my mic and worrying about how I'd have to edit all this later. Editing is fun and utterly absorbing work. You're perfecting the past, cutting out mucous moments, cough noises, awkward laughter, jokes that didn't work. But editing can also take a long time, sometimes as much as two-thirds again as long as the original recording. That foreboding sense of a time-intensive future can make you uncomfortable in the present moment of a leisurely dialogue.

What you're thinking about in that moment is what ancient rhetoricians used to call *arrangement*. Some of this arrangement of the content happens well before you begin the podcast, when you're mapping out the conversation or developing an outline. But much of it happens in postproduction when you're editing your audio, mixing the levels, folding in music beds, incorporating sound effects, etc.

I'm agnostic on what digital audio workstation is best. Mostly, I've used Pro Tools, which is the industry standard, at least for music production. But lately, I've been finding Audition easier to use for podcasts. Whatever you use, you'll be compelled to make decisions about what you're going to use the software to edit *out*.

- Do you want to get rid of verbal pauses? I tend to eliminate superfluous noises like "um" and other fillers. At the same time, those verbal pauses can infuse speech with vitality. To clean out the "likes" and the "you knows" can make speech sound undead.
- How hot do you want the music to be under the host? Matching voice and music levels is important for comprehensibility. But pushing one or the other can also be important for chemistry. You'll also want to think about how long to allow theme music to play, when to bring things up to full volume immediately and when to cross-fade gradually, and how long to play the closing theme.
- Are you trying for a lean or a maximalist aesthetic when it comes to what people say? My sense is that people often say their ideas two and three times in different ways. Sometimes each of their comments feels like a little impromptu speech, complete with an intro, a preview, two or three main points, and an outro. Should you cut the intro and outro and just get to the body of their address? Often people add little phrases like "Piggybacking on what you just said . . ." My own preference is to cut the lard. Given all the junk constantly orbiting each of your audience members, I'd recommend a minimalist aesthetic. But I have to admit that my lean preferences can eliminate the little noises that humans use to work out relationships with each other. Which brings us to role-play in podcast production.

Playing Roles.

There are formal roles to consider in podcast production: researching, hosting, editing, distributing, marketing. Some of those roles tend more towards the conversational and dialogic; some towards the broadcast and dissemination. But it helps with team cohesion if you each understand what other people's roles oblige them to care about.

- What concerns for accuracy or currency or plagiarism constrain what the writer/researcher is doing?
- What gifts is the host aware of in the group—and how does she need to curtail one talkative person and invite an introvert to speak?
- Why does the editor want you to pause for two seconds after you make a mistake? (So she can find it easily in the waveform.)
- Why does the distributor want an Mp3 file?
- Why does it matter to the marketer that you include the article "the" in the title every time you say it?

Answering those questions will make clear the modes the various participants are playing—and what opportunities or limitations those modes impose on the overall project. Sometimes, even when you're really "feeling it" in the mode where you're most at home, you'll need to adjust to the limitations of somebody else's mode.

But there are also informal roles that get played out within the podcast recording. These don't usually show up on name badges; they just happen. Somebody's really good at snarky comments or context setting or counterpoints or historical observation or connection-making. It's probably important to name these roles once you discern them. But call these informal roles whatever you like—they bring vitality and canniness to a podcast.

Role-playing involves knowing and being more than your part. Think about getting ready for a concert or a church service. Some people take technical roles (unspooling cable across the stage, hooking up mics and amps), while others play performance roles (introducing, singing, speaking, storytelling). Some of the best technicians I've worked with are people who understand what it's like to be a performer as well. Some of the best performers I've seen know at least a little about the technical details of mixing the show or the service. These people are not just good at switching modes; they're good at distributing their attention across modes. Even if they're primarily in one mode, they're able to adjust it to coordinate with other people's modes as well. Playing your roles well and clearly can help your audience keep their bearings in the conversation. *Oh, that's the comic relief guy.* Or, *I love it when she finds a way to tie everything to some current event.*

Making Sounds.

The subject of delivery is a touchy one because the way each of us produces sound is deeply personal. Your voice, your laugh, your grunts of agreement are all shaped by your family, by the county where you grew up, by your ethnicity, by your first language, by your body type. When you talk about somebody's ideas, it's not too hard to separate yourself from your position. But when you talk about somebody's voice, it feels like you're talking about *them*. I think this is especially the case when it comes to work done in the dialogic mode. In deep conversation, we use our voices to feel our way towards something reliable. To be criticized for how we're doing that can feel like a criticism of our whole way of being in the world.

But when it comes to the disseminative mode, you can afford to be more judgey. After all, the point of dissemination is to serve the other, not to express the self. Consider these cues as starting points. You'll have to come up with your own rules of thumb for making sounds.

Speak in such a way as to bring your whole self into the space.

We convey passion *first* not in our words but in our bodies. Ezra Klein is a skilled podcaster at *The New York Times*. When he talks with guests in his hour-plus episodes of *The Ezra Klein Show*, he walks around his studio, gesturing, stopping, starting up again, always on the move. Part of Klein's choice to go mobile, so to speak, comes from his need to deal with extra bodily energy, but that habit of bringing his whole body into the conversation gives not only his diction but his thought a keenness I've never heard paralleled. Most of us cannot pace a studio, because we're tethered to a tabletop mic or a boom arm. But you can gesture, sit with a posture that allows for full body swivel, and keep your feet in the game under the table. You have to pour the whole of your personality into the mic, and doing that (without slapping the table, clicking your pen, or making other distracting noises) will require more bodily energy than you might expect. Your voice, your gestures, your body form a net to catch what might otherwise pass by unheard.

Speak in a way that makes it easy for others to speak as well.

The goal of podcast delivery should be to speak with a range of force, pitch, quality, and rate that is distinct to you but responsive to your audience and situation. Usually, the host or engineer can pot down on your mic if you've got a loud set of pipes. But your inflections and your vocal quality are indispensable for inviting others to peg onto what you've just said. Think of it as pitching the end of what say to make an on-ramp for the next person's utterance.

Speak in language that is vivid and varied.

Arguably, the most important medium podcasters work with is language. Some people know how to shoot from the hip and come up with an apt phrase effortlessly in the moment. If you're not that kind of person, it's a good idea to have a notepad and a pen to jot down a three- or four-word phrase as it comes to mind. (Sometimes in the flow of what everybody else is saying, it's easy to forget the thing you wanted to say two minutes ago.) Make close friends with stylistic figures like antithesis and polysyndeton and simile and alliteration:

- Antithesis: the use of evenly counterweighted grammatical structures: "Ask not what your country can do for you but what you can do for your country."
- Polysyndeton: the inclusion of conjunctions in between items in a list: "When you go out to eat, you need to remember your tact *and* your taste *and* your timeliness."
- Simile: the explicit comparison of two seemingly unlike things: "She showed her tightly blanketed baby to the family like a baker showing off a newly made loaf of bread."
- Alliteration: the repetition of the initial sounds of words: "We need to oppose police brutality not with politeness or pretense but with power and possibility."

One final aspect of making sounds has to do with the style of delivery you use: impromptu, extemporaneous, manuscripted, memorized. My recommendation is to blend a couple of them. Scripting parts of the podcast ensures that you get across vital aspects of the content efficiently; loosening things up with impromptu delivery keeps the interchanges lively. Extemporaneous delivery blends the two, requiring thorough preparation without planning out every word. If you're working with a team, it's a good idea to rehearse the podcast, or a portion of it. It doesn't have to kill the vibe to do a run-through. Sometimes it shows you what moves work and what moves deaden the conversation.

And That's All for This Episode

One way to sum up everything said so far: mode craft for podcast production requires metacognition. (Perhaps we should call it modal cognition.) I guess we've all been a part of a group or a committee in which one of the team members is unable to see anything but their own tasks. They are myopic, preoccupied with their role, unable to see how their part interacts with other people's parts or how these parts constitute the whole. But being mindful of modes activates your metacognition.

Metacognition requires a simple but vital practice we might call *in-studio signaling*. When two or three people sit around a studio table, gabbing away, it can be little hard to keep track of where people are in the conversation. Are they ready to speak? Are they running out of ideas? Do they need to think out loud? Are they seeing a connection? It's a good idea to develop a roster of signals to communicate each person's status in the conversation.

1. Tapping your sternum: "I'd like to talk."
2. Waving your fingertips at your Adam's apple: "Not ready to talk."
3. Touching your ear and pointing to someone else: "Love to hear from him about this!"

You can, of course, develop signals that work for your team. But this underlayer of communication does more than convey a few clues. These signals cue metacognitive attention. In other words, they remind people to be reading the room at all times. It's tempting for external processers to play the talkative genius and miss the more introverted person's contributions. It's equally tempting for guests to monologue or hosts to imagine they need to interleave a comment after every other person's comment. But a practice of signaling can subtly redistribute attention and power. The practice equips podcast partners to adjust their performances to each other, coordinating with each other's contributions.

We can't each pay full attention to all the modes at play in a studio. We can't, for example, be utterly focused conversationalists and utterly competent audio editors at the same time. We can, however, keep contact with each other's contributions, allow each other to attend to different things, and thus diminish collective whelm.

All this talk of sending, receiving, attending, and adapting to signals brings us to the approach to communication discussed in the next chapter, the semiotic mode.

CHAPTER 4

Meaning Things

A chapter asking how to coordinate multiple meanings for work in the semiotic mode.

I HAVE KNOWN RYAN Wynia for nearly twenty years, ever since I was myself an early career professional. Every once in a while, I've caught sight of him on social media over the years, as he's made his way through early-to-mid-career professional life. He's always been a charismatic, quick-to-grin, entrepreneur type with a flair for thinking big thoughts about work and society. When I reached out to ask for an interview, he was glad to reconnect. Although he works in the insurance industry, he's always been a lover of research, a thought leader in the making.

In our interview, though, he came off as melancholic and subdued. He kept his face averted from the webcam, looking off to the side, sometimes keep the bill of his hat between his gaze and mine. When he did meet the eye of the camera, his eyes were heavy with indefinable emotion. Was it tiredness? Resignation? Caution? I kept registering this reticence as he narrated his career across several sectors in the knowledge economy, from real estate to the design space to brand strategy and health insurance. Much of his work—too much of it, he would say—has been for Blue Cross Blue Shield. At the time of our interview, he was employed by Anthem, or as he put it, "yet another Blue." He lamented that he has "inadvertently spent way too much time in health insurance."[1]

Responding to his cues, I asked him to tell me about breakdowns he's experiencing at work. He mentioned first that lately he spends too much

1. Ryan Wynia, interview by Craig Mattson, March 3, 2022.

time repeating himself to his team. These repetitive exchanges had him asking, "How many times are we gonna have the same conversation? Did we not just have this conversation a day ago? Two days ago?" He speculated that the problem might come from multitasking coworkers. But then, he asked if the problem was with himself. Could he, should he, be a better communicator? "How are we not getting this?"[2]

Later in our talk, Ryan said, "I think it's so hard in the digital space, because signaling and reading cues and receiving those signals and properly identifying them is so hard. I was thinking earlier today that our digital tools are task-oriented." But, he added, our work requires more than getting stuff done. We also need interpersonal connection in order to do our work well and creatively.

He went on to cite a second example of communication overwhelm, this time with his higher-ups. From them, it wasn't so much distractedness as *denial* that was causing the breakdown. "The gaslighting," he explained wearily, "is rampant at Anthem." He identified two kinds of invalidation that his administrators do. On the one hand, they will appropriate other people's ideas as if they, the administrators, had thought of them. On the other hand, the administrators will outrightly deny their own culpability in a company problem. Anthem, at one point, had transferred clinicians' information from one digital platform for another—without telling the clinicians. When confronted with this omission, they insisted they *had* contacted the clinicians. "Yeah, we did," they said. "We did that. We totally did that." And in a voice of utter fatigue, Ryan told me, "No, we did not."[3]

It was rapidly becoming clear why Ryan looked so pained as he spoke about his work. All these layers of everyday interaction, as Ryan notes, "can start to stack on top of each other" until "it all just feels overwhelming." At the nexus of technological density—all those distracted coworkers on their phones!—and affective intensity—all the fatigue from administrative gaslighting!—Ryan is suffering the migraine of digital overwhelm. And one of the consequences of the too-much-ness of it all is that his work loses its meaning—or what he refers to as its *mattering*. "[W]hen you're busting your hump," he says, "and you're not recognized for that value, mattering doesn't happen."[4]

---

2. Ryan Wynia, interview by Craig Mattson, March 3, 2022.
3. Ryan Wynia, interview by Craig Mattson, March 3, 2022.
4. Ryan Wynia, interview by Craig Mattson, March 3, 2022.

Asking Questions about How Work Matters

Who gets to decide what your work means? The market? Your clients? Your supervisor? Some other deity? My guess is, you'll answer that question by saying something like, *Um, I do. What my work means is not assigned by someone else. It's designed by me.*

And you're mostly right. It's a basic assumption of constructivist communication theory that meaning is not simply passed along, but is also constructed. (And in an age of nondestructive digital editing, the job's meaning probably feels intensely revisable.) It's a part-time job for you, just putting together what your job means. Your friends and intimates help, and so does your team. Your one-up probably *wants* to help establish what your job means, though, after that last 360, you may have some doubts on that score.

But it's a whole thing, isn't it, just figuring out what your work signifies?

You do this job curation with templates provided by the broader culture, too. Some culture-watchers talk about how work has become a sort of icon, before which even secularizing Americans genuflect.[5] Others discuss work's significance as a romantic symbol, as if your job were a significant other or maybe a sucky soul mate and your career a venture in codependency.[6] Still others see it as a sign of a kind of athleticism: your job gives you a chance to demonstrate your ability to win or lose the game.[7] But in any case, for millennials, who entered the workforce just after the 2008 economic collapse, and even for young professionals, who have since experienced the relentless jankiness of today's knowledge economy, there's a big gap between what the job is and what it signifies. If you're like the people I've spoken with, then you deal with live questions about whether your job means anything and, if so, what it means.

I should probably confess that I am not, by personal history or by temperament, inclined to see work as meaningless. I often enjoy the work I do. But this enjoyment is underwritten by my being a White guy, an overeducated middle-class academic, who has enjoyed relative institutional stability and has been able to rely on a close correspondence between doing work and getting benefits. Still, there is one voice in my life that has enabled me to hear something of what rising professionals refer to as the sometimes pointlessness of work—and that voice is the book of Ecclesiastes.

---

5. Chen, *Work Pray Code*, 213.
6. Jaffe, *Work Won't Love You Back*.
7. Sinek, *Infinite Game*; Carter, *Do Your Job*.

Qoheleth, the narrator of Ecclesiastes, despairs of meaning in work, in achievement, and even in acts of communication. As we saw in chapter 1 of this book, the book of Ecclesiastes tempers this despair by making space for a "weirdness" that keeps meaningful dialogue alive. But there's no denying Qoheleth's angry and fatigued tone: "Vanity of vanities, says the Teacher, / vanity of vanities! All is vanity." Or, as Cal Seerveld translates it, "It's all just a big fart."

But the pained voice (and the rank aroma) of Ecclesiastes has made it easier for me to hear how very diversely Gen Z and millennial professionals understand the point of the toil they do each day. I have always been a teacher, a vocation that has a certain psychosis when it comes to work and fulfillment, vocation and meaning. I've always done my professorial work with the assumption that the rising professionals I teach are entering a life of purpose and meaning. But Qoheleth puts the kibosh on that. "I have seen the business that God has given to everyone to be busy with," he says, groaning like an employee wiggling his mouse and staring at a spreadsheet.[8]

The Teacher in the book sets out on an experiment in vocational meaning, trying to learn what it might mean to do what he calls "great works."[9] Sounding a little Cal Newport describing what deep work can do, Qoheleth lists out all the projects he was able to complete by his magnificent industriousness: houses he built, vineyards he planted, parks he curated, transactions he made. "Then I considered all that my hands had done and the toil I had spent in doing it, and again, all was vanity and a chasing after wind, and there was nothing to be gained under the sun."[10]

Maybe You Should Try the Semiotic Mode

Qoheleth's experiment and Ryan's questions invite attention to the modes of communication we use when we ask what work means. Reading Ecclesiastes makes it clear that Qoheleth is a disseminator, a scatterer of wisdom, a popular author. And the editor who opens and closes the book compels us to think about the adequacy of that mode.[11] "Besides being

---

8. Ecclesiastes 3:10, NRSV.

9. Ecclesiastes 2:4, NRSV.

10. Ecclesiastes 2:11, NRSV. The litany of Qoheleth's accomplishments precedes this verse.

11. It's easy to miss the fact that, as the book opens, someone is talking *about* the Teacher in the third person. And whoever this editor is, he may not exactly share Qoheleth's skeptical outlook, as we learn in the conclusion of the book. Still, by framing Qoheleth's ideas, the editor shows deep attention to the Teacher's dark philosophy. After Qoheleth has conveyed his well-nigh despairing insights about the brevity and vanity

wise, the Teacher also taught the people knowledge, weighing and studying and arranging many proverbs. The Teacher sought to find pleasing words, and he wrote words of truth plainly."[12] But having noted this, the editor of the book goes on to say of this disseminative communication, "Of making many books there is no end, and much study is a weariness of the flesh."[13] Ryan's melancholy stories, too, point to modes of communication happening throughout his workplace. When he asks why his team members require overcommunication, he seems to be engaging the dialogic mode, asking questions about why interpersonal conversation isn't working. When he points out his administrators' gaslighting, he's noting their misuse of the disseminative mode. They send out their humbug and hope everybody buys it.

But notice that both Qoheleth and Ryan ask about how work *matters*. In doing this, they are engaging what this chapter will call the semiotic mode. Can you feel the strangeness of the jump there? These two communicators—the ancient sage, the contemporary manager—are fully engaged in speaking and listening, transmitting and feeding back—and then, all of a sudden, they shoot a glance at work itself and ask, "What's the point of it?" Most of the time, we look through our work the way you look through contact lenses. But when the lenses don't fit right somehow, you pop them out and study them. (*What's going on here? Is there some speck on them?*) That's the move Qoheleth teaches. It's also the move Ryan is making, the mode switch away from dialogue *with* or dissemination *to* and towards the semiotics *of*.

It'll help you to know a little history behind the semiotic mode. The semiotic approach comes out of a philosophical school known as structuralism, which said that we know things not by studying their essence, but by studying their relationship to other things.[14] (It's not about character; it's about connections, you might say.) Ferdinand Saussure (1857–1913) took this insight into the study of signs by urging the study of language as a system, not just as a pointing finger to something in the world.[15] Studying the parts of this

---

of everything, the editor concludes the book by saying, in effect, "You should listen to what the Teacher is saying here! But don't forget: there's more to life than what the Teacher says." Enns, *Ecclesiastes*, 110.

12. Ecclesiastes 12:9–10, NRSV.

13. Ecclesiastes 12:12b, NRSV.

14. "Above all, structuralism is a *method*. Its aim is to analyze isolated events or meanings in terms of their underlying structural laws. It seeks to comprehend the *particulars* by describing their interrelationship within the totality of *general* codes which govern them. It looks for the deep and often hidden structures beneath the surface manifestations of meaning." Kearney, *Modern Movements*, 240.

15. "In other words, he argued that language should be analysed in terms of its internal *structures* (what language is in itself as a formal system of relations) and not, as

system helped him distinguish the *signifier* (what a sign presents to the five senses) from the *signified* (what a sign evokes in human minds). You see a red octagon with white letters spelling "S-T-O-P." All those elements constitute the signifiers. Your brain processes those visual elements, and that processing creates a signified, a meaning, roughly translatable into "You should hit the brakes now." (Or, if you're like me, "You should slow down to five-miles-per for a few seconds.") Usually, the signifier and the signified merge so quickly that you don't notice anything but the sign.[16]

Saussure's concepts help explain the weird thing we're trying to do when we treat our work like a sign. But what does the sign *mean*? That depends, say C. K. Ogden and I. A. Richards, on how you understand *The Meaning of Meaning*. They get right down to work whiteboarding the concept with a triangle model, something like this:

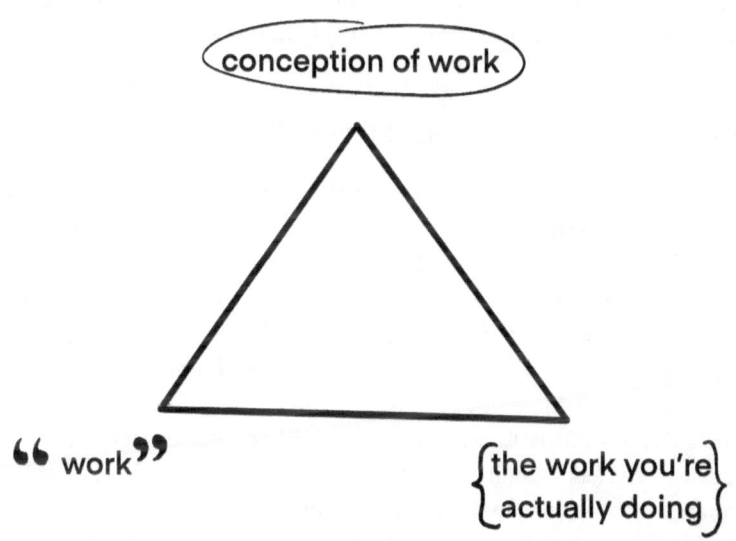

The dotted line is Ogden and Richards's graphic indicator that there is no direct connection between a word we use (the *symbol*) and the thing we're referring to (the *referent*). Everything depends on the top part of the triangle, or what's in somebody's head (the *reference*) when they hear you say "work."

---

had traditionally been the case, simply in terms of its *content* (what language is about, that is, what it refers to)." Kearney, *Modern Movements*, 240.

16. My account of semiotics in general and Saussure in particular is dependent on Berger, *Signs in Contemporary Culture*, as well as the already cited Kearney, *Modern Movements in European Philosophy*.

The reference you have in your head for "work" is probably different from what I have in my head and what your coworkers have in their heads.

Ogden and Richards wrote *The Meaning of Meaning* in 1923. But they echo three-thousand-year-old insights from Ecclesiastes, naming the dangers of multiplying words with complacent assumptions about meaning.[17] Writing in 2023, I think they'd have to deal with meaning in a different way, asking how digital media disrupt significance. Ogden and Richards make referents sound easy to examine, like pebbles in a rock garden. Sometimes that feels right—on a quiet Sunday morning, drinking an espresso, wondering what it's all about. In a contemplative moment, asking what your work means feels like picking up a Petoskey stone and fingering its edges. But most days, the job's potential meanings are whitewater rapids, rushing past us in images and sounds on phone screens, on laptop screens, on the little TV that blares on the gas pump, in your one-up's latest DM. We're not standing comfortably on the banks of this rushing river; we're riding inflatable rafts, rowing like mad, trying to avoid puncture and upset.

How to Talk about Semiotics in This Economy

Seth Godin sees the crazy-fast pace of the attention economy as an opportunity to find meaning in your work. Although he doesn't get deep into the particulars of communication theory, he does discuss how understanding "Semiotics, Symbols, and Vernacular" can enable you to discern the meanings people carry around in their noggins and then to use those meanings to help them thrive in their work, or at least to make good money.[18] Semiotics can help do good *and* do well, in contrast with old forms of mass communication, which his book *Purple Cow* describes as "obsolete" because those approaches are self-interested.[19] Godin notes that today, thanks to the precise targeting of digital messaging, jobs in the attention economy can become "the generous act of helping others become who they seek to become. It involves creating honest stories—stories that resonate and spread. Marketers offer solutions, opportunities for humans to solve their problems and move forward."[20] All this optimism is based on "the magic of online advertising," which enables you to "reach people more precisely online than in any other medium" and quickly: "You can decide to run an ad at 10 a.m. and have it reach people

---

17. Ecclesiastes 3:7, 5:2, 12:12, NRSV.
18. Godin, *This Is Marketing*, 145–56.
19. Godin, *Purple Cow*, 3.
20. Godin, *This Is Marketing*, 6.

beginning at 10:01 a.m."[21] For Godin, mastering the semiotic mode is like learning to see an optical illusion both ways: the duck that's also a rabbit that's also a duck. You look at the work of marketing one way, and, by gum, it looks effective, strategic, smart, savvy. You're selling things as fast as a rabbit can run. But look it another way, and it's pure altruism, pure duck all the way down. That's Godin's optimistic take on the semiotic mode.

Todd Gitlin sees today's media environment in a similarly semiotic but in a much less optimistic fashion than Godin. Gitlin writes that "because there are so many clamoring signals, and because they interfere with one another, everyone must learn one particular cognitive skill. . . . Everyone learns not only to see but not to see—to tune out and turn away."[22] You must find ways to navigate "the torrent" of the digital through what he calls "styles of navigation," some of which he lists as "fans, critics, paranoids, exhibitionists, ironists, and jammers, all churning within the currents of image and sound, trying to keep our heads up; and sometimes, also, as secessionists or abolitionists, conscientious objectors trying to clamber to dry land."[23] In contrast with the Godin, Gitlin doesn't see the attention economy as a meaningful site for work.[24] What he describes as styles of navigation might be good for discerning which streaming platforms to subscribe to, but my research suggests that rising professionals are doing more with the semiotic mode than simply coping.

Notice that Godin and Gitlin each focus on part of the whelm. Godin sees the digital disruptions of online communication as an opportunity to find meaningful work but underplays the dark side of the attention economy. Gitlin makes money on the attention economy by being a pundit and an author but underplays work opportunities. My research among early-to-mid-career professionals, however, suggests that early careerists have found at least four different ways their work matters in digital environments.

---

21. Godin, *This Is Marketing*, 168–69.
22. Gitlin, *Media Unlimited*, 118–19.
23. Gitlin, *Media Unlimited*, 119.

24. Gitlin tells a fascinating story about how he tried to finesse the media by giving blood to support the troops in the first Iraq War, while at the same time criticizing the administration sending the troops. His plan doesn't work. See Gitlin, *Media Unlimited*, 121–26. Anand Giridharadas joins Gitlin's critique of Godin-styled optimism. Giridharadas calls out do-gooding businesspersons like the "gazillionaire" who "is appropriating the language of movements and love, solidarity and selflessness, and even the therapeutic language of sharing being caring, and using it to dress up the naked truth of his oligarchic visions." See Giridharadas, *Winners Take All*, 68.

Four Postures Towards Work's Meaningfulness

The Therapists.

Donna Veitkus manages a quick service restaurant in Holland, Michigan, and her cheerful, upbeat manner suggests that she loves the work even when it's crazily stressful. But what strikes me about the stories she tells is how pastorally she positions herself in her managerial role. She told me a story about a time her restaurant joined a local parade, passing out some three thousand sandwiches. Even in the chaos of all that work, some of her team members weren't behaving professionally and required coaching. "And so I walk in. This is the day of the parade. We've been up for twelve hours and just cranking out work . . ."—and there's all this immaturity and discontentment. But Donna is down for coaching these younger coworkers. "It's very exciting," she says of her complicated work. "We're super happy about it"—and then adds, "It's still really stressful."[25]

Adam Frankenfeld works for an enormously successful video game company. If you know gaming, you would know this company immediately. But because Adam's place within the brand is complex, he felt cautious about having me name it explicitly. During our several interviews, I've noticed a shift in his thinking about what his work means. In our first conversation, he spoke mostly about the logistics of putting out a video game. Any one project is so massively complicated, involving dozens of technicians, that a bottleneck in one division can cause frustrating constrictions elsewhere. That was the nexus of the digital and the affective that Adam focused on in our first interview.[26]

But when I interviewed him later, he was speaking about what his work meant in quite a different way: instead of focusing on project management, he was speaking much more about people care. Needing to meet a project deadline, he said, felt like you have something you can't quite swallow. Needing to care for people, in contrast, feels like breathing out slowly. There's still plenty of digital overwhelm. Sometimes in remote meetings, the chat fills up with all sorts of superfluous stuff, which makes him want to tell everybody to just please shut up. But he doesn't do that; he's trying to help them enjoy the work. He's finding meaning in his work by practicing a therapeutic approach to management. Before wrapping up our interview, he asked me if I've heard of a book called *Radical Candor*. I jotted down the

---

25. Donna Veitkus, interview by Craig Mattson, May 18, 2022.
26. Adam Frankenfeld, interview by Craig Mattson, January 3, 2022.

book title, and we hung up—he to attend to his team, and I to ponder the therapeutic meanings Adam seemed to be deriving from his work.[27]

Donna and Adam are hardly alone among the workplace Therapists that I interviewed. I might, for example, have told you about Caleb Hughes, whose work as a pastor literally involves counseling other people—but who also finds it therapeutically essential to make sure he avoids his own burnout. ("Pastors are just really busy," he explains with a smile, "and I'm not.")[28] But I wanted to know if these professionals' stories were idiosyncratic—or if this therapeutic posture was a "thing" in contemporary work culture. Turns out, there's a whole industry of what you might call Therapists for the Therapists in the knowledge economy—gurus, TED Talkers, book bloggers like Simon Sinek and Donald Miller and Kim Scott. For young professionals cultivating a pastoral or therapeutic attitude towards their teams, these authors provide the reinforcing insights.

Simon Sinek's books and talks and LinkedIn videos position him as a square-jawed, squinty-eyed life coach in today's attention economy. Figure the heck out of your "why" is his constantly reiterated insight in a spreading empire of talk.[29] Similarly, Donald Miller's "Story Brand" positions the knowledge worker not as the hero of their own story, but in a supporting role for the client's stories. Your work isn't about you, he insists. It's about being the "trusted guide" for other people's work. Kim Scott provides "radical candor" as a framework for avoiding, on the one hand, being too nice to be productive and, on the other, being too blunt to be pastoral. Why do so many people today see work in therapeutic terms? That's a question that's driven the work of sociologists from Nikolas Rose to Jonathan Crary to Nigel Thrift, each of whom analyzes how management has come to mean shaping the inner lives of employees.[30] But in any case, this culture-wide impulse is propelling many millennial managers and Gen Z team leaders to listen well, to discern problems, to make connections, and to provide nonjudgmental solutions.[31]

---

27. Adam Frankenfeld, interview by Craig Mattson, June 3, 2022.
28. Mattson, "Barefoot Burnout."
29. See, for example, Sinek, *Find Your Why* and *Start with Why*.
30. Rose, *Governing the Soul*; Crary, *Suspensions of Perception*; Thrift, *Knowing Capitalism*.
31. Miller, *Building a Storybrand*.

The Skeptics.

"What do workers gain from all the toil at which they toil under the sun?" asks Qoheleth.[32] And many of my interview subjects would echo the Teacher's skepticism by saying, "Same." Here's one such case. Chicago-based marketer Andrea Munday runs Gold Soul Marketing. She enjoys what she does: even in the sometimes craziness of online advertising, she keeps her sense of humor. And she's had enough success to build a viable clientele. But even so, she's not sure that any of her work means anything. The question reflects a painful decade after college, struggling with questions of work and fulfilment. Graduating in 2007, she took a job at Christianity Today International, a move that made sense to her as a then practicing Christian and as an ambitious professional glad for work in what she now wryly refers to as a "big company." As a talented vocalist, she was also trying to break into the music business, doing as many as fifty to sixty gigs a year. But then, things started falling apart. Her marriage to her pre-high school sweetheart broke up. Her music career burned her out. And her Christian faith disappeared. Her new religious agnosticism meant, in turn, that she had to quit her faith-based job. No partner, no artistic path, no career—it was such a terribly painful time that, to this day, she wishes deconversion on no one.

But for her, the struggle gave her a new way to talk about what her work meant, perhaps because, for the first time she could remember, she was able, as Frederick Buechner might say, to listen to her own life. She started to rebuild what she came to call Life #2—a second marriage, kids, a vigorous political engagement, a bespoke marketing company. When I asked her about what role spirituality plays in her work, she warned me that her answer was "going to sound very atheist." She said that although she enjoys her work a great deal, she doesn't get much meaning from it. It puts food on the table for her kids and gets them school supplies, and it gives her a chance to collaborate with her husband. But as for vocational meaning, she explained, "I think it's unfindable." At the core of human life is an emptiness that no job will satisfy.

> And I think that was a big part of my sort of breakdown when the marriage and God went away and all of that—was that I thought something was gonna fill that void, and I still get stuck in that. What is the purpose? What is the meaning? What's gonna fill the void? And I think probably—and maybe this is just where I am in my life right now—the answer is nothing. We will live with this void until the day we die, and that's the

---

32. Ecclesiastes 1:3, NRSV.

human condition. And that's like—we just have to enjoy the little moments in life. There is no giant purpose or meaning. You're just here to live and to love people.[33]

Andrea's stories reveal a consistent and skeptical posture towards the question of work's meaning. It even shapes the product she creates. On the one hand, you can see that she's not completely dismissive that work has meaning. As an online marketer, she's developed an advertising campaign for Kaboo snacks that celebrated the various vocations of people who carried the snacks in their everyday backpacks. The result was the Be You With Kaboo campaign, a series of videos that Andrea speaks of to this day with satisfaction.[34] On the other hand, as we finished our interview, she asked herself, "Should I be finding more meaning in my work?"[35] Andrea's skepticism about work is somewhat agnostic. Work *might* be ultimately meaningful, but she has not so far discovered precisely how.

Look around a little, and you'll quickly find that Andrea's perspective is not an isolated one. A growing discourse of pundits, journalists, and cultural theorists strengthen and extend the Skeptic's posture towards work. Being a true believer in work just might be very bad for you, these authors say. They critique the way that work has assumed quasi-cultic significance for Americans, especially in the upper echelons of society. Perhaps the preeminent voice here is Derek Thompson's in his persistent exhortations to give up "workism," or the misplaced faith that work can and should provide the transcendent meaning once proffered by organized faith.[36] In her book *Work Pray Code*, Carolyn Chen describes a transposition of two very different symbol systems in the tech sector. Lots of Silicon Valley folk aren't going to church, but they are going to work as if it were church—or, more specifically, a Buddhist temple. Chen writes,

> One firm I visited sponsors weekly "dharma talks," where employees meditate and reflect on the teachings of the Buddha. Google sponsors Search Inside Yourself, a program that brings in Buddhist teachers to teach Googlers meditation, which employees affectionately call "church." The tech giant Salesforce

---

33. Andrea Munday, interview by Craig Mattson, March 14, 2022.

34. See, for example, Nubu Snacks, "Rita—The Inspired Artist—Presented by Nubu."

35. Andrea Munday, interview by Craig Mattson, March 14, 2022.

36. Thompson, "Workism Is Making Americans Miserable." You can find similar arguments in the work of writers like Anne Helen Petersen, Malcolm Harris, and Amelia Horgan. See, for example, Petersen, *Can't Even*; Harris, *Kids These Days*; and Horgan, *Lost in Work*.

invited over thirty monks from Plum Village, the order of the famous Buddhist leader Thich Nhat Hanh, to chant and teach at the meetings of their annual conferences in 2017 and 2018. At companies such as LinkedIn, Buddhist virtues such as compassion and mindfulness are celebrated as part of a company culture that supposedly gives them a competitive advantage. "The workplace," one tech executive told me, "is the hotbed of spirituality" in Silicon Valley.[37]

My own research among social entrepreneurs turned up very similar findings, as I asked company presidents, program directors, and solo-preneurs what spirituality is doing in their organizations. Quite a lot, it turns out—although some of the most fascinating stories came from people who had serious questions about infusing religion and spirituality into company mission.[38]

These Skeptics, no less than the Therapists, inhabit the semiotic mode, but they tend to do so deconstructively. They watch the powerful shape that work takes as a mythology, a term proposed by the semiotician Roland Barthes, who provided critical machinery to examine the constantly evolving symbolic action of late capitalism.[39] He would note that mythologies tend to reinforce the cultural power of a dominant cultural groups like the CEOs and the shareholders and the super wealthy. Truth be told, though, Barthes would also have to deal with the weirdness that Derek Thompson has pointed out: elite workers in the attention economy worship their work more than blue collar folk do.[40]

37. Chen, *Work Pray Code*, 3. Tara Isabella Burton has mapped similar corporate pieties in *Strange Rites*. Jonathan Crary describes nineteenth-century efforts to manage the inner lives of workers. My spiritually focused research among social entrepreneurs shows how organizational leaders add "spiritual capital" to economic and social capital. Burton, *Strange Rites*; Crary, *Suspensions of Perception*; and Mattson, *Why Spiritual Capital Matters*.

38. Mattson, *Why Spiritual Capital Matters*, 37–56.

39. Barthes's writing makes for fun reading. His semiological analysis shows how an established sign (job-as-a-way-to-provide-for-the-family) gets cashed in, so to speak, as a new signifier with another signified so that a new sign (job-as-path-to-success) emerges. But then *that* sign becomes the signifier of yet another signified, with a newly emergent sign (job-as-personal-quest-for-transcendence). See Barthes, *Mythologies*. I depend for my understanding of semiological analysis upon Griffin, Ledbetter, and Sparks, *First Look at Communication Theory*, 320–31. But you can find an up-to-date semiological observation in Derek Thompson's observation that in twenty years he might be writing, "'Here is a history of work in eight words: from jobs to careers to callings to . . .' Except I'm not sure what the eighth word should be yet." Thompson, "Why Americans Care About Work So Much."

40. Barthes, *Mythologies*, 219. "The economists of the early 20th century,"

The Survivalists.

If you spend much time on Gen Z TikTok, you'll hear plenty of voices who say, not so much that they have deconverted from work, but that they think about work as little more than a way to get by. Sometimes my interviewees said this explicitly; sometimes they merely implied it. Dyvon Melling told me stories of getting a great job right out of college, wanting to set the world afire with his work—and then discovering that he was unqualified and needing to leave the work for other less impressive employments. He then spent some time in a kind of anti-capitalist mode, working as a bartender, just trying to eat and get by. Today, he makes good money working for a stealth company owned by a prominent but infamous CEO—so infamous in fact that Dyvon had been compelled to sign a nondisclosure agreement and felt that even the name of the company he worked for might be under that agreement.

I appreciated Dyvon's blunt style of communication; he conveyed the raw difficulty of being a Black man in corporate America and the challenges of managing other colleagues of color. (Just before our interview, he had had to fire a Black coworker.) But I think the thing that most struck me about Dyvon's disposition towards his work was his no-nonsense dismissal of work's mattering. The Skeptics recognize the possibility that work *could* mean something, even if they're sadly sure it doesn't. Dyvon, in contrast, is apathetic about work's significance. He reminds me of a friend who describes himself not as a theist or an atheist, but an apatheist. Dyvon doesn't believe in work or disbelieve in work; he just doesn't care. The whole thing is so broken that it just needs to be replaced.[41]

It was in talking to Olivia Winkowitsch that this Survivalist position within the semiotic mode came most clearly into focus. In narrating her professional and personal experience of the COVID-19 pandemic, she had to unearth what she called "layers of why I'm feeling so burned out."[42] Although she's making it economically in a tough, fast-paced industry in

---

Thompson notes, "did not foresee that work might evolve from a means of material production to a means of identity production. They failed to anticipate that, for the poor and middle class, work would remain a necessity; but for the college-educated elite, it would morph into a kind of religion, promising identity, transcendence, and community." See Thompson, "Workism Is Making Americans Miserable." On the other hand, Chen uncovers how work-as-religion tends to reinforce the power of corporate leaders "in knowledge-intensive industries, such as technology, that faced both global competition and frequent labor shortages." Chen, *Work Pray Code*, 8–9.

41. Melling, "I Can Be Too Transparent," interview by Craig Mattson, *Mode/Switch*, April 30, 2022.

42. Olivia Winkowitsch, interview by Craig Mattson, January 28, 2022.

Hollywood (as a manager in a company that creates key art for movies and streaming TV shows), she registers some pain in her work. Part of it is a felt loss of personal efficacy: "Everything that I do, I could have done this ten times faster and better with more assurance a long time ago and I don't feel like I can do that right now."[43] She concedes it looks like laziness, but then adds that "that's not the problem here."[44] What's wearing her down is a densely layered sense of predicament. "It's not just things that are happening in the world. There are things that are happening with me personally. There are things that are happening with my own health, and then there's a job that is working in a very turbulent industry."[45]

Olivia is a gently spoken person, inclined to smile a lot, always attuned to the other person in the conversation. It was startling to hear her expressing this raw, almost dystopian picture of things. "I think for me there's also just a general sense of—it feels like the world is ending, and so it's so hard to care about small work. . . . It's very hard to care right now about business. Because that just doesn't seem to be what is important right now, but we have to keep on keeping on."[46] Past Olivia might have been inclined to tell herself to step up, step out, get stuff done, work harder. But Present Olivia's job "just feels so small in the grand scheme of things right now."[47]

You noticed Olivia's mention of health problems. Like other of my interviewees, she deals with the fragility of the body—in her case, a chronic disease—that shapes the whole of professional life. Nothing necessitates the Survivalist posture like the fragility of bodies. So powerful is this concern that Survivalism doesn't even seem to belong in the semiotic mode at all. Work is about what it takes to be a body and to keep a body *going*. Doesn't that take these survivors outside the semiotic mode altogether? This is an important question, one that points to a sometimes flaw in communication theory in general, a tendency to exaggerate the power of language, symbols, and meaning in human life. But communication scholar Celeste Condit would still say that, although humans are powerfully shaped by material processes, "our distinctiveness arises from the fact that our lives are so thoroughly governed, and enabled, by our symbolizing activities." The survivors, in other words, are vulnerable animal creatures, but that doesn't mean they cease to be symbolizers.[48] Dyvon and Olivia may be see-

---

43. Olivia Winkowitsch, interview by Craig Mattson, January 28, 2022.
44. Olivia Winkowitsch, interview by Craig Mattson, January 28, 2022.
45. Olivia Winkowitsch, interview by Craig Mattson, January 28, 2022.
46. Olivia Winkowitsch, interview by Craig Mattson, January 28, 2022.
47. Olivia Winkowitsch, interview by Craig Mattson, January 28, 2022.
48. Condit, *How Should We Study the Symbolizing Animal?*, 8. Condit is a student of

ing work as a mode of Survival, but there's still a meaningful narrative in the background. Call this the postcapitalist narrative. Even the Survivalists who want to detach us from work as it is normally done today do not want to detach us from meaning altogether. It's not that work means too much or too little, but that it means *something entirely different.*

You may have heard of postcapitalist movements like the mutual aid discourse of Dean Spade and others.[49] Spade's work lays out tactical steps towards constructing a new kind of society, one not grounded in the crisis saturation of late capitalism, but in the long-honored practices of communities caring for themselves.[50] Similarly David Graebner writes in *Bullshit Jobs*, "There is something very wrong with what we have made of ourselves. We have become a civilization based on work—not even 'productive work' but work as an end and meaning in itself."[51] These discourses offer a cautionary note to the cruel optimism of professional success seminars.[52]

Burke, who famously described humans as symbol-using animals. Burke, *Language as Symbolic*, 3. For our purposes the words *sign* and *symbol* are interchangeable, although linguists will tend to use one or the other.

49. Authors like Jaffe—and, to an even more radical extent, Dean Spade, Nick Srnicek, and Alex Williams—inhabit a radical corner of the semiotic mode. Their postcapitalist postures towards work and its meanings range from better worker organization to universal basic income to automation of labor, and alternative communities of mutual aid. See, for example, Spade, *Mutual Aid*, and Srnicek, *Inventing the Future*.

50. Speaking very much in the postcapitalist vein, Spade writes, "Mutual aid projects work to meet survival needs and build shared understanding about why people do not have what they need" (italics and bold removed). Spade, *Mutual Aid*, 9. I think that a modal perspective such as I'm describing in the book both has some kinship with this perspective (in that both perspectives are aimed at the disempowered), but also could tend towards Lynn Twist's perspective as well—that what the current system needs is not abrupt replacement but hospice care—as something new is midwifed into the world. See Twist, *Soul of Money*, 252. My theological reasons for resisting revolutionism are grounded in the practices of the early church as described by historians and exegetes like C. Kavin Rowe in *World Upside Down*, 150. I think something like what Rowe describes of Paul's stance towards empire is the most sustainable challenge we can offer to late capitalism today.

51. Graebner, *Bullshit Jobs*, xxvi. Graebner here shows overlap with the posture I described above as the Skeptics. But he is not just trying to raise good questions about workaholism; he's trying to create a whole new kind of society.

52. The phrase "cruel optimism," I understand, traces to Augustine, though I have not been able to locate its exact source. A more contemporary use of the phrase emerges in the work of Lauren Berlant. See Berlant, *Cruel Optimism*.

The Coordinators.

Although each of the three postures just described enacts a good way to engage the semiotic mode at work, this fourth posture represents this chapter's recommendation for semiotic engagements at work. My reason for recommending it is that, in contrast with the other three postures which focus on the rising professional's own mattering in relation to work, the posture of the Coordinator is focused on *other people's* meanings in work. This approach draws on the communication theorists Barnett Pearce and Vernon Cronen's theoretical framework for hard-to-reconcile positions, which they call the Coordinated Management of Meaning.[53] Instead of trying to make sure someone else is picking up exactly what you're putting down, this theory would recommend creating a pattern of behavior in which multiple meanings can cooperate. Here are two stories to illustrate what this might look like in the workplace.

Javairia Taylor works for a security firm called GardaWorld, where she started out as a human relations manager. One of the company's security guards was a delightful human, quick to chat, and always ready to help out clients and coworkers. But this woman had also gotten on the wrong side of Javairia's boss, a tough, militaristic ex-cop, who was always looking for excuses to fire her. And Javairia had to say, no, they couldn't just issue firings without documentation.

One day, the guard came into work and found that an elevator camera wasn't working properly. She spent her shift working on that camera, completely neglecting to lock the doors. When a guard came for the next shift, he found a door unlocked and reported it. Here, finally, was a fireable offense, and this time there was no way for Javairia to protect the guard.

> I don't think I slept the night before we had the call. I knew just how much of a dedicated person she was. She loved her job—super happy all the time. Having to tell her that we had to separate ways was really hard. Just hearing her plead for her job—she started crying on the phone. I had to tell her, "I'm going to hang up now."[54]

Javairia felt like she was losing the meaning at work, even though she sometimes felt like the only person playing by the company rules. After firing the guard, she felt dissatisfied with her own actions: "The woman's been at the site for ten years!" she told me. "How about we allow her some grace

53. For this account of Pearce and Cronen's theory, I am dependent on Griffin, Ledbetter, and Sparks, *First Look at Communication Theory*, 66–74.

54. Taylor, quoted in Mattson, "When It's Your Job to Fire Your Coworker."

to change these habits?"[55] Malfunctioning tools and a pained phone conversation make this an overwhelming situation. Instead of playing Therapist (helping the boss and the guard to understand their feelings better) or Skeptic (trying to convince the boss and the guard that they were exaggerating the importance of things) or Survivalist (urging both of the boss and the guard to be self-protective), Javairia was clearly taking the role of a *Coordinator* of workplace meanings, trying to negotiate a kind of synchrony between the boss and the guard.

- The authoritarian boss believes that organizational life is meaningful when it functions like a well-oiled machine, all the parts sending and receiving and feeding back properly. He wants to send directives out and see the consequences follow. What if Javairia could have convinced the boss that he did not *need* minute feedback on compliance issues to confirm his authority? What if she could have convinced him to focus on larger company goals instead, attending to the company's vision, its engagement with community members, its profitability? Doing that would help him to retain his own sense of how mattering happens in the company but would also leave room for Javairia to coach the security guard in a more leisurely way.
- The affable security guard understands work as meaningful in terms of helping people and maintaining a friendly, almost family-like atmosphere. Basically, everybody loved her for it, except the boss. What if Javairia could have persuaded the affable guard to see procedural compliance as what her coworker-friends most needed from her? The best way for her to have a good time with her coworkers, in other words, was to make sure that the workplace was secure. Alternatively, Javairia might also have encouraged the guard to pursue friendship outside of work. This new set of actions, without the guard's knowing it, might have achieved coordination and compliance.

Javairia's story makes clear that nobody is sovereign in a communication situation. She really tried to coordinate their meanings, but sometimes breakdown is unavoidable. There are times, however, when meaning can be coordinated successfully. Ben Hoekstra's story is a witness to that.

Ben runs a small consulting firm, a side hustle after hours from his PR job for a major medical organization. His business is something of a social enterprise: his mission is to offer marketing help for overwhelmed companies with small budgets. Once, at a mix-and-mingle fundraising gala, he casually mentioned to a gala-goer that he was running a marketing

---

55. Taylor, quoted in Mattson, "When It's Your Job to Fire Your Coworker."

consultancy. She responded that, hey, she knew a guy who needed consultancy. (It happened to be her dad.) Ben was quietly ecstatic: at that point in his career, he desperately needed clients to build out his body of work so that he could get more customers. But as he made arrangements for the initial consult, he was puzzled about one thing: nobody would say what it was that this company exactly *did*. When Ben finally asked that blunt and slightly embarrassing question, he learned that the organization was a payday loan company.

I imagine Ben inhaling slowly, trying to keep the dissonance at bay. Here he was, thinking about building a website for a company that he knew could be bad for everyday citizens, especially, as careful research makes clear, for Black and Brown citizens.[56] No matter how skillfully he did his design work for this company, would he be imprinting on his record that he'd made a website supporting online sharks? But on the other hand, could he, *should* he, tell the client (as he put it to me), "I despise what you do, so I can't tell your story"? Ben decided to have dinner with the business owner and see if they could coordinate their meanings.

At this consultation, Ben was a little relieved to learn that the president was trying to run an ethical company. But, of course, he also needed to pull in clients and make money. The next challenge, then, was to figure out how to tell the story persuasively, using principled payday-loan messaging that doesn't endanger vulnerable clients. The story Ben came up with was low-key. No hard-sell glitz. Lots of candor. Here's an edited transcript from a critical point in a podcast interview we conducted about this experience:

> Ben: The way that this company did things—they had ethical and even legal constraints for how they would do things. So that checked off one box. But then there was another one. I'm building this company website: normally, as a marketing professional, I'm going to build the most compelling, convincing website that I can. I wasn't sure if I wanted to do that here.
>
> Craig: If you did the hard sell, if you worked hard to make this website super persuasive, then you could lure somebody into a harmful service. So, how'd the story end?
>
> Ben: I worked a lot with the client making sure there wasn't any possibility of someone's getting far in this process and then getting blindsided by the interest rate. This is a company to meet actual if temporary human need.[57]

56. Hawkins and Penner, "Advertising Injustices."
57. Hoekstra, quoted in Mattson, "On the Art of Being Good People."

Notice how Ben managed and coordinated the meanings here. He recognized that in the digital venues of many payday companies, there's a dark manipulation of two kinds of desperation—that of the company trying to make a profit and that of a customer needing grocery money in the middle of the month. Instead of saying to the company owner, *Don't do this work—it's essentially unethical*; instead of saying to the potential customer, *You should figure some other way to get grocery money*, Ben coordinated their meanings differently. He built a website without heated, excessive, deceptive language that would allow the company to put their brand in front of needed audiences *and* inform those audiences exactly what to expect from the company.

Conclusion

Nothing has so helped me to listen to the stories I've shared in this chapter as the book of Ecclesiastes. Qoheleth's cries against cheaply held convictions and oppressive injustice and existential emptiness enable me to hear the sometimes pointlessness of toil. At the same time, the book cues me to notice life and work and people as gifts. Qoheleth is everywhere and always talking about gifting. Work may be meaningless, but it carries gift.[58] People act like jackholes, and then they die—but you need and should treasure their company.[59] Youth is fleeting, old age is wretched, but you should hold your life like a present from God.[60] There's also attention to the gifts of sex, friendship, wine, fine clothing, and days full of sunshine.[61] The Teacher says, "I know that there is nothing better for them than to be happy and enjoy themselves as long as they live; moreover, it is God's gift that all should eat and drink and take pleasure in all their toil."[62]

Qoheleth somehow manages a vocational paradox. Our work is ephemeral; we should do it with gusto. He avoids, in other words, just offering people bromides to make them feel more comfortable about the toilsomeness and injustice of so much of human life. I'm sometimes uneasy that those who posture themselves as workplace Therapists might simply give their team members better feelings about being paid too little. I am uneasy about how Skeptics might be oblivious to harm sometimes caused by their profitable work (*At least, I have critical consciousness about my privilege*). I'm uncomfortable that Survivalists might be ignoring the ways that already

---

58. Ecclesiastes 2:24, NRSV.
59. Ecclesiastes 4:9–12, NRSV.
60. Ecclesiastes 11:8, NRSV.
61. Ecclesiastes 9:7–9; 11:7, NRSV.
62. Ecclesiastes 3:12–13, NRSV.

existent governmental, corporate, and philanthropic systems could partner better for the common good. Even the posture I think wisest, the Coordinator, may be negotiating people's meanings without asking hard questions about why such coordinations are so necessary in late capitalism. (*Why do we have an economic system in which payday loan companies feel necessary?*) But even so, Qoheleth commends finding the gift embedded in work. I think these postures often manage to do that.

Qoheleth adopts each of these postures throughout the book, and he is surely right to do so. Organizations need those who posture themselves as Therapists, because they keep an eye out for win-win situations, even in overwhelming conditions. But that way of mattering at work can burn through the available oxygen quickly. (Sometimes, we all need a break from self-help techniques and community-building exercises.) So, we also need the Skeptics, those people who are constantly putting the scale of the work into proportion. (*Hey guys, we're not going to save the world by getting this logo right.*) But even skepticism isn't enough, when it comes to people whose work bears down on them cruelly or unjustly. We need the vocational Survivalists to ask impertinent questions, to stoke a righteous impatience, and to strive for a better world. Finally, organizations need the Coordinators, who are well-positioned to cultivate an environment in which all these postures can collaborate.

One of the great strengths of the semiotic mode is that it makes room for very different potentials at work—or what Ryan, in the opening story, might call different matterings at work. In the Christian tradition I use to make sense of things, sacraments do not turn bread and wine into something else; they make the bread and wine more truly themselves.[63] I think that's what we do when we take up our meanings and walk them into each other's workspaces. We make those matterings, and each other's, more what they are, and we transform our disappointments and failures into meanings more fully speakable in each other's lives.

---

63. Julie Canlis writes of Irenaeus's view of the sacraments: "Creation under the impact of the Spirit, does not give way to a higher reality that is other than itself; rather it becomes more itself as it participates in the new creation." See Canlis, *Calvin's Ladder*, 240.

CHAPTER 4.5

How to Work Like You Mean It
Mode/Switch Workshop

Goal: To help you address pesky and profound questions about the meanings you are making with your work.

Synopsis:

Throughout much of this book, I'm urging you to recognize the mode you're stuck in and to switch to another that is more apt for your context in the moment. But when it comes to the semiotic mode discussed in the last chapter, I don't need to urge you to make the switch. You're just there whether you want to be there or not.

What do you make of your job? You might answer that question therapeutically or skeptically. You might answer it as a survivalist or as a coordinator. But, look, you're a symbol-using animal, as Kenneth Burke would say. You're going to face the question.

It's annoying and distracting, frankly. You're trying to get stuff done, and your crazy brain pops out questions like a college kid after one too many energy drinks.

Let's say it's 3 AM, and you're working on an end-of-month report at an all-night coffee shop. One table over, you hear four people talking. Gradually, you figure out that the quiet-spoken African American woman is Chakena (Perry), and she works as a policy advocate in Chicago. The super articulate White guy, who takes a *long* time before he says anything, is Kaleb

(Nyquist)—he seems to be a data analyst in the nonprofit sector. You've been eavesdropping for a while, so you've figured out that Andrea (Munday) with the amazing glasses is a business owner, quick to laugh, quick to drop an F-bomb, quick to empathize. There's a trim, smartly dressed guy at the table, too, Carlos (Lemagne), is it? His faint accent might be—Cuban? You're not sure. Anyway, he keeps talking about grad courses and his nonprofit work in Grand Rapids. (The comments you're overhearing have been edited from individual interviews for clarity and brevity.)

If it feels weird just sitting there and snooping on the conversation, grab a pen and do some journaling in the space provided below. It'll be the perfect eavesdrop cover.

Let's start things off by asking, does your job have meaning for you?

Carlos:

It's a question that I don't think about a lot. I think I'm lucky because I am in a position where I'm able to combine a lot of things that I studied. But you know, it's also challenging work. When you look at all my friends who are financially better off, it's hard to see that. And you're like, *How am I going to make it?* I feel like every year there are parts of the year where I'm thinking, *Is this it for me? Should I move on?* And then something else happens, reminds me this is why I like this, and this is where I should keep doing it.

Chakena:

Every job I take relates to my Why. So, who am I fighting for? Why am I fighting for it? What intrinsic connection does it have to my personal story? Who am I trying to create access for or help liberate in the process? So, the meaning is always there. Because I work in government, because I work in nonprofit that's more policy- and research-driven, sometimes the direct impact isn't always there. We're doing the back-end work of trying to do strategy and drive policy decisions. That stuff doesn't come together immediately. It takes a few years for a good policy proposal to even get heard, and sometimes it takes five years to get implemented. And then, there's another few years after that, before you actually start to record the results, see how you can scale it and how it's making an impact. I only work jobs that I know I can make a difference.

Kaleb:

I spent my twenties doing work that I was very passionate about. Climate change work. I've understood this season of my life to dial back the passion and to have a job that makes ends meet, so I can take work that compensates myself well so I can pay off my debts, live a lifestyle that's a little more healthy than before. But with the idea that I have a season of life coming up that would be more challenging or more sacrificial.

Andrea:

I don't need there to be meaning. In my mind, it's like, "Oh, does your job have meaning?" No, absolutely not. Like, this is totally pointless. I just need money. I enjoy my jobs. It enables me to do things with my kids. It enables me to travel, you know, that sort of thing. It gives me some way that I'm contributing to society and things like that. That prescriptive meaning thing—that feels like too much pressure. And like if you missed it, you f—ed up. Excuse my French. I don't assume that this person is who I'm gonna be forever, that these ideas won't change, that this job will suit me forever or provide for me the same things that it provides now.

| Questions to ask yourself: | How has your job's purpose changed in different seasons of your life? |

Survival is a repeated theme in the conversation. What meanings can you give your work when you just need to make money?

What passions does your current job connect you with? Or do you see your values as something to primarily pursue outside of work?

How does your life's story shape the way you understand your job's meaningfulness?

Chakena:

My parents, grandparents, and uncles were like, *Hey, if you find a good job that has good benefits, that's paying you well, you're happy, you're not stressed out, somewhere you can retire from*—I'm in my twenties, and you're talking about retirement! This is a weird conversation to have. That's how they were raised. My mom stayed at places for twenty-some years. My grandma retired from the place that she worked for thirty or forty years. My uncle has been doing similar work all of his life, and you know that's just how those conversations go.

I've had the privilege of being able to pick and choose when I'm ready. If something's no longer serving me, I can, you know, start looking elsewhere to do other things. If I feel I'm not being stretched or challenged, or if this is not interesting anymore, I recognize that's a privilege to be able to move in and out of those spaces.

Andrea:

After my divorce I went through probably a good year of just feeling like I was living somebody else's life, because nothing around me was familiar. I wasn't with the person that I was with since I was fourteen. I had to move. I didn't believe the same thing. I didn't have the foundation of God and the church and sort of laid down my music career, which had been a huge driving factor for me forever. I lost a lot of friends. Nothing looked familiar. I had an actual existential crisis. I thought I was dying. I was having panic attacks on the floor every day. It was horrible, but I do feel like I've come out of that with an understanding that I don't belong to anybody and nobody belongs to me.

I do struggle with this because I have read research that essentially says that we live longer if we live in community or if we have strong relationships. So I have that on one hand, and then on the other hand, I'm grappling with the fact that my son could be killed today. Yes, it brings up a ton of fear in me, but I do believe I have full agency over what my life is and means, and I don't belong to anybody. Nobody belongs to me. But then, that's kind of beautiful, because we're just choosing. We're choosing each other. And that feels better to me.

Carlos:

Back home, we don't really think about work as a vocation. And this Cuban model, it's very European when it comes to work culture. I don't think we think of us as meant to live for work, but we're more meant to live, to enjoy life. And so you go to work so that you can do all the things. And of course, you have people that love their jobs. Like my dad: he does physical education. He adores that. My mom, she was a teacher. Hated it. But then since I got to the States, it's a big thing to start thinking about your vocation and why you're doing this and why you are taking this or that direction. Why do you feel that way? I don't think a lot of my background necessarily influences the way I see it now because of that difference.

Questions to ask yourself:

What were the taken-for-granted assumptions about work in your family of origin? How do you think differently about work today?

How has loss and trauma shaped your understanding of work?

How do race and ethnicity shape your understanding of work? What do you have to give thanks for in those cultural assumptions? What do you want to resist?

What advice would you give for other early career professionals coming along behind you?

Kaleb:

Even in the years since I've graduated, the technology landscape has changed so much. Look at artificial intelligence—the promise and the peril of this technology. I had this realization that you could go seek the highest possible paying job right after graduation. That is not necessarily going to be the highest paying job five years from now. There's a lot of venture-capital-driven bubbles right now. If you take the mindset of getting an education for a job that doesn't even exist yet—that might exist in five or ten years and you would be happy doing—it's OK if you're not on the current hype train. We don't know what the workplace is going to look like five or ten years from now. And so maybe we fret a little less.

Carlos:

America has so much focused on doing so much so you're ahead, and there's not a lot of time to just chill and go through life in a different way. When you get out of college, there's always the pressure: *Where are you headed to?* I'd say, take your own time. It took me five years to graduate—I ended up adding business marketing, which was not in my plans, but the music was not going to get me a long way. But for me that was a good balance. I still did what I wanted to do and added something else that allowed me to keep going. Feels like I am doing meaningful work with room for other things. Don't just focus on one or the other. I know friends of mine who are accountants or finance people who are basically working for the money. But they're not happy with what they do at all. They hate it. For me, it's more important to do something that—even though I know I could be better off somewhere else—it's still work that is doing good for me and good for other people.

Andrea:

The most helpful thing for me has been to find the ways that I was critical of myself. I get bored very easily—that's why I job-hopped. I'm not the most organized person, things like that. I've slowly moved myself into a position where I don't have to feel like a failure every day because I'm bad at details or because I get so bored working on the same product or for the same company year after year. It takes time. I had to go through a lot of jobs. I needed to go through that to not be so hypercritical of myself. And I think that's what I would tell somebody: *What are the ways that you feel like this is not working for you? And what's something that could be a better fit?* I do feel like my advice is very anti the idea you're failing if you're doing something you don't absolutely love. It doesn't even matter that much to like what you're doing. It's about the practical fit.

Chakena:

Even jobs that we enjoy—it's still work, right? You still have to move things around in your schedule. You still have to deal with people. It's emotionally taxing to show up every day, showing up well for other people, sometimes suppressing anything going on in your personal life. Sometimes you're going to get jobs that you know you are doing good work, and you are supporting people in positive ways, but it's not gonna always be exciting. But that doesn't mean that the job is not worthwhile or the job is not a good fit. Everyday looks different and I think that's the beauty of just a human being. We don't feel the same every day. We don't have the same energy level.

Questions to ask yourself:

What job that's not even been invented yet would you like to get ready for?

What are ways that you're overly critical of yourself? How might a different posture towards your work make more room for grace and chill?

What's taxing about your current job? How can you give a very human thanks for the ways your energy for your work ebbs and flows?

CHAPTER 5

Fixing Things

This chapter on the tacit mode seeks to cultivate shared attention when equipment breaks down.

When Tools Malfunction . . .

WHAT DO YOU DO when you hear someone say those dreaded words, "We seem to be having technical difficulties"—and it turns out that the voice is yours? Do you start yelling at your equipment? Do you curse it in a sweet and deadly tone of voice? *Why you lovely, lousy, *#@%-ing piece of #2^*!* Do you treat your tech like a rascally partner who's pulling a prank? Do you stiffen up like you're facing a hostile? Do you complain to others how out-of-date it is? Do you get panicky? For me, technological breakdown feels like choking on water. *This shouldn't be happening*, is all I can think in the moment.

Kenneth Burke once said that humans are "separated from their natural condition by instruments of their own making."[1] What he meant by that was that we use our tools to do more than survive; we use them to build out a reality that we come to depend on. Think of how you build out a multi-platform marketing campaign. You research the audience, you build out the website, you capture video and images, you draft content unique to each platform, and you launch. Through this whole process, and then as you're checking notifications by the hour, the campaign separates you from your

---

1. Burke, *Language as Symbolic Action*, 13. I'm changing the pronouns here to bring this into our own parlance. Burke's actual words were that "Man . . . is separated from his natural condition by instruments of his own making" (13).

natural condition as a merely biological creature. The campaign feels, in a sense, as if it has its own reality, its own taken-for-granted set of conditions. It's just *there*, like sun and shade, breeze and soil. But when the website goes down, when the event scheduler crashes, when the server has a power outage, it feels like something fundamentally unnatural has happened. *This shouldn't be happening* is all you can think.

We need to talk about the digital overwhelm that comes with technological breakdown.

Here's what I'd like to suggest in this chapter: moments of technological breakdown bring gift with them. They jolt us out of complacency and inattentiveness and startle us into an awareness of awareness that this chapter will call the *tacit mode*. Among the six modes discussed in this book, this one may be the hardest to speak of adequately, partly because "tacit" means "unspoken," partly because the mode obliges attention to attention itself. In our distracted times, that feels like a heavy lift. Usually when we think of tools, we think of the cybernetic mode or the disseminative mode. But when our tools break down, those modes are inadequate. We need a mode switch that will allow us to pay attention to technology with others. Too often, we're stuck in an efficiency-driven mode—looking for some sort of quick fix, some sort of hack—to fix the presenting problem. But if we can look at our looking and attend to our attending, we can begin to see the breakdown in a different way. This chapter will call it the tacit mode.

. . . And All the Feelings Happen

Latifah Williams is a Chicago-based media technician who agreed to talk with me on a very cold February night. I don't think our interview was uppermost in her priorities: just the night before she had postponed so she could throw on her pottery wheel. But I could hardly hold it against her. She holds a stressful job at an advertising agency called Gravity Well Studio. Being a production coordinator means, in part, that Latifah has to be careful to protect her personal time.

She told me a story about an internship she once held, doing shoots for season four of the TV show *Chicago Med*. It had been an intense day full of the thousand details of design and preparation that take a show deep into the night. (You can make good money on a fifteen-hour-a-day job, Latifah notes, not just through overtime, but because you don't have any time to spend what you make.) But on this particular night, something went wrong while she was doing lights, and Latifah felt strongly that it was her fault. "I remember I messed up on something, and—that was the last straw for me."[2] She assured me it wasn't a cataclysmic thing. "I didn't ruin anything," she added.[3] But in a setting where time itself is very expensive, a malfunction can make a technician feel conspicuous. "It's a fast-paced industry, so even if nobody is in my face saying, 'Hurry up,'—it's that pressure to perform well quickly."[4] All she could think was, "I don't like this . . . this is frustrating . . . it shouldn't take me this long."[5] Some technicians, Latifah told me, respond to situations like this by saying, "I'll deal with my feelings later."[6] Not her. Latifah left the room, found a bathroom stall, and had a good, hard cry.

Latifah's story of emotional breakdown at work is hardly unusual. But what makes it stand out for me is how her mistake was embedded in a setting of intense, collective attention. As an electrician assigned a specific set of tasks on the set of a big TV show, she could have obsessed on the error itself. This was the one thing she needed to get right—and she didn't. But I noticed in her story that she didn't even tell me what the mistake was. Was that omission due to my inability to understand technical jargon? Maybe. But I think that, at some level, Latifah was also aware that her mistake was entangled in the way everybody else on the set was paying attention together.

"When you roll in Black and a woman," as Latifah put it, you notice the way others notice things and notice *you*.[7] Her identity as young, as female, as a person of color means that her actions bring a different surveillance than the actions of a White guy in a ball cap. When a mistake happens, when stress mounts, when people pointedly do not look at you, you might not know if the trouble comes (as Latifah herself put it) from being young or Black or a woman. You just know, in that moment, that a tech problem is not *just* a tech problem.

Fortunately, Latifah has a resilient sense of humor. My guess is that, as a coworker, she's a quiet teaser, someone who is watchful enough to extract something funny from the mayhem of a TV production set. But I also noticed that for her, what's funny on a set has to do with the intersections of technology and identity. She told a story about a guy who was always subtly flexing, showing off his detailed technical knowledge of cameras. This device, he'll say, has an ISO range up to 25,600 and has a mad optical viewfinder and a dope megapixel sensor and—Latifah laughs: "They're just

---

2. Latifah Williams, interview by Craig Mattson, February 4, 2022.
3. Williams, interview by Craig Mattson, February 4, 2022.
4. Williams, interview by Craig Mattson, February 4, 2022.
5. Williams, interview by Craig Mattson, February 4, 2022.
6. Williams, interview by Craig Mattson, February 4, 2022.
7. Williams, interview by Craig Mattson, February 4, 2022.

looking at him at that point, like, *Can you take pictures with it?*"⁸ But she also found a way to tease him about his know-it-all-ness. One day when she was having trouble working the team's coffee machine, he offered to make a video to show her how to do it. She laughed and asked if he was seriously going to "mansplain coffee"?⁹ But when she eventually took his advice anyway, she added, "I can't even be upset about it, because it did help me make better coffee."¹⁰

Latifah's stories have me thinking about the terrible awkwardness that settles in when our technologies malfunction at work. It's tempting in the moment to say, *How do I fix this thing as fast as I can so I can get back to my task?* But Latifah's stories about taking the time to cry at work and spotting the humor in a sexist coworker suggest the wisdom of never wasting a breakdown. For people of nonconforming or non-majority identities, and, come to think of it, for all rising professionals, it's tempting to look for a hack to get you beyond the mistake and out of the awkwardness. But maybe that in itself would be a mistake.

Emily Bosscher, a generational researcher, works every day to help early careerists get leverage in workplace culture. "We talk a lot about hacks for this younger generation. They do love finding shortcuts. . . . They've always had the ability to go to YouTube and TikTok—I think it started with video games, where you could find ways to get through levels. And that idea of 'Yeah, how do we do it easier?' has just become standard."¹¹ But, Emily says, some kinds of problems require more than hacks; they require awkwardness. That is, they require patience for the knotted details of complex situations. Author Sheila Liming, the author of *Hanging Out*, has noted,

> Awkwardness is part of our emotional landscape. There's no real way to avoid it. It's just something you are going to run into at various points in your life anyway. So, I think the idea of shielding anybody, a kid or anybody else, from awkwardness is itself sort of silly, because that awkwardness is just going to take place all the same under different circumstances.¹²

As in all the other chapters of this book, there's a wisdom voice I'm listening to as I write. But this time, it's not a biblical voice. Instead, I'm hearing Socrates in my head as I think with you about how

---

8. Williams, interview by Craig Mattson, February 4, 2022.
9. Williams, interview by Craig Mattson, February 4, 2022.
10. Williams, interview by Craig Mattson, February 4, 2022.
11. Bosscher, quoted in Mattson, "Is There a Hack for Awkwardness?"
12. Liming, "'Quiet Catastrophe' Brewing in Our Social Lives."

communications technology promises to eliminate human awkwardness. In Plato's *Phaedrus*, the character of Socrates makes gradually clear that we *need* awkwardness. But when technology breaks down, as it inevitably does, we also have an opportunity to practice an attentiveness that Michael Polanyi calls tacit awareness. This tacit mode can help us deal with the digital overwhelm of technological breakdown.

Why Awkwardness Is Essential to Human Life and Work

"My friend!" calls out Socrates in the opening lines of the *Phaedrus*. "Where have you been? And where are you going?"[13] From the get-go, Plato depicts his teacher as cagey, funny, skillful, ironic, and utterly committed to what Michael VanderWeele might call "the difficult gift of human exchange."[14] But above all, Socrates is exhaustively attentive, missing nothing. So, when he asks where you are and where you're going, you might as well tell the truth. He's going to figure it out anyway.

As it happens, Phaedrus has been downtown taking in a talk given by Lysias, a thought leader in Athens. Phaedrus is gushing about Lysias's insight, the way you might urge someone to read Malcolm Gladwell's latest book or catch Brene Brown's latest post. The guy can't say enough about how the speech was "simply superb, especially in its choice of words."[15] But Socrates, as usual, is paying attention to something other than the bright lights that have so impressed Phaedrus. The philosopher is noticing a piece of technology under his friend's cloak, much in the way you might catch someone checking a text on their Apple watch. It sounds strange to us, but for people in predominantly oral culture like ancient Greece, paper and pen were late-breaking technologies. When Socrates sees papyrus under Phaedrus's tunic, he says, in effect, "Pull that thing out and let's download Lysias's speech."

Today, Phaedrus would probably hold up his phone, and the two of them would just watch Lysias's TED Talk together. But the available tech being what it was, Phaedrus reads the speech to his friend. It doesn't take long to figure out Lysias is recommending sex with strangers. That's put

---

13. Plato, *Phaedrus*, 227A. Throughout this discussion of the dialogue, I am indebted to hermeneutic help from Reppmann, *Truth of Love and the Love of Truth*, and Peters, *Speaking into the Air*.

14. VanderWeele, "Marilynne Robinson's Gilead and the Difficult Gift of Human Exchange."

15. Plato, *Phaedrus*, 234C.

too strongly: it's not *strangers* so much as *non-lovers* he's recommending. On the one hand, Lysias is smooth, never explicitly naming anything embarrassing or awkward; on the other hand, he is as direct as a business contract. "I don't think I should lose the chance to get what I am asking for," he notes, "merely because I don't happen to be in love with you."[16] It's much less awkward to sleep with people who don't care about you. People who love make things messy. Sex goes better, and so does everything else, conducted in a businesslike fashion—or so Lysias argues.

What Phaedrus doesn't notice is that, in reading Lysias's speech, he is doing with communication what Lysias is doing with sex: mediating an effortless transaction. Or trying to. Just as Lysias recommends scattering one's sexual favors without regard to love and passion, so Phaedrus is broadcasting the speech without regard to place or person, as if "Lysias himself is present," as Socrates jokes.

Socrates isn't so sure that Phaedrus's technology is working so well as the lad seems to think. In some ways, Socrates is a bit of a techno-minimalist, like Cal Newport or Sherry Turkle. He can use the tools of his day just fine, but he'd rather have a meaningful conversation, sitting knee to knee, face to face. But the old teacher is cagey enough to know he can't just tell Phaedrus to stop fanboying Lysias. Besides, Socrates really wants the young man to own his own life.[17] So the teacher lands on a way to show Phaedrus the actual complexities of communication and technology: he gives an oratory of his own, making the same argument about sex that Lysias did, but with much more skill, and then just as the young fellow is getting into it, Socrates hits the stop button. "That's it, Phaedrus. You won't hear another word from me, and you'll have to accept this as the end of the speech."[18] In contrast with the easy transfer Lysias's speech had conducted, Socrates's speech ends in an awkward silence.

---

16. Plato, *Phaedrus*, 231A.

17. One of the most striking things about Socrates's conversational gambits in *Phaedrus* is how much leeway he leaves Phaedrus to opt in or out. Even after the conversation begins and Socrates has begun to press his questions home, he still wants the guy to take active leadership in the conversation. Over and over again, he expresses willingness to submit to the younger man's guidance, saying things like, "you can lead me all over Attica or anywhere else you like" (230E). When Phaedrus raises a point that Socrates disagrees with, he will still say that "what you just said, in particular, must not be dismissed" (260A). It sometimes sounds like cajolery, but by encouraging Phaedrus's active participation in the conversation, Socrates is enacting an indispensable dynamic of the dialogic model of communication: the egalitarian invitation that seeks consent and involvement.

18. Plato, *Phaedrus*, 241E.

Phaedrus is baffled; things had been going so well! Socrates gradually reveals that he has questions about Lysias's proposals. *Should* intimacy be so transactional? Probably not. Should communication be indiscriminately scattered like a friends-with-benefits arrangement? Can't a contract adequately convey the world of human relationship? Isn't human life about sending out seed every which way and hoping somebody, somewhere catches it? Yeah, maybe not. The philosopher offers some counter-insights in the form of a take-it-back speech, which functions like a prayer for forgiveness from Eros, the god of love.

Although the Palinode, as this third speech is sometimes called, is gorgeous, what obliges our attention is the speech's defense of awkwardness. Socrates doesn't call it that, of course; he calls it *madness*. But whatever its specific name, it's a condition that's diametrically opposite to the cool, frictionless, chill approach to sex and, implicitly, to communication that Lysias proposes and that Phaedrus enthuses about. Socrates argues that what seems irrational and impractical is actually essential to human society: "in fact the best things we have come from madness, when it is given as a gift of the god."[19] Music? Poetry? Art? All these, Socrates insists, depend on madness. Get rid of awkwardness, in other words, and you get rid of the human in human life.

From there, Socrates moves on to describe what he calls "the painfully difficult business" of being a human soul, especially a soul in love.[20] To be a person, he says, is to struggle, as you try to keep on the way of wisdom. He uses imagery of a chariot with two struggling horses, one pulling the vehicle upwards, the other down. But to be a person in love with another is no less a painful and overwhelming condition: "when he sees a godlike face or bodily form that has captured Beauty well, first he shudders and a fear comes over him. . . . his chill gives way to sweating and a high fever."[21] What Socrates describes here is far from transactional and far from manageable. But the awkwardness and overwhelm of impassioned desire, he believes, offers guidance for life with others in the company of our technologies.

You remember from the Introduction of this book that Socrates and Phaedrus discuss how well writing, as a technology of communication, does what we're hoping it will do. Although Socrates prefers dialectical conversation, he is open to ways to align okay tools with excellent goals. But he also envisions a kind of technological breakdown for the pen—when one's writing gets scattered to the wrong audiences, much as a reply-all

19. Plato, *Phaedrus*, 244B.
20. Plato, *Phaedrus*, 246B.
21. Plato, *Phaedrus*, 251A.

email might arrive in unintended inboxes. Given his conservative take on technology, he suspects that the work of using a stylus will be laborious and prone to error. It's a good thing that Socrates's student, Plato, seems to differ on this point: if Plato weren't such a generous writer, we wouldn't be discussing this dialogue at all.

This is the text that comes to mind with Latifah's story about slumping in a bathroom stall on a cold January night, trying to get herself together after a technological error. It's also what comes to mind as she tells about laughing about the coffee-making videos of her mansplaining colleague. From across the millennia, Socrates speaks to us of the discomfort, woundedness, and excessive emotion that are elemental to the human condition—so elemental, in fact, that not even the latest communications technology can eliminate them. I think we can build on Socrates's wisdom with the help of Michael Polanyi, whose thought gives us access to the tacit mode, a manner of engagement that might help us be overwhelmed better when our tools get tricky on us.

What the Tacit Mode Is and Why It's Needed

I first encountered Michael Polanyi on a Walkman portable cassette tape player, a chunky little piece of communications technology that even in the 1990s was beginning to feel passe. After listening to an audio documentary about Polanyi's theory of tacit knowing, I tried to find this thinker's ideas in the graduate textbooks I was assigned in theory courses. I quickly discovered that "Polanyi" is not a name you'll find in communication texts, even though he himself tried to make his ideas widely accessible in a quirky confessional of a book called *Personal Knowledge: Towards a Post-Critical Philosophy*.[22] What has kept me reading and studying Polanyi's thought over decades of teaching and researching communication practice has been his attention to attention, and, in particular, his attention to the role of language and tools in the practice of shared attention.

Although it's hard to separate language and tools—Polanyi sees language as a kind of tool—let's talk about language first. Polanyi insists that "we know more than we can say."[23] He doesn't mean that it's *impossible* to say what we know, only that it's *difficult* to say it. My favorite example of knowing more than you can say has to do with riding a bike. Let's say you're trying to teach your niece how to ride her new two-wheeler. You'll probably start by offering a few cues. *Turn your handlebars whichever way your bike*

22. Polanyi, *Personal Knowledge*.
23. Polanyi, *Tacit Dimension*, 4.

starts to tip! Pedal faster when you're going to fall! But one thing you probably won't do is to tell her exactly, precisely, scientifically, how to ride a bike. Polanyi shows how ridiculous this would be: "A simple analysis shows that for a given angle of unbalance the curvature of each winding is inversely proportional to a square of the speed at which the cyclist is proceeding."[24] Imagine telling your niece, *All you gotta do, honey, is keep the curvature inversely proportional to your velocity squared!* You know good and very well that your niece has to learn to ride a bike in the risky space between the tool she's trying to use and the fun she's trying to have. Super-precise language offers only the illusion of control. But Polanyi didn't stop with *we know more than we can say.* He also insisted that *we say more than we know.*[25] Language, as we will discuss in the chapter on the performative mode, is always taking action, and some of that action is unintended.

These ideas that knowing > saying and saying > knowing have implications for technology usage, too. In the same way that words and intentions get out of whack, so do tools and goals. Polanyi argued that when we interact with tools, we practice what he called from-to awareness. One level of our attention is *attending-to*. This is your intentional focus, like the nail you're trying to pound into the board. But that act of attending-to also requires an act of *attending-from*. The *from* is your contextual awareness. I'm no carpenter, but even I know that if you want to pound a nail, you have to look at the nail—but you also need to have a good feel for the hammer. Polanyi would say that you practice successful from-to attention when, without taking your eyes off the nail, you adjust your grip on the hammer, adapt to its heft, and pound the thing home. Polanyi uses this distinction between the *to* and the *from* of tool-using awareness to explain the gap that opens between what we intend to do with our technologies and what we *actually* do. In that gap between tool use and goal achievement, we practice the complex attentiveness of the tacit mode.

Let me share a story that illustrates the complexities of from-to awareness in the work of marketing and strategic communication. I've already talked to you about Liv Winkowitsch, who works for a design company in Los Angeles and who embodies a quality of contemplativeness that feels indispensable in the frenetic work of digital communication today. But being a mindful person does not, of course, mean that everyone around her practices the same tacit awareness. Would that it were so.

She told me about a time when she and her designers needed a vector image for a graphic project they were working on for a Hollywood client.

---

24. Polanyi, *Personal Knowledge*, 50.
25. Polanyi, *Tacit Dimension*, 95.

(Vector images are indispensable to design projects because they maintain their quality at every size.) Liv thought at first that she could solve this problem quickly by shooting a note to the client, asking for the image again. She was focused, quite understandably, on the "to" needed for the project: the missing file. And nothing, one would think, could be simpler. The other party owned the image; they needed only to send an email attachment. Sure enough, Liv soon received an email with an attached file. *Phew. The design process could continue.* But when she opened the email, she found that the executive had sent, not the requested vector image, but a video file instead. Presumably, this emailer was technologically proficient enough to send the vital scalable vector graphic. Hollywood is a guild built on visual imagery, after all. Instead, what had arrived in Liv's email box was—an mp4 file? What level of detachment, hurry, and disregard could have resulted in this mistake? And what should Liv do to get the design processes running again? It was a face-palm moment for Liv.

But it was also a moment for her to pull back and consider the "from" of the situation. It no longer seemed smart to treat this problem as simply The Case of the Missing Vector File. Something about the miscommunication with the client had alerted Liv, spreading out her memory into the network of relationships in which this sort of work always has to be done. Over her years with this design firm, Liv had learned that more attention from a client does not necessarily mean better relationship with that client. Lots of "back and forth" (a term I heard more than one of my interviewees complain about) can create needless work that the company has to somehow negotiate.[26] For example, Fred Walls, another millennial professional, told me about the dumb ideas that clients come up with when they get too involved in the process. "A lot of times clients will suggest things that are awful, and I know they're awful. But they don't know that. And the only way for them to know it's awful is for me to give it to them. And they're like, 'Wow, that's terrible.' And I'm like, 'I know, so let's do something else.'"[27]

I like to think of that moment when Liv pulls her face out of her palm and stares out the window for a moment, contemplating the network of relationships and possibilities in which her work for that day is embedded. Dismissing overcommunication as a hack, she instead turned to her team, explained the situation, and proposed that they recreate the vector image themselves. It would be a time-consuming project—a day's work that would eventually reach deep into the night—but they had the skills

---

26. Mattson, "Question: Why Do Clients Require Overcommunication?"

27. Walls, in Mattson, "When Clients Dispute and Colleagues Disparage." This quote was edited for brevity and clarity.

and the tools to do it. So they got to work. I'm struck by the amplitude of attentiveness here. By practicing this from-to awareness, Liv and her team located unobvious resources to solve a problem and, by deft and patient work, got the design process back in motion.

How Rising Professionals Use the Tacit Mode

You can find your way into the tacit mode by way of three postures towards technology. Although I draw on Polanyi's ideas here, I find his terminology a little dense.[28] Instead, I'll refer to three postures of tacitness: *rapport*, *tracking*, and *breakdown*.

Rapport.

Polanyi notes that people have skills for which they have no words, or few words. You probably can't explain how you float on your back in a swimming pool, for example. Polanyi refers to this tacit awareness, a little grandly, as "the ineffable domain"—but, he hastens to add, ineffability doesn't mean something super-spiritual or mystically transcendent. As a posture towards technology, this is a way of inhabiting the digital that has worked through the difficult stuff, the awkward stuff, and has come out on the other side.

Perhaps because the focus of my interviews was professional overwhelm, I didn't hear a lot of stories of technological rapport, although I think such a relationship with communication tools was often implied in stories of success and generosity at work. But one such narrative showed up explicitly with my daughter Emma, who was a speech pathology master's student at the time, doing virtual tutoring on the side. I asked her

---

28. I'm drawing here on Polanyi's discussion of three ways that speech and thought interact. Language, after all, is itself a kind of technology developed to deal with the world. Of course, words are more than tools, as Burke notes. They're ways of acting in the world. To say that words are just tools is like saying that because water can generate power, it is just an instrument. "But though instrumentality is an important aspect of language, we could not properly treat it as the essence of language. To define language simply as a species of tool would be like defining metals merely as species of tools" (Burke, *Language as Symbolic Action*, 15). I am transposing Polanyi's account of how speech interacts with thought to describe how technology interacts with intention. The first interaction he calls "the ineffable domain" because in it "the tacit predominates to the extent that articulation is virtually impossible." In the second domain, "the tacit component is the information conveyed by easily intelligible speech, so that the tacit is co-extensive with the text of which it carries the meaning." And in the third domain, "the tacit and the formal fall apart, since the speaker does not know, or quite know, what he is talking about" (87). See Polanyi, *Tacit Dimension*.

about working with the GoPeer platform she shares with tutees, and she described the establishment of rapport, not just with the students but with the technology itself. She noted that, at first, there's some awkwardness as the students are gauging "how much of an agentic role they're going to take in the session, and which of the Zoom room tools we'll be using." After that, though, Emma notes that a cadence settles in, especially when she and they get to laughing.

> I genuinely think that my connections with these kids are just as strong as if they were meeting me in person at the library for a hour each week or at an in-person tutoring meeting. Actually, I think they're stronger. The kids themselves have more agency because they're in their spaces, they're not meeting me on my turf. Now that I'm thinking about it, I think that's a real boon for them—and for us clicking. They ask me about my background, where I am, if Peaches [the cat] is going to make an appearance; I get to see the kind of decorations/fandoms in their bedrooms ("Is that Ahsoka Tano from the Mandalorian??" etc). So my feelings about the virtual calls mostly relate to whether or not we've successfully cultivated that "click."[29]

Emma's term *clicking* depicts a posture open to rapport with the shared technology. What she seems to have figured out with her students is a way for the tacit mode to work through awkwardness towards a shared and productive awareness.

Tracking.

Polanyi describes the experience of reading several letters at breakfast, some of them in different languages. When he's finished the stack of correspondence, he can't remember what languages they were written in. So perfectly was he tracking with the letters that he was able effortlessly to attend *from* the language *to* the meaning the language carries.[30] "While I read the letter, I was consciously aware both of its text and of the meaning of the text, but my awareness of the text was merely instrumental to that of the meaning, so that the text was transparent in respect to its meaning."[31] You track similarly with technology when you follow GPS directions on your phone. If you're like me, after you hear the phone voice say, "You have arrived," you may not remember

---

29. Emma Mattson, personal correspondence with author, November 10, 2022.
30. Polanyi, *Tacit Dimension*, 16.
31. Polanyi, *Personal Knowledge*, 91.

how you have arrived—so transparent were the instructions you received. I tend to simply make the turns, follow the roads, and get there.

One example of tracking closely with technology showed up in an interview with Adam Frankenfeld, who works for a video game company. When a video game hits the market, many players are thinking about the game at one level only, following the reward structures of the game to complete it more or less as the designers intended. There are, of course, multiple ways to do this. You could repeat a move over and over, picking up points, getting the tokens needed for winning the level. You might also get the needed tokens from another player through a kind of economic transaction. You might "grind" like the Starbucks district manager Adam told me about who, when a game came out, would play it from 5 PM to 1 AM every night till she had finished the game. You might take a saner, slower approach, finishing the game in months. The point is that, if the game is well-designed, the player can track with it steadily.

Adam can tell me all this because he doesn't track with games on just one level—at least not at work. His job requires him to test the game's weaknesses, finding its bugs, anticipating how someone might complete in a few days a game that was designed to take three weeks. To do that, Adam has had to cultivate a weird objectivity about the game. He's looking *at* a given game rather than *through* it, like a composition teacher who can't help listening for somebody's grammar errors. But Adam's skill as a tester only shows more clearly how a game's normal play is usually trackable.[32]

Breakdown.

Polanyi identifies a domain of technology and attention in situations where your tools and your experience refuse to coordinate. In what he calls "*the domain of sophistication,*" he notes, what we're saying and what we're intending to say fall away from each other. You've had the experience, surely, of saying something and not knowing if it was ingenious or idiotic. Sometimes a child says something without understanding what they're saying, and yet somehow the words manage to be profound. This happens with technology as well, when a bug invites complex attention, resulting in a solution that might be elegant or might be, as Em Orendorff puts it, trash.

---

32. So powerful is the text as it is designed, he says, "We can't hire a tester and then just throw them at something and say 'Log any bugs you find,' because they don't know what to find yet. And I can't just list everything out for them." Adam Frankenfeld, interview by Craig Mattson, January 3, 2022. The "at" and "through" language comes from Lanham, *Economics of Attention*, 158–162.

Em used to work at a specialty coffee company, and they hated it. In a way, it was good to get laid off during the pandemic. They'd been pretty burned out by all the emotional labor of politeness to rude customers. What a relief, then, to switch guilds entirely and find work as a software developer. Em enjoyed the older, more mature colleagues. They also enjoyed *not* dealing with customers directly. "I do the ticket and that's really all I do." Frustrations arise from problems with the code, not so much with entitled clients. "A lot of our problems can seem really small, but then they're so chained together that any little thing can mess up a whole system."[33] It is tricky, admittedly, to work with brilliant people, as Em does. What a seasoned colleague can do in minutes may take them *hours*. "There are times when I'll have a problem that I feel like I cannot fix, and I feel like I've tried everything, and I get so frustrated and literally will just walk away or I'll sleep on it or something." That moment of walking away to sleep on it is, I think, the domain Polanyi refers to as "sophistication"—and what we would call "breakdown."[34] It's a liminal space in which Em doesn't know how or when the solution will show up. They go away from the screen, take a walk around the building, come back, and—there it is, as if "something's been standing right in front of you."

Although Em did not foreground it, more questioning from me turned up the fact that problem-solving does involve some emotional labor. They sometimes compare their abilities negatively to those of others. But not always. Mostly Em enjoys seeing all the solutions coders can come up with. There's an intriguing openness to the work. Even if Em's own solution works, it might not be as elegant as someone else's:

> It's fun to watch other people's solutions to the same thing, I think, because there's not one right answer in development. I'll do something, and I'll be like, "That's pretty good, I think," and then I'll see someone else's solution, and I'll be like, "Mine is trash." But I like that. It's cool.[35]

Sometimes, collegial interaction can be tiresome, though. Em notes, "I think for me being non-binary and using they/them pronouns and working with a range of people—I think that certainly has been challenging in and of itself."[36] Em likes remote work, because it provides a chance to do some convenient identity signaling by putting their pronouns on a Zoom name. Even so, "That's a lot of emotional labor in itself. Feeling the need

---

33. Em Orendorff, interview by Craig Mattson, May 2, 2022.
34. Orendorff, interview by Craig Mattson, May 2, 2022.
35. Orendorff, interview by Craig Mattson, May 2, 2022.
36. Orendorff, interview by Craig Mattson, May 2, 2022.

to correct somebody on who I am is a weird dynamic to navigate. And a lot of times it's not worth it to me to have a random coworker misgender me, let's say. It happens. It happens all the time, and it kind of sucks. But at the same time do I want to further engage somebody like that, to try to tell them why that's wrong?"[37]

I asked if workplace discrimination slows down cognitive speeds while problem-solving.

> Yeah, definitely. There are some days are better than others . . . It often depends on the amount of times it happens in a day or how I feel about that particular coworker to begin with. I think that always is a thing. I feel like I can operate on a "strikes method." . . . You know, first time? I get it. It happens. Are you going to correct yourself? Are you going to be conscious enough to know that you made a mistake? Self-aware enough, I guess? Am I going to have to say something? And if it keeps happening repeatedly, then it makes me more angry. Those days, I think, are harder.[38]

Here's what I'm hearing in Em's testimonials. Moments of technological breakdown alter our awareness: they push us into complicated in-between spaces where we have to practice a sophisticated awareness. It's *sophisticated* in the sense that the solutions that come from that awareness may turn out to be ingenious or mere *sophistry*. But here's the thing: even in a rather secluded industry like software engineering, people don't do problem-solving in isolation. The problems they deal with are always a part of a milieu, a complex set of interactions, partly machinic, partly social. Practicing the tacit mode, then, obliges an attunement not just to lay hands on a The One Right Solution, but rather to engage with emotional wisdom with a highly interactive ecology. The mode switch pressed upon us by the tacit mode is one from extraction to attunement.[39]

Who Needs the Tacit Mode? (Hint: Not Just the Rising Professional)

Everybody has to practice tacit awareness to do their work. Everybody has to recognize the fullness and interactivity of collective attention in order to do their work. Comedians have to work with audiences to turn an ordinary

---

37. Orendorff, interview by Craig Mattson, May 2, 2022.
38. Orendorff, interview by Craig Mattson, May 2, 2022.
39. Rickert, *Ambient Rhetoric*, 160.

situation into a funny story. Detectives have to fan through a crime scene together, attending to subtle patterns in the wake of violence. Mystics and other worshippers have to gaze together upon the invisible. All these situations require fanned-out awareness not just for hacks for an isolated problem, but for networked attunement for a shared context.

For rising professionals after the pandemic, remote work can generate technological breakdowns hard to work through. Brittany Minnesma was hired remotely as a marketer and, at the time of our interview, was still doing her work remotely without ever having met her managers or coworkers in person. "I think that most of the breakdown that I've experienced so far is being remote and not having as easy access to my colleagues, my boss, not being able to get answers as quickly, especially if I'm just communicating via a platform like Teams or Slack," Brittany noted. "Everyone is on different schedules. Everyone is remote, mostly, and very spread out. So, it's hard to get answers sometimes."[40]

It is tempting to say that the problem here is a technological malfunction. The tools are failing Brittany. She should find a way to meet in person with her team. There's some truth to that: Derek Thompson, writing for *The Atlantic*, has discussed how hard it is for remote communicators like Brittany to get acclimated to the hard-to-talk-about details of an organization's culture.[41] But after this chapter's analysis and storytelling, I think it would be more accurate to say that the malfunction Brittany senses *involves* technology but is not isolatable *to* technology. In fact, the managers' inability to engage the tacit mode with Brittany online suggests that even if everybody came back to the office, there would still be a tendency to ignore contextual and relational "from" issues in a managerial hacking of "to" strategies for efficiency.

But what interests me most about Thompson's discussion—and what gives me hope for Brittany—is that the tacit mode can also be practiced in remote work. "One school of thought says face-to-face interactions are too precious to be replaced," writes Thompson. "I disagree. I'm an optimist who believes the corporate world can solve these problems, because I know that other industries already have."[42]

Thompson cites a study by Carl Benedikt Frey and Giorgio Presidente, exploring the impact of new communication technologies on collaborative scientific discoveries. It used to be the case that scientists who were "co-located" (i.e., working in-person) made new discoveries more

---

40. Brittany Minnesma, interview by Craig Mattson, February 9, 2022.
41. Thompson, "Biggest Problem."
42. Thompson, "Biggest Problem."

often than those who were "distributed" (i.e., working remotely). The advantage provided by accidental conversations at the water cooler Frey and Presidente refer to, rather nerdily, as "the onsite collaboration premium." But things have begun to change. Frey and Presidente note that remote collaboration has, in the past decades, been making startling strides—so much so that the researchers note "evidence that the onsite collaboration premium has become more muted over the decades, suggesting that the benefits of co-location have diminished."[43]

In other words, remote working groups used to do science less well than in-person collaborators. Today that ratio has flipped so that in-person collaborations are losing ground to digital collaboration. Some of this is surely due to people who knew each other offline coming together online with great relational capital in hand. But these teams have also able to improve communication with people they've never met. With the spread of Skype, Zoom, and Teams, "individual scientists in distributed teams are likely to present and discuss their research with faculty in their respective departments"—because they know them well and communicate easily whatever the medium. So "spillovers from the local networks of members might benefit not just the individual, but also increasingly the wider team," including people they don't know very well.[44] Thompson summarizes these findings by saying that "After decades of trial and error, they've learned to combine their local networks, which are developed through years of in-person encounters, and their virtual networks, to build a kind of global collective brain."[45] That's the tacit mode: recognizing the actual fullness of interactivity and attention across a network of in-person and remote communities.

What is the gift of the mode switch this chapter recommends? Switching from the efficiency-driven cybernetic mode to the highly attentive tacit mode brings with it awkwardness, to be sure. But that awkwardness affords human exchange in moments of technological breakdown. And this, in turn, gives us the gift of moving forward in stronger collaboration with each other and with our machines. But we can't make this tacit awareness a requirement for millennial and Gen Z professionals alone. Everyone, and not just quarterlife careerists, can and should *guess across the gap* between the explicit and the tacit. In fact, the tacit mode can be a gift that managers give their teams and leaders their organizations.

43. Frey and Presidente, "Disrupting science."
44. Frey and Presidente, "Disrupting science."
45. Thompson, "Biggest Problem."

CHAPTER 5.5

How to Get Unstuck from Technical Difficulties

Mode/Switch Workshop

Goal: To recover and improve your coping mechanisms when digital tools break down.

Synopsis:

LET'S START THIS WORKSHOP about dealing with the digiwhelm of tech-failure with a quick story from Robert Pirsig's *Zen and the Art of Motorcycle Maintenance*. He tells a story about a guy who takes his seized-up bike to what turns out to be a bad mechanic.[1] The bike owner watches as the repairman beats the motorcycle with a hammer and a chisel, until the only thing to say is "Just stop" and then to wheel the bike out of the shop as quickly as possible.

The character wonders later what went wrong. "There was no obvious reason for it. And I tried to remember back into that shop, that nightmare place, to try to remember anything that could have been the cause."[2] He remembers that they were playing music loudly, that they were in a tearing hurry, and that everybody acted like they were watching TV. "But the biggest clue seemed to be their expressions. They were hard to explain. Good-natured, friendly, easygoing—and uninvolved. They were like

---

1. Pirsig, *Zen and the Art*, 24–25.
2. Pirsig, *Zen and the Art*, 26.

spectators. You had the feeling they had just wandered in and somebody had handed them a wrench."[3]

I bring up Pirsig's story to start off this workshop because it has so much to do with the tacit mode discussed in the last chapter. His musings align with the wisdom of Plato and the analysis of Polanyi: technological malfunctions are never just about the tools themselves. They are about people's attentiveness as they use the tools.

In what follows, I conduct a conversation with four working professionals about tech breakdowns, asking them how they cope. They all work in different sectors of today's knowledge economy. Andrew Holmes was at the time a warehouse associate for UPS. Tyler May-Gruthusen is a hardware engineer at Allegion. Rosalia Portillo is an executive assistant at the Walgreens Boots Alliance. Javairia Taylor is an employee relations specialist at GardaWorld.

(This interview was first published in the *Mode/Switch* newsletter on Substack and has been stitched together from four separate interviews and edited for clarity and brevity.)[4]

Craig:

I think when we use the phrase "technical difficulties" as in, "We seem to be having technical difficulties," we use the phrase a little ironically or wryly. Does that sound right to you—and why do you think that is?

Tyler:

Well, I'm just gonna muse. I don't know how else to answer your question. My guess is that at one point it was a serious thing—"Hey, this is what's happening." And then at some point, the way that we said it was infused with how we all felt.

Craig:

So, the phrase has a vibe. It's naming an affective experience more than a literal reality.

---

3. Pirsig, *Zen and the Art*, 27.
4. Mattson, "How to Get Unstuck."

Javairia:

I would say it's serious business, but also a joke. "Oh, good job. You broke the machine."

Rosalia:

I would add *jokingly* and *lightheartedly*, but also *somewhat apologetically*. Especially in my line of work, I'm scheduling my boss for a lot of thirty-minute time slots, so even taking five minutes figuring out your mic or your camera—there is a desire to cut that off at the pass with apologies. It could be a very Midwestern point of view: "Oops, sorry about that!" Maybe as a woman, too—that might be a part of the dynamic of it.

Craig:

That's interesting—the role of gender norms in problem-solving.

Andrew:

There's an expectation that males are mechanically inclined and that they have this magical commonsense that just descends on them all. I don't know exactly where that mythos comes from, but it's a pervasive feature. I was tempted to feel an immense amount of shame about the fact I have never worked on an engine before, and these expectations are placed upon us unwittingly.

Questions to ask yourself:

When tools break down at work, what is your immediate emotional response? (Try to name the feelings as precisely as you can.)

Are there factors about who you are—where you grew up, your gender, your trade or guild—that incline you to feel that way?

Craig:

We rely a lot on artificial intelligence in our everyday work, even when our office spaces or warehouse floors look nothing like Tony Stark's lab. When your tools and systems at work take on a mind of their own, do you experience them as willing partners or outright hostiles or misfit oldsters or mischievous collaborators?

Tyler:

Oh, I definitely get hostile. I have always been this way and I have no idea why. I have to go walk it off or something. I guess, if it's one of those things where I have zero control over it, that's when it becomes hostile. I have to actually leave the situation. Stop thinking about the problem. Distract myself. And then, I can come back to it.

Andrew:

I would mostly align myself with the *mischievous collaborator* in the sense that, especially at UPS, while we do deal with a lot of simpler machines, there's lots of computer processes on top of mundane mechanical—telescoping lifts and things like that. But my capacity to troubleshoot the system is so limited because they don't train me to troubleshoot—that's not something that they want to pay me to know. So there's a lot of times when it's like, OK, *How do we do this without having what we actually need to do this?* Things break. It's the entropy. Whether it's miscommunication from people or the breakdown of actual physical components, things go awry. From a certain perspective in the chain, for me, the only thing that that can look like is black magic at work. I don't know who has it out for me, but all I know is that I have to start improvising. So I think the "mischievous collaborator" feels very right to me.

Javairia:

When I think about tech, I think about systems that we use. I would say, *Willing Partner*. Now as far as helping someone set up their tech, I would say *Mischievous Collaborators*. Part of my job is virtually helping someone set up their computer. I'm very anxious. I can't say, "Okay, I'll look at your screen" and, "Click here, do this." I have to say, "Walk me through what you're seeing." I *think* we're on the right path, but I'm not sure exactly.

Rosalia:

My boss uses touch screen a lot and so she'll end up in meetings where it's like this [showing just forehead and eyes at the bottom of the screen]. "How do you *not* realize that I can't see you?" Technology isn't very black and white. Sometimes it can be gray, and there's like funk to it. It's almost like a horse you're riding that you have to kind of keep on track. And if you don't pay attention to it, sometimes it'll veer and you have to bring it back.

Questions to ask yourself:	How do you experience some of the critical technologies of your job? Willing partners? Outright hostiles? Misfit oldsters? Mischievous collaborators?
	Do you experience technology as having a funky willfulness? Does it ever seem to have a mind of its own?

Craig:

In *Zen and the Art of Motorcycle Maintenance*, Robert Pirsig describes: "This is the zero moment of consciousness. Stuck. No answer. Honked. Kaput. It's a miserable experience emotionally. You're losing time. You're incompetent. You don't know what you're doing. You should be ashamed of yourself. You should take the machine to a real mechanic who knows how to figure these things out."[5] When things break down, we have to find a certain headspace to get through the stuckness. What does that look like for you?

---

5. Pirsig, *Zen and the Art*, 251.

Rosalia:

I think I can empathize with that feeling. But I feel like, when we're talking about technology with work, I don't give up very easily. Even if we need to switch to a cellphone to get us through this meeting—there's always a different way of going about it. I feel like that has been an ongoing thing for me through mindfulness practice, particularly. "What's going on right in this moment? How can I work with what's going on right now, sit with it?" And in doing that, I find that you allow yourself to be open to other possibilities. In general, taking things with humor, like when bad things happen—I like the word "mischievous" because I think that's the light-heartedness everyone has experienced. It's a commonality that we share. So even if someone is frustrated, if you acknowledge it and name that—people know that you're dealing with this little thing that doesn't want to work. I'm sure that just happened to them yesterday.

Craig:

What do you do when you get into stuckness with tools and systems?

Andrew:

It sounds like he [Pirsig] is kind of alone with his machine. But for me the biggest lesson that I've had to learn is how to ask for help. He's describing the judgmentalism that will arrive in those moments. And that's part of the reason that it has been important for me to lean into collaboration, to get a new set of eyes, to shake up the way I'm looking at it.

Javairia:

Phone a friend.

Craig:

Right, phone a friend. Rosalia, you brought up mindfulness. What about that practice has been helpful to ease you into an appropriate attentiveness?

Rosalia:

I still get upset. Mindfulness is all about allowing yourself to be in the moment. If sounds happen or a feeling comes in your body, instead of investigating it and saying, "What can I do to fix it?"—just allowing it to pass through you. "I know that this was an issue in the past, but frustration from the past is not gonna be helpful in the moment." So allowing yourself to say, "OK, what's going on, and where can I start to see what some solutions might be?"

I constantly have to remind myself that I don't have to stress myself out. Work is important, and I should take pride in my work, but I shouldn't feel the urgency of life or death with work, because it really just stresses you out to the point that you almost can't function. You get that feeling of stuckness because you build up such high stakes.

I just got a performance review: "Rosie is weirdly able to stay calm." The crazier things get, the calmer I get. But that's after years of practice. In your day-to-day when things aren't working, instead of choosing frustration, take a deep breath and chill out and give yourself a break. Which is difficult to do.

Andrew:

I had to learn to take a look at my history. Learning to contact my actual history and say, "What is reasonable for me to expect myself to be able to do right now?" I'm not supposed to be some island, this self—totally self-sufficient.

Javairia:

You know, when issues go wrong, everything seems like an emergency. Super important. And one time, it was as simple as turning on and off the computer. "Oh, OK, there's everything!"

Questions to ask yourself:	What practices do you find help you when you feel stuck between tech breakdown and the tasks you have to do?
	What parts of your own story, or your family's story do you need to remind yourself of when tools malfunction?

Craig:

I love that phrase, "Oh, there's everything." So, the mindset change can be, "Maybe this isn't an emergency. Maybe this isn't a crisis. Maybe it's a simple thing." That sounds like the wisdom of the low-key. OK, last question: Is there anything that you feel like you've had to unlearn in order to resolve technical problems?

Javairia:

That's a really good question. I've had the tendency to rush through things. "OK! Spent an hour trying to figure out how to get your computer fixed, when it probably should have taken thirty minutes. Now we have to make up for lost time." Which doesn't make a good experience for everybody, because they feel like they're getting gypped of information.

Tyler:

I have always been a solo learner. You have to sign off on stuff. You're always thinking. You're always questioning. You're always pushing the envelope. At the same time, you can overdo that and hold the team hostage to your own thoughts.

Andrew:

I was listening to psychologist Hillary McBride talk about her concept of "the man box." There's this closed system of expectations and those create certain types of fears, certain patterns of behavior. In some ways, I was positioned to feel like a fake man because of those expectations about how men are technically competent and work with their hands and all this kind of stuff. That's been the process for me.

Questions to ask yourself:	What's your social habit when it comes to tech breakdown? Do you isolate? Do you step back and let others take charge? Do you collaborate on repairing the tool? How could you improve that habit?

> Are you dealing with a "box" of other people's expectations? How have you managed to get out of the box? What helps other people see that you don't really belong there?

One thing I'm thinking about after that conversation is that technical difficulties aren't just freak conditions, like a hurricane that blows in all of a sudden, decimating the day's plans. No, technological breakdown is where we live. Because we find ourselves immersed in infrastructures, because we indwell technologized environments, we endure the stress and intensity of relating to artificial intelligence constantly. And as a friend of mine used to say, "Machines break down. That's what they do." After this conversation, I'm also thinking that what breaks down is not just our machines, but our collaboration with machines. We forget to exercise the subtle wisdom of tacit knowing. We forget to be attentive, to move slowly, and to be digitally circumspect. To keep the tacit in play, we need the wisdom that Andrew, Tyler, Rosalia, and Javaria have brought forward. Don't isolate, and don't panic, for starters. But there's also the uncanny awareness that relating well to our technology requires us to relate well to ourselves. Know yourself and your background, and keep that knowledge close when technological assistance gives way to digital overwhelm.

CHAPTER 6

Signaling Things

A chapter on the performative mode, which exercises indirect communication in workplace life.

Why You Need Another Mode Switch

STOCK ART IS KIND of terrible, but it can also tell us a lot about cultural taken-for-granteds. One day, I searched for "Conversation with a Manager" on a stock art site, an experiment you can try for yourself on a browser near you. But in case you are stock-art allergic, I'll tell you what the image-seeking algorithms churned up for me.

- In many of the images, the conversations were twosomes: workplace interactions were depicted as dyadic, featuring communicator A talking with communicator B.
- The images showed people involved in reciprocal exchange: that is, you could see the images playing out the familiar drama of turn-taking conversation.
- The depictions looked soulful. In other words, you could see the play of compassion and concern in people's gazes, expressions, and postures.

This stock art thus evoked an ideal of professional conversation that is one-on-one, equitable, and mutual. If we can see these images as both reflecting and projecting workplace realities, we might reasonably guess that the people imagined as users of the image feel underwater at work and wish for the reassurance and guidance of direct conversation with an empathetic manager. These images depict our yearnings to stop the world of digital hyperactivity so we can hop off and have a thoughtful conversation.

At the same time, a thoughtful interchange with your manager is complicated by the fact that she also evaluates you and thus affects how much pay you take home and how long you hold the job at all. (How *do* you communicate your need for help without coming off as needy or inept?) We can't stop the world, obviously, any more than we can eliminate the risk of conversation with the boss.[1]

But there is a zone of choice-making here that's easy to miss but affords you a chance to engage your workplace wisely. So, here's the mode switch I propose in this chapter: a toggle from direct to indirect communication. If you assume that the "real communication" in your organization is happening directly, explicitly, and pointedly, you'll miss out on another just-as-important mode of communication across the workplace. This chapter recommends that you learn to angle your communication from many angles in the performative mode.

My Own Reason for Making This Chapter's Argument

That's my agenda for what follows: to convince you to make another mode switch. But behind that agenda item, there's a backstory that comes out of my spiritual formation. Long before I read the performative theorists we'll discuss later in this chapter, I had already encountered performative communication in the Psalter of the Old Testament. As a kid, I didn't know how to read these psalms. I mean, I *did* read them, even memorized some of them verbatim, but I didn't know what to do with them. Occasionally, I was encouraged by information they seemed to contain. They told me, for example, that God was a rock, a shepherd, a shelter, a stream for which I thirsted.

But for every piece of apparently reliable information, there was plenty of what seemed like misinformation. The psalmists were smugly self-righteous ("I was blameless before him . . . The LORD has recompensed me according to my righteousness"), prone to vindictiveness (asking God to "break the teeth of the wicked"), keen to call down unthinkable violence ("Happy shall they be who take your little ones / and dash them against the

---

1. Not to mention the fact that "malfunctions in turn taking, miscues extrapolated into gigantic webs of faulty assumptions" make our communications less direct, dyadic exchanges than "a jumble of voices." Peters is talking here about the miscommunications depicted emblematically in modern drama and sociology as well as in the literary theory of Mikhail Bakhtin. Peters, *Speaking into the Air*, 264.

rock!"), and proud of how good they were at despising people ("I hate them with a perfect hatred").² What was the inspirational information I was supposed to derive from these passages?

It wasn't until I was well into adulthood that I encountered an approach to the Psalms not in terms of meaning, but in terms of action. The Psalms aren't like secret codes, containing pellets of data about the divine. Instead, they conduct actions: they bless, curse, lament, confess, praise.³ You might even say the Psalms take on interactive roles: the sage in one psalm is countered by the complainer in the next who is responded to by a devout worshipper in the next who is, in turn, rejoined by the desolate griever in another song or the aging and anxious in still another.⁴ Not only has this approach to the Psalms made them more understandable, but it has also made them actionable. The Psalms have thus become a way for me to take action in settings where I have limited agency. They are, you might say, acting on me, propelling me to new kinds of communicative action—like writing this chapter.⁵

Even if you are not yourself inclined to read, much less rely on, the wisdom literatures of the Bible, you may find that the raw voices of the Psalms—so eloquently testy about injustice, so brutally candid about hostiles, so blissfully happy on sunny days, so joyously grateful for good food—speak from recognizably hot human experience.

But enough about my story and my reasons for noticing the performative mode. Let's turn to the experience of rising professionals.

---

2. Pss 18:23–24; 3:7; 137:9; 139:22, NRSV.

3. This insight derives from biblical scholarship that classifies the psalms, using a pattern like the one developed by Hermann Gunkel. See Crenshaw, *Psalms*, 80–95.

4. "The dialogic interaction of voices—the *complainer-become-truster* and the *instructor* is characteristic of Israel's faith. . . . In this psalm [Psalm 4], the dialogue is between *settled, confident faith* and the *restless protest* that is grounded in troubled experience. The interaction features human honesty down to the bottom of reality. But that interaction is more than psychological interplay. It is a theological practice in ancient Israel, for YHWH is the *God of peaceable well-being* but also the *God of disputatious interaction*. In Israel's faith—so congruent with lived reality—neither impulse is permitted to veto or overcome the other." Brueggemann and Bellinger Jr., *Psalms*, 42.

5. My account of a performative reading of the Psalms relies on Brueggemann, *Praying the Psalms*, xiv–xviii. But I should note that although Brueggemann uses the language of performativity sometimes (cp. Brueggemann, *Materiality as Resistance*), he prefers the language of dialogue as a way to understand the Psalms. That use of the term *dialogic* would seem to take us back to this book's first chapter and its discussion of the dialogic mode. But in this chapter, I am moved by this dialogical way of reading the Psalms as they *act on us*. The Psalms do things to us, propel us outward into the world, activate our complaint and demands of God.

A Story of Direct Communication—That Wasn't

As a special education classroom assistant, Cecilia Franklin tried to be ready for whatever her job would ask of her. I noticed that she was a quick-to-smile and good-humored interviewee. She told me she likes to call out "Good morning!" to coworkers and that when she feels stress, she tends not to show it. And, as it turns out, these are qualities her job demands of her. One day, a student prone to cussing out the assistants clambered up onto a table and did a stomp. The action wasn't wholly unprecedented: Cecilia described her job as a scene where chaotic things happened fairly regularly. But this particular stunt was funny enough that she whipped out her phone and captured the table-top shuffle as footage to share with her family in the ongoing saga of My Crazy Job. I'm guessing that phone-recording a student doing a table-top dance probably isn't on the list of best practices for assistants, much less sending the video to an external party. So, it was probably a good thing her supervisor wasn't patrolling at the moment. Truth be told, Cecilia wasn't on the best of terms with the supervisor.

Part of the difficulty, from Cecilia's standpoint, is that the boss isn't sufficiently attentive to what's happening in the classroom. Instead, the supervisor is forever issuing unilateral directives: *here's how the bus routes are working today, here's a room change you need to deal with, tell your students to keep their masks up!* Sometimes these unilateral performances left Cecilia nonplussed, like the day when the supervisor accosted her in the hall with the words, "I'm mad at you, Franklin." The supervisor's disconnection from classroom experience sometimes had troubling consequences. One day a big student started spinning around near Cecilia and then, to everyone's surprise, jumped on her and pinned her down. The attack happened so quickly that Cecilia was overpowered, and a coworker had to drag the student off her. Cecilia left the scene bewildered and disconcerted. Eventually, she felt she had to report the incident and request the student be moved to another classroom better suited for handling violence-prone students. When she described the attack, the administrator dismissed the seriousness of the event and told her to grow a pair.[6]

There's a lot to unpack in this truly upsetting story. But it's such a chaotic scene that we might be tempted to throw up our hands and say, "What just *happened*?" Here are two ways communication theory might make sense of the scene.

---

6. Name changed, interview by Craig Mattson, January 3, 2022.

What happened was information breakdown.

Back in the middle of the twentieth century, one communication theorist, Harold Lasswell, said we can understand human interaction better by asking the question "*Who* says *what* to *whom* by *what channels* with *what effect?*"[7] It's a clean and clear heuristic for describing some of what's going on in Cecilia's situation.

Think first of the *who* and the *whom* in this situation. Who are the transmitters or the senders here? The guy dancing on the table. In a sense, he wants to convey something about who he is and how he experiences the world. There's something colorful and hilariously excessive about his table-top messaging, but also something urgent: you have surely seen people who are also *dancing who they are*, so to speak, because they don't know how to speak of their identity or their experience adequately to others.

And then, there are all the other *whos* involved: the assault perpetrator, the coworkers, the supervisor, Cecilia herself. But each of these people are just as describable as *whoms* as well—that is, recipients of communication. They're objects of communication in the room, but not because they're taking turns talking to one another. It's a complex, open-ended, multidirectional situation. Lasswell's analytic compels us to notice the rather un-Lasswellian point that everybody's a subject and everybody's an object at the same time.

How about the *what* in this situation? Is there a content to be conveyed? We've already noticed that the table-top dancer doesn't have an explicit message to share. Does the troubling attack convey meaning? Perhaps a sense of frustration and hostility. Cecilia does have some direct communication with her boss. But that message feels like a fail. The supervisor dismisses her report as essentially meaningless. It begins to feel like each time Lasswell's question helps us to get our hands on an element in the communication situation, it dissipates into empty air.

But what about the *channel*? There's a smartphone, recording the table-top dance. There are social media, too. But it explains only the merest sliver of this situation to say that Cecilia is a sender using a medium to interface with receivers. The communication situation is larger than that, involving a lot of factors. Think, for example, of Cecilia's coworkers wrestling and fighting to pull the violent student off her. The communication they're doing in that feverish scramble doesn't channel meaning so much as induce cooperation and enable coordination.

---

7. Lasswell qtd. in Rogers, *History of Communication Study*, 12.

Finally, there are the *effects*. Lasswell's question trains us to look for resolution. But in Cecilia's story, most of the communications don't resolve into isolatable effects. It's hard to identify that *this* caused *that*, in other words. I suppose we could think of the supervisor's response to Cecilia's report as a kind of effect. But it seems better to think of that as an unfortunate joke that falls hard and flat. The supervisor's non sequitur has the feel of a line in a bad sitcom.

Lasswell's analytic question implies that nothing could be more transparent than direct communication of content, so long as there's a channel available between the who and the whom. This is good news for you when you are trying to navigate workplace culture. Lasswell's framework suggests that the interactions essential to organizational life function simply and directly. The employee sends a question via an email to a manager, who responds with an answer.

But Cecilia's story is also a parable for the ways that organizational life can be so atmospherically pressurized that human communication doesn't feel like a clear and direct interface. Her story cues us to look instead for how everyday exchanges involve the drama of indirect communication—the embodied hustle (the dancer), the desperate scramble (the coworkers), and even the showy non sequiturs (the supervisor) that constitute what communication historian John Durham Peters describes as the diverse ways that "we humans caress and harass each other."[8] Given the spectacle of all this communicative action, we might need a second set of theorists to help explain what was happening in Cecilia's story—and in your organization as well.

What happened was a narcissistic spectacle.

In Cecilia's story, it initially appears that the digital has only a small role in what's happening with her students, her coworkers, and her supervisor. The only piece of digital technology in the story is her smartphone whipped out and then stuffed back in her pocket. But media sociology from Nicholas Abercrombie and Brian Longhurst suggests that the digital infuses all human interaction today. When Cecilia approaches her manager looking to report an incident, she and her one-up form a more complicated community than first meets the eye. Due to the omnipresence of digital devices, everybody feels more guardedly cautious or more recklessly theatrical. Given all the ways that an interaction can be surveilled, recorded, and shared, speaking and listening feels like a diffuse activity.

8. Peters, *Speaking into the Air*, 264.

Abercrombie and Longhurst note that a part of that diffuseness comes from the way that communication adopts private and public qualities at the same time.[9] They also point out that one's role in a given interaction shifts constantly between being spectator and performer: there's an intensely and even bewilderingly performative quality to conversation such that you're never quite sure whether you're putting out as a performer or taking it all in as an audience member.

Think of what it's like being on a Zoom call where you can't stop checking to see how you look onscreen. Something like that oscillating focus—checking one's own image, checking others' expressions—back and forth, back and forth—intensifies your sense, online and off, that you should constantly readjust words, expressions, and scenery. Abercrombie and Longhurst trace a culture-wide narcissism to this diffuse awareness: "People simultaneously feel members of an audience and that they are performers; they are simultaneously watchers and being watched."[10] These simultaneous roles generate something like stage fright, or at least an ongoing uncertainty about what's supposed to happen next. The upshot of this for Cecilia's story is that indirect communication plays a surprisingly large role because the digital infuses all that's happening with the energy of performance.

Both of these explanations tell us *something* about organizational communication today. Lasswell's analytic question might point to the need for transparency and accountability, although his goal is mostly descriptive rather than prescriptive. Abercrombie and Longhurst may imply a need to slow down "the show" in everyday life, although they, too, are primarily interested in explaining and predicting rather than exhorting and persuading.[11] But for our purposes, what seems most helpful about these theories is not what they describe so much as what they make visible. As we look at the intersection of information flow and digital spectacle in everyday workplaces, we can begin to make out a zone of action that this chapter will call the performative mode. It's a zone that has some affordances—some gifts—but also some limitations.

9. Abercrombie and Longhurst, *Audiences,* 44, 39.

10. Abercrombie and Longhurst, *Audiences,* 75. About narcissism, Abercrombie and Longhurst speak of "a cultural condition, diffused widely, rather than a personality disorder" (92). They argue that we all feel, to one degree or another "the difficulty the narcissist experiences in distinguishing the boundaries of the self, in separating him- or herself from others" (90).

11. Abercrombie and Longhurst's work is not prescriptive so much as descriptive. Any corollaries or exhortations have to be deduced from their sociology.

The Gifts That Come with the Performative Mode

That term is problematic, I know. Performativity often refers to a theatrical but deceptive messaging like "virtue-signaling" or "greenwashing." But the first thing this chapter will need to make clear is that the performative mode isn't necessarily about communicating in an artificial or vacuous fashion. Sure, sometimes the game of performativity results in what Harry Frankfurt defines (with humorously precise care) as *bullshit*.[12] But with the help of J. L. Austin and Judith Butler, we'll see how this mode of engagement flips our usual models of communication so that human exchange includes not just content but also conduct. The performative mode uses communication to try to make something happen. But because it flies under the radar of explicit awareness, it's easy to ignore—or to treat it as a last resort when more conventional approaches are not working. Instead, this chapter aims for skillful use of the performative mode at work.

You do a lot of signaling at work. Everybody does, in part, because it's difficult *not* to make use of what Peters calls "the variety of shrugs, grunts, and moans that people emit (among other signs and gestures) in face-to-face meetings."[13] Signaling can function directly: someone nods their head to signal the affirmative. It can be a transmission of the content of a message; it can convey a person's intentions. But even though you signal that way all the time, you may have to blink once or twice to spot how signaling also operates performatively: by that, I mean those cases when signaling doesn't just *mean* but also *acts*. If you nod your head at an auction, you not only indicate something about your intentions, but you do something. By nodding, you accept a price and a purchase. The performative mode thus shifts our communication model from the *content* of a message to its *conduct*.

But if we often use performative communication without paying too much mind, we also take in quite a lot of performativity, especially in marketing and advertisement. Here's a quick example that might make performativity recognizable from your own experience of streaming television. Today, with so many streaming platforms competing for our viewership, competition for your spectatorship is intense, which is why these platforms engage you through the performative mode. Here's how one critic explains it:

---

12. Frankfurt, *On Bullshit*. The word "bullshit" means something very like "humbug," in that the bullshitter is essentially concerned with coming off well, but has no concern for the truthfulness of the communication. It's not that bullshitters wish to deceive; they just don't care about the truth one way or another.

13. Peters, *Speaking into the Air*, 34.

Nowadays, brands doggedly attempt to present in an "authentic" way to users, typing like a woke friend. They present themselves informally, often communicating with other users through the likes of jokes and memes. It undoubtedly works: while the façade is recognized, it still remains engaging to many users who then retweet and share these memes further, quoting "that's so me" and "#relatable." Ultimately, Netflix's social media strategy tries to distract you from remembering it is a brand making profit, by instead becoming just another person on your feed.[14]

The content of Netflix's message here is potentially cheesy and easy to see through, but the conduct of the message can be hard to resist, especially in a lonely world. Our TV networks thus use performativity not just to get their content into our living room but also to *befriend* us. Notice, though, that what marketers have figured out about dealing with digital overwhelm has a certain practical wisdom: given all the information that circulates through our lives, how else can we deal with overload but by communicating less informationally and more performatively? Treating every communication as a potentially direct conversation—characterized by reciprocity and mutuality—would be like trying to greet every passenger on a Boeing flight as you head to your seat at the back of the plane.

Performativity, then, is a kind of efficiency move for dealing with digital overwhelm. It takes advantage of a phantom power source in human communication. It infuses our exchanges with extra energy—the charisma of performance that an actor feels on stage or that audience feels in watching. Understanding humans as performers isn't a new thing in human thought: as far back as the sixteenth century, Shakespeare was talking about how all the world's a stage and all the men and women merely players. Much more recently, the sociologist Erving Goffman described "the presentation of self in everyday life."[15] Our challenge in this chapter is to take advantage of the infusion of energy that the performative can bring to workplace communication, especially in situations where direct communication is tricky or impossible. If you're open to becoming more skilled with the performative mode, you will find some help, I think, by learning a few concepts from the work of J. L. Austin and Judith Butler, two of the great theorists of performative communication.

14. McKune, "Don't Be Sucked In By Netflix And Performative Activism."
15. Goffman, *Presentation of Self in Everyday Life*.

Words Do More than They Mean . . .

Professor Austin gave a set of talks, eventually entitled *How to Do Things with Words*, at the William James Lecture series at Harvard University in the mid-1950s to a group of professors who were suffering a slowly spreading vocational crisis related to the direct use of language. Richard Rorty has noted that these mid-twentieth-century philosophers of language had inherited their job description from the eighteenth-century thinker Immanuel Kant, but that by the twentieth century this job description was in doubt. Their job as they saw it was to "divide culture up into the areas which represent reality well, those which represent it less well, and those which do not represent it at all (despite their pretense of doing so)."[16] They were trying to decide what language enabled people to see about the world, with the result that words were good if clear and less good if smudged. This seemingly worthwhile project, as it turned out, had proved a dubious job description.[17] They had thought they had found a seam in the universe, but as it turned out, their understanding of rational, explicit, transparent language use had missed a sizeable part of human communication.

You might have some sympathy for Austin's audience, if only because you may well intuitively share their model of communication. When you say something a little risky at work, for example, you fall back on that old hedge, *I'm just saying*. In other words, *I know that the statement I just made might sound awkward or cocky, but for me, this thing I'm saying is patently obvious. I'm just saying.* When you use an expression like "just saying," you reveal your underlying model of communication. You show in other words that communication is about transmission and that language is about reporting. As Austin notes, this *constative* function of words treats language like a medium for transferring meaning and direct content. Language is for just saying things.

Austin's goal is to get his audience (and maybe you, too) to stop talking one way—*Is the language clear or smudged?*—and start talking

---

16. Rorty, *Philosophy and the Mirror of Nature*, 3.

17. Rorty, *Philosophy and the Mirror of Nature*, 4. As Rorty notes about early-twentieth-century philosophers, "there was a note of desperation in their voices," because the clear need for this role was less and less apparent. With the decline of religiosity, "the philosopher could no longer see himself as in the intellectual avant-garde, or as protecting . . . against the forces of superstition" (4). Whether or not Rorty's way of telling this story is entirely correct, his story does help to explain why Austin is giving his talk to a vocationally threatened crowd. Rorty subscribes to a theory of secularization now widely discounted. See Habermas, *An Awareness of What Is Missing*, and Taylor, *Secular Age* for thorough discussions of why Rorty's secularist narrative needs rethinking.

another—*What is language doing and achieving?* So, he changes metaphors. Instead of using the visual figures of speech so beloved by his fellow philosophers, he uses theatrical metaphors.[18] Many supposed statements of fact are, he suggests, "masqueraders" in that they are dressed up as descriptive assertions or what he calls "constatives."[19] But beneath their costumes, these report-like statements are utterances of a very different sort.

Here's a story from a rising professional's digital overwhelm, a story that illustrates the performative role of language Austin is referring to. Courtney Kalous told me that her family motto growing up was "Kalouses Don't Quit," a slogan she took with her into her work at a faith-based nonprofit, going a hundred miles an hour. "I have this personality that's like, *Oh my gosh, I have to knock it out of the park. I have to answer the email the fastest. I have to really prove myself.*" Her family's slogan got her up at 5:30 AM and sent her crawling to the end of her bed where her laptop lay buried in throws. Half an hour of emailing later, that slogan sent her to the shower and then off to work at a dead run. At work, her bosses' energy would take over. She describes them on a ten-point scale: "one being the detail-oriented, nitty-gritty people and ten being high visionaries. I wanna say they're probably a fifty-two."[20] Their fast-moving ideation kept her hopping all day until she'd connect with a volunteer over dinner and turn to more laptop projects till late into the evening. The alarm the next morning sent her crawling to the end of her bed and the waiting MacBook all over again. This clearly wasn't sustainable—but who could she tell? Everybody in the nonprofit seemed just as busy as she. Then COVID hit, and Courtney discovered the unexpected happiness of not working all the time. Pandemic-induced rest taught her how to guard her boundaries better. Recently, a coworker had asked her to do a task, and Courtney responded with an evenly voiced no. There was a moment of startlement, and the coworker asked what had happened to the colleague that had always been so available. Courtney shot back with unaccustomed bluntness: "She's dead."

From one perspective, the words "Kalouses Don't Quite" are nothing more than a slogan. But notice the propulsive effects of that slogan. The phrase isn't a report on a family's diligence; it is a catalyst for Courtney's workaholism. Notice, too, that the phrase "She's dead" sounds like an exclamatory statement checkable with a pulse. But when Courtney says, "She's dead" in response to her colleague's question, the utterance takes on

---

18. Rorty discusses the overreliance on visual metaphors by philosophers of language in *Philosophy and the Mirror of Nature*, 11, 13, 28, 38–39.

19. Austin, *How to Do Things with Words*, 4.

20. Courtney was referring to the Paterson Wavelength. See, for example, Gray, "Paterson Thinking Wavelength Process."

a different character entirely. Instead of offering a report on biological viability, Courtney is making a joke. Although the phrase "She's dead" conveys some information, these words are not primarily reporting. They are primarily performing. They are doing things. They are acting. Look again at the phrase, "She's dead"—the words cannot truly be understood as the wry joke that they are if the coworker treats them as verifiable information. Courtney has, after all, made a move. In response, her coworker isn't supposed to verify it, but to *deal* with it. Her utterance performs a good-natured but determined assertion of new work/life boundaries. Austin would call Courtney's communication actions not constative but *performative*.

You know from ordinary workplace exchanges that language doesn't just say things; it does things. Take a look at the following examples:

- When an HR manager says, "Welcome to the team."
- When a coworker says, "I wouldn't say that around here."
- When a supervisor reads from your evaluation form the words, "Exemplary in all categories."
- When someone tells you in the breakroom, "Betcha twenty bucks he's in trouble."
- When you say to a custodian, "The recycle bin is full!"
- When a manager tells an employee, "You can do that, but if you do, we're going to have to have a talk about your long-term status in this organization."

Do you see what all these utterances have in common? They're performances. They're actions: welcomes, warnings, wagers, reminders, threats. They might convey some information, sure. But you know from watching people's expressions that these performatives also carry a lot of energy (Austin calls this *illocutionary* force) and bring about certain results (he calls this *perlocutionary* force). Austin insists that performative "do not 'describe' or 'report' or constate anything at all, are not 'true or false,'" but instead "the uttering of the sentence is, or is a part of, the doing of an action."[21] This doing-of-an-action is a way of carrying forward energy.

Austin proposes that instead of judging the truth or falsity of an utterance, we should judge its *felicity* or *infelicity* as an action. Austin notes that what determines if a word is felicitous or not depends on its

---

21. Austin, *How to Do Things*, 5. Such an utterance, as Austin puts it, "is not to describe my doing of what I should be said in so uttering to be doing or to state that I am doing it: it is to do it" (6).

appropriateness to the "total speech situation."[22] In other words, language takes on a great energy and power as it follows the rules of its context. If the president of a college announces in chapel, "Classes are canceled today," that's felicitous or satisfactory language, because the president, within that context, has the authority to say that. If the president of a college shows up at on Wall Street and says, "The Stock Exchange is canceled for the day," he's using infelicitous or unsatisfactory language.

So, how does Austin's theory of performativity describe what's going on in the workplace? Here's a quick story from a rising professional, Jessie Synerges, a non-binary employee at a nonprofit. They told me they used to be a quick-to-respond, always-on-the-ball worker. When the organization started a zine to publish stories about wellness, Jessie stepped up, volunteering to do the research and to gather the stories. They loved the work, showed an aptitude for it, and found it infused the job with meaning. But it was also overwhelming, and eventually Jessie had to quit the zine. That move provided needed rest, but it also caused Jessie to lose interest in their job. Perhaps it was a good thing that the manager so readily accepted their resignation from the zine. But it might also have been a better thing for the manager to recognize something like, "Hey, Jessie's good at the zine, and the zine's good for the org! Let's shift responsibilities around so Jessie can keep up the zine." But the manager missed the cues. Jessie started experimenting with quiet quitting soon thereafter. At the time of our interview, they were planning to leave the job altogether. What the manager missed there was that even when a team member isn't saying anything directly, communicative actions may well be occurring.[23]

. . . But Words Can't Do *Everything*

Have I managed to persuade you, with the help of Professor Austin, that language has power to carry out actions in human life? Think about what it feels like to get hit by someone else's language. In a time of digital overwhelm, when performativity saturates our everyday lives, Austin's theory points to a terrible vulnerability to the power of words and images. This vulnerability may be exacerbated or diminished depending on your various social and political identities. I'm thinking of a Black friend and colleague who has spent much of her career trying *not* to reinforce White stereotypes about people who look like her. She can say all the right things, in other words, and everybody can be nodding and smiling at her. But still, the

22. Austin, *How to Do Things*, 52.
23. Name changed, interview with author, May 2, 2022.

performative mode she shares with them handicaps her. I'm also thinking of a Black interview subject who was himself a manager of a team, and who told me that he'd noticed just how hard it was for people of color to ask for help on the job. Being in any sort of minority position can make you feel like you have to guess a lot about ways that language might hurt you or simply create awkwardness for you. Many of my research participants and interviewees over the past few years have been people holding some kind of minority status and who, therefore, disproportionately experienced the performative effects of other people's language choices.

But note that Austin sometimes makes language seem sovereign. The language used by the people around us can feel like the weather. What else can you do when it's raining and cold but put on your coat and trudge through the miserable conditions? But is our vulnerability to language absolute? Does language make the speaker all-powerful and the hearer necessarily a victim? Cultural theorist Judith Butler's arguments suggest that we may need to qualify Austin's theory of performative language a bit. Words can do things, Butler notes, but they can't do everything. The speaker engaging the performative mode doesn't hold a superpower. The hearer in that same mode can act back on the oppressor.

The problem, Butler notes, is that our sense of what Austin calls the total speech situation is rarely total enough. The more you think about the cultural complexities of everyday talk in the workplace situation, the more complicated they become. If you're a member of a majority culture, you can resort to a kind of self-victimization: *All these DEI workshops—all this political correctness—makes me walk on eggshells!* If you're a member of a minority culture, you may resort to another sort of victimization. *I can't do anything in this warehouse without evoking microaggressions!* I don't mean to create a false equivalency between these experiences of majority-culture and minority-culture employees. But I do want to name the fact that language in Austin's performative theory is always doing its thing in our workplaces and that many of its consequences feel hurtful. What's a body to do? Butler has ideas.[24]

In her book *Excitable Speech*, Butler concedes that, yes, words do have a rather weird capacity to injure people—"weird," because we language-users give language that power and yet are somehow ourselves made by that power.[25] Using an Austin concept, she notes that words

24. "There is . . . no easy way to decide on how best to delimit that totality." Butler, *Excitable Speech*, 3.

25. "Could language injure us if we were not, in some sense, linguistic beings, beings who require language in order to be? Is our vulnerability to language a consequence of our being constituted within its terms? If we are formed in language, then that formative power precedes and conditions any decision we might make about it, insulting us from the start, as it were, by its prior power." Butler, *Excitable Speech*, 1–2.

carry force—which is why, in the 1980s, Catherine MacKinnon argued that pornography did something to women's bodies by objectifying them. Still, MacKinnon did not succeed in making pornography illegal. Why? Maybe because it's hard to demonstrate that sexualized imagery always injures a person—the way that throwing a wrench would unfailingly hurt a person. Butler notes that such cases focus necessarily (as Austin would suggest they should) on which kinds of communication should be made illegal—"which words wound, which representations offend," when "linguistic injury appears to be the effect not only of the words by which one is addressed but the mode of address itself."[26]

But Butler notes that things are rarely so simple when it comes to what language is doing in human life. Austin would say that what gives language performative force is its context. Butler responds that, well, sometimes language works by eliminating context. In other words, one of the tendencies of hurtful speech is to communicate, in effect, *You have no place here*. Austin bases his sense of what's fitting and appropriate on (supposedly) clear rules for a given situation, "one that might be defined easily by spatial or temporal boundaries."[27] But says Butler, "To be injured by speech is to suffer a loss of context, that is, not to know where you are."[28] Remember Joycee Black's story about crying after watching the DEI video with her unperturbed coworkers? Those colleagues were communicating, in effect, that she didn't belong. Or so Butler would say: such moments of pain reveal that "one can be 'put in one's place' by such speech, but such a place may be no place."[29] Austin, thus, is both right and wrong: he's right that language has power, but he's wrong that the power is solely centered in a total speech situation.

If you're not careful, Butler argues, you can learn the wrong lesson from Austin's theory of performativity. You can, in short, imagine yourself to be more stuck than you are. Think about this experience: someone can speak of you in demeaning language without your feeling demeaned. How is this possible? How can you, in some situations, actually be amused by a nasty thing said against you? Why aren't you inevitably injured by what other people say? Butler reminds her readers that although language carries some force, its force doesn't always bring about what its user intended. Utterance, says Butler, is not sovereign: "To act linguistically is not necessarily to produce effects, and in this sense, a speech act is not always an efficacious action."[30] Language works like an unpredictable weather system. Earlier in this chapter's discussion, Cecilia's manager might have been trying to rain on her by

---

26. Butler, *Excitable Speech*, 2.
27. Butler, *Excitable Speech*, 3.
28. Butler, *Excitable Speech*, 4.
29. Austin, *How to Do Things*, 4.
30. Butler, *Excitable Speech*, 17.

using a sexual slur ("Grow a pair"). I suspect Cecilia initially felt the force of that insult. But the fact that she was able to repeat it to me suggests that she wasn't *wholly* disempowered by it. In a way, her repetition of the insult in another context deprived the language of some of its power.

Butler would say it's a good thing that language can be satisfactory without being successful—but not because she wants "to minimize the pain that is suffered as a consequence of hate speech."[31] Words can sting, or worse. But Butler's also mindful that, if we exaggerate the power of the performative, we may end up depriving people of agency.[32] She notes the fact that, very often, people struck by language whip around and wield that same language against their oppressors. The term "Christian" was an insult at first, and so was the word "queer" and many other belittling or condemnatory terms. But the victims of the language turned around and used the language in unexpected ways.

Think of Courtney's story. You might conclude that the language she was given as a child—"Kalouses Don't Quit"—had an unfair and outsized impact on her. And at first, those words did drive her to workaholism. The slogan was law. Those were the rules. Being a working professional mandates an ethic of total work. But eventually, gradually, Courtney was able to pick up the phrase in a new way and wield it differently than her family had intended. She was able to use it, even in the course of our interview, as a weapon against overwork. The performative mode is constantly complicated, constantly shifting, especially in the digital spaces where Courtney does so much of her work. But the very shiftiness of digitality—the way it compels us to toggle constantly between being a performer and a spectator—can provide unexpected leverage. Even the phenomenon of quiet quitting is taking a performative tactic. Just as managers have been unresponsive to employees, so employees are using subtle unresponsiveness to detach from the job.

What Language Could Do in Your Workplace

The basic task of this chapter has been to help you recognize an easy-to-miss mode of communication and to learn its possibilities, gifts, constraints,

---

31. Butler, *Excitable Speech*, 19. It's a good thing, in other words, that language can strike a body blow without bringing about the pain it seeks to give. Butler insists that "the assertion that some speech not only communicates hate, but constitutes an injurious act, presumes not only that language acts [which is what Austin has been saying all along], but that it acts upon its addressee in an injurious way [which doesn't necessarily happen]" (16).

32. She wants, in short "to leave open the possibility that its [language's] failure is the condition of a critical response." Butler, *Excitable Speech*, 19.

and deficiencies. We started with Austin's account of language's relationship to its context—although he does sound too much like the psalmists on a smug day: if you follow the rules of the given situation, your communication will be effective. Fortunately, Butler—also sounding like the psalmists, but in a more imaginative mood—emphasizes the way that language does unpredictable stuff, sometimes for a person's good, sometimes not. Together, these thinkers make the performative mode visible and show why it's needed for organizational communication. If you assume that communication is primarily about the transfer of meanings, says Austin, you'll miss a great deal of what language is doing. If, on the other hand, you assume that language is sovereign, Butler adds, you'll miss a great deal of what *you* could be doing with it. The performative mode requires a constant watchfulness. It asks managers and their teams to engage language as something we can't control and can't do without.

Without this mode of indirect communication in your sights, or at least on the periphery of your sights, you could just so easily keep minding your communicative business, so to speak: sending things as fast as you can, emailing logistics, texting how someone has misunderstood your message, conveying the intentions of a policy. But you'd be missing out on some important relational dynamics. Mode-switching to the performative mode is like being in a restaurant, preoccupied with what the person across the table is saying. But suddenly, you become aware of some background music that's been playing the whole time. Shifting your awareness back and forth between the music and the conversation takes some dexterity, but it keeps you present to the ambient context in a rich way. Or think about trying to learn a new language: if you can only translate what the other person is saying word for word, you're stuck at a literal level of exchange. But as you become more fluent, you also become more willing to take in the conversation holistically without worrying about the direct meaning of individual words. After all, learning all those individual terms won't help you understand what the other person is *doing* with the language. What you're sensing when you become aware of the performative mode is what I think Cecilia and Courtney and Jessie had learned to see, or perhaps I should say, learned to *hear* in the indirect and performative energies in a situation.

I began this chapter with the question of how you ask for mentoring from a busy manager without coming off as inexperienced or needy. But now I'm thinking that, when you're trying to navigate workplace culture, that might be the wrong question—or at least not the only question. The query assumes that what you can learn about your job is primarily learned through the direct back-and-forth of asking and answering. Its attention to the flow of information (from those in power to those disempowered) tends to reinforce the hierarchies and bureaucracies it should be critiquing.

But one of the benefits of learning about indirect communication is beginning to discern and deconstruct the ways our uses of communication subtly reinforce inequitable power arrangements. And that, finally, may be the most important reason to make this mode switch from direct to indirect communication.

I began this chapter by reflecting on the ways that my Protestant tradition's reading of the Psalter all too often obscured the performative dimensions of this wisdom literature. In my case, that made it difficult for me to imagine any other way of praying than as a heartfelt conveyance of pious information about my heart to God. Breaking out of this direct reading of the Psalms—"What is the psalm telling me specifically about God's character?"—allowed me to participate in the feisty and often demanding communication the Psalms enact. The psalmists "do things with words," to use Austin's phrase—and they invite us into that action as well. Not only does this motivate my seeking to understand better performative communication wherever it happens in human life, but I think this prayerful language activates imaginative and critical communication with your supervisor and with your team. In other words, the psalmists take things further than Austin's performative theory does.

In keeping with the performative theorists we've discussed in this chapter, Walter Brueggemann contrasts conventional ways we understand language—whose basic purpose is "to report and describe what already exists"—with the language of the Psalms, which "evokes into being what does not exist until it has been spoken."[33] What Brueggemann has helped me to see in the Psalms is, in a sense, what I'm trying to help you see in your workplace—that the performative mode of communication is a way to critique and resist the boring, power-infused explicitness of so much organizational communication. Learning to pay attention to this indirect but more imaginative mode of interaction gives you a politically granular view of your organization.

But it's not enough to simply be able to see this mode at play in your workplace. Once you've learned to recognize it as an affective space where vital action is happening, you'll need to ask how it relates to the larger organizational context. The larger and more important question is what it equips you to do—which is why this next chapter turns to the mode craft of indirect communication.

---

33. Brueggemann, *Praying the Psalms*, 18.

CHAPTER 6.5

How to Survive Video Chat

Mode Craft for the Zoom Room

THE PREVIOUS CHAPTER ARGUED that you should pay closer attention to indirect communication via the performative mode. But how to do that will take some serious and subtle skill.

What professional communication seminars teach is something that Richard Lanham has called C-B-S model of communication. Clear. Brief. Sincere.

> Words are like things and ideally should be things. You have a message that you want to send to someone else. It must be clear: you don't want the wrapping to obscure the stuff. It must be brief. You don't want to waste anybody's time. That's why UPS delivery persons run from the truck to your door. And you must be sincere. You must not, that is, have any designs on anybody, try to persuade them of anything. You must say exactly what you mean, neither more nor less. You owe the whole truth to everybody.[1]

A few minutes thought will make clear why this model of communication is so bad for employees and managers. Clarity is hard because it depends on seeing what's going on in a workplace transparently well. But workplaces are not transparent. Workplaces are weird. To communicate clearly may be easy for people who run the place and for people who accept all the taken-for-granteds of the place—but not for those employees

---

1. Lanham, *Economics of Attention*, 137.

just trying to get their bearings. Brevity is tricky, too, especially on video calls, where the whole game (at least for rising professionals) is to get and give as many cues as possible through the narrow keyhole of the webcam. It takes a lot of time to manage and to be managed well in remote work conditions. Brevity isn't just hard; it can be unfair. Sincerity is unreachable, or nearly so. The essence of being a rising professional is *needing other people to do things so you can do your things*. To act as if all we're doing is moving information around, sending our emails, shuttling our spreadsheets—nothing to see here, folks!—is to ignore all the ways Gen Z and millennial employees (and, really, employees of any generation) have to convince their coworkers to take action.

All this to say, the values of clarity, brevity, and sincerity all tend to reinforce the practices of hierarchical communication. After the last chapter's argument, I hope, you're hankering to practice indirect communication within the mode of performative communication, if only to resist the occasional power abuses of direct communication. With the help of a fascinating study about Zoom fatigue by social scientist Jeremy N. Bailenson, I'm going to recommend some performativity for your next remote meeting.

Why Are Zoom Calls So Tiring?

Let's start with Bailenson's diagnosis of remote-meeting fatigue. You would think that video chat work would be less stressful and more liberating than in-person meetings. But it's often the case that people often find videoconferencing to be exhausting.[2] Bailenson identifies four potential causes for Zoom fatigue. I'll follow each with some performative action steps.

Energy Suck: Exhausting Eye Contact.

He notes, first, that strangers on an elevator avoid each other's gazes. On Zoom, in contrast, strangers have to endure "long stretches of direct eye gaze and faces seen close up."[3] Joycee Black's need to get off camera in order to weep, followed by her adopting of a strong and stern facial expression seems to bear out the exhaustion Bailenson describes in the dynamics of digital conferencing.

---

2. Bailenson, "Nonverbal Overload."
3. Bailenson, "Nonverbal Overload."

Action Step: Vary Your Eye Contact.

Few communicative choices are more integral to how people carry social and emotional information in a video chat than what they do with their gaze. The hardest element of eye contact online is that you have to look *away* in order to look *towards*. Mode craft in the Zoom Room involves switching up your focus regularly. Doing so may, in some moments, feel like an act of self-giving, as you look at the green dot rather than at the image on the screen, but such generosity is an important part of wisdom in the Zoom room.

Still, you don't want to give too much eye contact! When you're standing and talking with someone in the same physical space, you don't stare deeply into their eyes, unless you happen to be a vampire. It's a good idea to take that practice into the remote meeting as well, not only so other people don't feel like you're scheming to snatch their souls, but also so that you (and they) suffer less exhaustion.

Energy Suck: Wearying Nonverbals.

Communication theorists distinguish between direct and phatic communication, the latter category referring to all the little noises and nods that we use to cultivate an air of being a friendly person. But online nonverbals are cognitively tiring. "Users are constantly receiving nonverbal cues," notes Bailenson, "that would have a specific meaning in a face-to-face context but have different meanings on Zoom."[4] Take the familiar experience of standing in a small group and noticing that someone has made a sidelong glance. That might be a signal that the side-long glancer wants to leave—or a warning that there's an eavesdropper to an otherwise exclusive conversation. But in a videoconference, that same eye movement means something else. Even if you know that glance just means their toddler strolled into the room, "it is often difficult to overcome automatic reactions to nonverbal cues."[5]

Action Step: Nod Your Head Less.

During the pandemic, we all felt it necessary to offer as much encouragement as possible through our webcams. We bobbed and grinned and waggled and waved like we were all gazing at each other through the back car window of a vehicle departing forever. But if, by the time this book has

---

4. Bailenson, "Nonverbal Overload."
5. Bailenson, "Nonverbal Overload."

come to press, we haven't manufactured another global pandemic, I would recommend that you stop being (to adapt Stanley Hauerwas's great phrase) a quivering mass of agreeability. Maybe you're nodding so that everybody knows you're a nice person. I am happy to report that you *are* a nice person. The rest of us have met and voted on the point, and the motion carried. So you can stop nodding right about now.

You might also shift attention away from the nonverbals by emphasizing your verbals. It's tempting on a video call to speak with as few inflections as possible or with as flat a vocal quality as possible. Maybe you do this to diminish ethnic or gendered or regional differences. But sharing your voice fully can feel complicated in any case by your environment: either there may be a lot of ambient sound in your workspace, or you may be leery of disturbing others in your immediate vicinity. Even given all those things, I think it's a good idea to share your voice as fully as you can.

Some video call platforms include automatic filters and suppressors. But check your settings and experiment with which noise suppressant works best for your voice. A high noise suppression, for example, may cut out the clattery sound of your keyboard, but it will also cause some breaks in your vocal production. To further enrich your spoken delivery, you may want to utilize a USB microphone, which will allow a broader range of your sounds to arrive in the Zoom room. In any case, one thing I almost invariably notice about good speech craft online is that its practitioners put a great deal of vocal energy into their delivery. The best way to share yourself in a video call may be simply to speak up.

Energy Suck: Fatiguing Self-Monitoring.

Next, Bailenson notes that Zoom tires us out by confronting us constantly with our own facial expressions. "Imagine in the physical workplace, for the entirety of an 8-hr workday, an assistant followed you around with a handheld mirror, and for every single task you did and every conversation you had, they made sure you could see your own face in that mirror."[6] That's the exhaustion Zoomers experience all the time.

Action Step: Hide Self View.

If the media sociologists discussed in the last chapter are right, we constantly feel like we are spectators and performers at the same time. Let's agree that this is tiring, always buying tickets to see ourselves. Abercrombie and Longhurst describe this as narcissism, not in a clinical or condemnatory sense,

6. Bailenson, "Nonverbal Overload."

but simply in the sense that the self feels like it doesn't exist apart from the other person.[7] But here's a small piece of good news: you exist outside the Teams call. I could help you locate empirical proof for this reality, but I suspect you know it's true already.

Both Teams and Zoom offer the three magic dots, which, if clicked upon, allow you to Hide the Self from View. You and I should do that. Performative communication is not fundamentally about self-expression. It's about adopting the persona that creates coordination on the team or that serves the needs of the other person. Hiding Self View sometimes helps you keep an other-centered view. It also enacts confidence in the other person. You are relying on the other people's goodwill, believing they will see you with the kind of care that makes perpetual self-checking unnecessary.

Energy Suck: Claustrophobic Frustrum.

You might not use the term *frustrum* very often, if at all; but you know the thing itself all too well. The frustrum is the range of things included in your camera's view. Video conferences force us to stay in a narrow space. Social media reels sometimes joke about getting caught in uncomfortable situations by a video call. (E.g., you're about to board for the Bahamas on a day you called in sick—and your boss Teams-calls you.) But even when you're at your kitchen counter on a video call, you will likely feel pressure to stay close enough to your webcam to keep visible. That pressure to stay in a fairly tightly circumscribed space is an unexpected cost in remote work.[8]

Action Step: Lead with Your Toes.

In other words, stand during the video call. Standing desks and highly mobile laptops make it easy to join a meeting in a full-bodied way. Your frustrum might not change much, but the fatigue will. Another benefit that comes from this practice is that it makes multitasking harder. Being mindful that your feet are about shoulder-width apart, that you are standing on the balls of your feet, that your toes can wiggle, that your knees aren't locked, that your diaphragm is open, that your shoulders are resting back—all that helps you to carry the conversation of the meeting forward with less fatigue.

Take time to compose your onscreen frame. Make sure you have good lighting to illumine your features, but don't neglect where you *put* those features in your frame. If you divide your screen into thirds, you might position yourself in a different third at different points of the meeting. You

---

7. Abercrombie and Longhurst, *Audiences*, 92.
8. Bailenson, "Nonverbal Overload."

should also think about your head room (how much space there is above you in the frame): if you're too close to your camera, the top of your head will be chopped off and you may appear invasively close, like someone peering through a private porthole. If you're too far away, you may appear a little detached or disempowered. My recommendation would be to switch up your position. Just as good speakers vary their relationship to their podiums or to the edge of the stage in order to refresh their relationship with their audience, you can make analogous choices in the Zoom room.

Wisdom on the Teams Call

My hunch is that it's tempting to deal with the digiwhelm of Zooming by cutting back on direct communication or avoiding indirect communication. But if you're looking for a maximalist, not a minimalist recommendation, I'll recommend a quirky maxim derived from reading Lanham: communication should keep the *through* connected to the *at*.

Think of direct communication as the *through* and indirect communication as the *at*. Skilled communicators, Lanham notes, have always known how to communicate in a way that is straightforward, plain, and simple. Such a speech doesn't draw attention to itself; instead it invites audiences to look *through* to its content, focusing viewers' attention in a transparently functional fashion.[9] That's direct communication in the C-B-S model. But to try out this chapter's advice requires another model characterized by aesthetic intelligence, bold obliqueness, and gentle irony. That's where it's *at*.

These binaries can be blurrier than this discussion makes them sound. In fact, you can't have substance without style, directness without indirectness. They're always sneaking up on each other and switching places.[10] But mode craft attends to the interaction of the *through* and the *at* not only for the sake of attractive effectiveness, but also for the sake of a larger, moral concern that we might best call wisdom. To be wise, in this sense, is to exhibit an attention that is both simple and complex, direct and indirect, caring for both self and other, at the same time and in the same Google Meet.

9. Lanham, *Economics of Attention*.
10. "If you are a car designer, for you the style of the car will be the substance. If you are a philosopher, 'what you think about things' will be the 'things' of your world." Lanham, *Economics of Attention*, 156.

CHAPTER 7

Advocating Things

This chapter discusses how to persuade people to share a project and its tasks. The rhetorical mode pursues the good of inducement, convincing coworkers and oneself to take needed action.

IT WASN'T A GOOD sign that the phone was ringing this late at night. Lauren Hughes eyed the device skeptically for a minute, looking at the caller ID. *Great,* she thought, *my supervisor—also not a good sign.* But it wasn't as if she had a choice about taking the call or not. Graduating with a public relations major a few years earlier, she was feeling all the usual precarity of early careerism. She and her partner had crisscrossed the country, sometimes not knowing what the next job would be. She'd worked at a boutique agency, doing public relations for Sullivan & Associates in Huntington Beach. She'd worked for Whitworth University in Spokane as a media manager. Then, she'd taken a position at a faith-based nonprofit in Orlando as a communication specialist. She asked me not to name the organization, because they're quick to sue people. But I am allowed to say it was a manager calling her at this late hour.

Lauren took the call. As the sole wage earner in the house, while her husband was in graduate school, she needed this job. But as she swiped to accept the call, she immediately knew it would be a hard call to get out of her head. The manager's voice on the line was loud and irate, which wasn't shocking, unfortunately. Lauren had been forced to get used to power-driven thinking among her organizational leaders. She'd been doing social media for them for a while now. She had overhauled their website content;

she had developed advertising copy for them; she had live-tweeted their events. But through all her work, she was never able to build trust with them. Every tweet had to be approved before it was sent, which sometimes required Lauren to hunt for the manager who was designated as the tweet-approver. It felt silly.

We're revoking your posting privileges, the voice on the line said. Although the supervisor's voice was tight with anger, Lauren told herself to respond neutrally. She inhaled and exhaled slowly. She wondered what could have provoked such a passionate outpouring of managerial wrath. *What has gone wrong?* The answer, when it came, staggered her: in a recent post, she had used straight quotation marks instead of curly ones. *That* was the offending move? Lauren took another deep breath and then apologized. If she hadn't abased herself before the manager, she felt quite sure she would have been fired.

It's not always immediately apparent to rising professionals what's going on when power is being misused in the workplace. They're in the middle of things, trying to look professional and do the tasks and not mess up. But by the time of our interview, Lauren, having found better employment, could name the power abuse that was endemic in the nonprofit. It was, she told me, a terribly stressful place to work. Her higher-ups had come out of the business, financial, and military sectors, and their approach to leadership seemed out of keeping with the pastoral mission of the place. They were distrustful. They scrutinized small things and responded harshly to mistakes. They kept a tight clamp on dress code, requiring business formal attire every day. One of her coworkers was hospitalized for heart palpitations, a disconcerting experience that Lauren later traced to the claustrophobic stress of the organization.

I don't think Lauren would put her experience on par with the assault described in a previous chapter nor the harassment cases discussed later in this chapter. She simply had to deal with a manager's overreaction. But the Case of the Sinful Quote Marks proved a decisive moment for her nonetheless. She was burning out, a condition she'd been hearing about from other social media managers as well, and she knew she needed to quit. But before she went, there was one more thing she had to do. She had to advocate for change within the organization.

She went to her one-up and described the trouble she'd experienced. When the supervisor was dismissive, Lauren thought about letting it go. Her style tends to be nonconfrontational. She's quick to agree, quick to please, and speaking up made her feel estranged from herself. But her conscience bothered her. Sure, she could leave and find a better job, but her manager would still be around creating trouble for the next media manager. She checked out the processes for mediation within the organization—and then went to Human Resources and asked for a conversation with the offending supervisor. The mediation did not go well. The HR manager felt responsible for one thing: protecting the organization. For her part, Lauren wasn't the whistleblower type. But in this case, she felt she had no choice.

Lauren was able to name for me some of the darker dimensions of organizational communication. She'd spent enough time in the shadows of organizational life, and then enough time in therapy, to name abuse clearly and to give thanks for the healthier work cultures she was now enjoying. But she felt worried for the rising professionals entering the workforce now. She knew what it is to simply need a job to eat. She knew what it was not to be able to pick and choose your organizational culture. It bothered her that the sages in her life had not warned her about watching out for abusive employers and toxic workplaces. How, she wondered, are Gen Z and millennial professionals supposed to comport themselves towards toxic environments that they can't afford to leave?[1]

You May Want to Skip This Chapter

Perhaps the pages that follow should lead off with a medical warning—something like, *You may be allergic to this chapter's argument if you experience any of the following symptoms or conditions:*

1. You're a woman professional whose male boss ignores your email suggestions, nods absently at your comments in meetings, and only communicates at you in early morning cellphone texts.

2. One team member in your nonprofit spends every video chat talking about how every strategy proposed "lacks push" in comparison with what he used to do in the for-profit sector.

3. Your partner at home has a chronic illness affecting your performance at work.

4. The only person of color on your production crew tells you that his coworkers say they hate DEI workshops because they "don't have a racist bone in their bodies."

5. You're a manager with two non-binary team members, but the vice president of your division refuses to pay attention to their preferred pronouns.

---

1. Lauren Hughes, interview by Craig Mattson, March 31, 2022.

Those are conditions where advocacy is needed but painful. Even so, I aim to persuade you to step up, step out, and speak up. In other words, I'm going to make a case for the importance of *the rhetorical mode*, an approach to organizational communication that sees all human exchange as fundamentally persuasive. I don't think the rhetorical mode is just for attorneys and activists. I think it's for you, too. But a part of what makes advocacy so difficult is that the mode is easy to fall into without noticing. You might think you're in one mode—*we're just having a conversation here*, or *I'm just trying to get the word out*, etc.—and all of a sudden, you realize you're in an argument. It's an uncomfortable realization, and one that causes some people to try to hop out of the mode and into another one that feels less rocky.

Despite all these allergies and aversions, though, I'd like to persuade you to practice persuasion in your workplace. We'll start by trying to get some clarity on why advocacy is so hard, first, from the organizational perspective and, secondly, from a technological perspective. Then I'll share some stories with you from Gen Z and millennial professionals whose experiences, I think, make the importance of this mode clear.

The Problem Is the Politics

Stanley Deetz, a University of Colorado researcher who's been theorizing and writing about organizational communication since the 1970s, would say that what makes advocacy hard within an organization is also what makes it necessary: the abuse of managerial power. Such exploitation and manipulation feels jarring in organizations like Lauren's with pro-social missions: how is it that a nonprofit can be seeking the good of a society while treating its own workplace society so poorly? Unfortunately, it's not an unusual tension.[2] Deetz would emphasize that cultivating a healthy internal culture requires a lot of communication—not just information transfer, but advocacy, attention, argument, and collaboration. Employees and managers like Lauren who care for organizational operations *and* organizational community have to figure out:

- how to persuade those above them to take steps they believe to be necessary.
- how to persuade those around them to join the work.
- how to persuade those reporting to them to act in cooperative fashion.
- how to persuade themselves to—well, do the work of persuasion.

[2]. I've explored a similar tension in Mattson, *Why Spiritual Capital Matters*, 37–56.

The challenge in each case, Deetz would say, has to do with the distribution of decision-making. It's all too easy to think of workplaces as primarily machines for shuttling information around, as if what's needed in a workplace is to get the right data to the right nodes in the system as efficiently as possible. But this, says Deetz, is naïve. Worse, such an information systems approach to interaction can reinforce top-down corporate-styled thinking about workplace community by ignoring power's role in human exchange.

What's needed instead is what he calls a "communication perspective," which sees organizational interaction not simply as a transmission of data from A to B to C and then on to D—what Deetz calls "the conduit metaphor of communication"—but rather as productive of the social setting in which A and B and C and D all contribute to meaningful decision-making.[3] That requires an organization animated by two communicative ideals: participation and effectiveness. "*Participation* deals with who in a society or group has a right to contribute to the formation of meaning and the decisions of the group—which individuals have access to the various systems and structures of communication and can they articulate their own needs and desires within them."[4] In Lauren's case, the nonprofit administrators were chary of sharing power with their teams. People low in the company hierarchy were simply not trusted to contribute to the work of meaning-making and decision-making. But alongside participation, *effectiveness* should also guide an organization's communications: this ideal "concerns the value of communicative acts as a means to accomplish ends—how meaning is transferred and how control through communication is accomplished."[5] Lauren's nonprofit devalued their employees' communicative actions through micromanagement, all the way down to questions of straight and curly quotation marks.

Deetz contrasts participatory and effective decision-making with *managerialism*, a top-down administrative strategy driven by "one-sidedness and domination" in contexts where people are using communication tools to zip messages to one another.[6] Often such managerialism relies on *consent*, where disempowered people *think* they are serving their own

---

3. Deetz, *Democracy in an Age of Corporate Colonization*, 81, 91. Deetz discusses this perspective in "Corporate Governance, Communication, and Getting Social Values into the Decisional Chain." In discussing how corporations can address social problems, he writes, "To me, this is not a philosophical debate over the grounds for ethical behavior or a regulation issue but a question of corporate governance—who and what shall be involved in making decisions. To the extent that it is a governance issue, it is a communication issue—based on the interaction processes by which we incorporate values and make decisions" (607).

4. Deetz, *Democracy in an Age of Corporate Colonization*, 94.
5. Deetz, *Democracy in an Age of Corporate Colonization*, 94.
6. Deetz, *Democracy in an Age of Corporate Colonization*, 224.

interests, when they are being manipulated by those in power.⁷ For a while, Lauren may have felt she was involved in the company's decision-making; she was a manager of their media after all. But again and again, she found that her voice did not matter, that her decisions were distrusted.⁸ What Deetz recommends is to infuse a company's communication culture with values that can feel foreign to efficient bureaucratic management, but which are indispensable for human well-being: "care, emotion, relationships, and communities."⁹ It seems likely that Deetz would have supported Lauren's self-advocacy as "a micropractice" indispensable to organizational well-being, or what he called "a democracy of the insides."¹⁰ Lauren found it hard to advocate for herself and for the employees who would succeed her. But the difficulty is more than personal. Advocacy is hard, because across the organization the work of persuasion is quite simply never done. Deetz would say, "the project is endless."¹¹

The Problem Is the Media

Agreed, Zac Gershberg and Sean Illing might say. But then, these media theorists would also likely add, *But have you thought about what the digital is doing to organizational communication?* Unlike Deetz, after all, Gershberg and Illing are not organizational communication theorists; they are media ecologists, studying the effects of digital mediation on democratic values and practices.¹² Whereas Deetz advances a micro-perspective, at-

---

7. Griffin, Ledbetter, and Sparks, *First Look at Communication Theory*, 263–65.

8. Griffin, Ledbetter, and Sparks, *First Look at Communication Theory*, 265–66.

9. Wieland, Bauer, and Deetz, "Role of Entrepreneurialism in Colonizing Identities," 117.

10. Deetz, *Democracy in an Age of Corporate Colonization*, 333.

11. Deetz, *Democracy in an Age of Corporate Colonization*, 333.

12. It's not hard to spot complementarities within Deetz's ideas and Gershberg and Illing's theorizing. Both see communication not as primarily about information transfer, but about culture formation. Just as Deetz says it's not enough simply to make sure there's equal representation of women and minorities in upper levels of an organization, so Gershberg and Illing say that democracy is not preserved simply by having certain institutions (universal suffrage, e.g.)."The first issue must concern how such groups are produced within or in relation to the closed, self-referential system of the corporation," Wieland, Bauer, and Deetz write in *Democracy in an Age of Corporate Colonization* (351). Similarly, Gershberg and Illing say, "So many accounts of democracy emphasize legislative processes or policy outcomes, but these often miss the depth of connection between communication and political culture" (Illing and Gershberg, *Paradox of Democracy*, 10.) What matters for both sets of theorists is the culture of communication. "[D]emocracies are defined by their cultures of communication. If a

tentive to life within an organization, Gershberg and Illing's book *The Paradox of Democracy* adopts a macro-perspective, which makes it useful for understanding the trickle-down effects of democratic society on smaller-scale societies like Lauren's workplace. They identify the "paradox of democracy," in which "a free and open communication environment . . . because of its openness, invites exploitation and subversion from within."[13] Why is it hard for Lauren to practice advocacy within her organization? Quite simply because her managers are concerned to cut off all possibilities for "subversion from within."

Lauren's managers appear to have a firm grasp on the paradox that Gershberg and Illing identify in open societies: the more freedom you allow, the more admirably democratic your community will be—and the more vulnerable to wild cards like Lauren to subvert the company's mission. Ridiculous as it sounds—especially given Lauren's nonthreatening and eager-to-please comportment—the managers appear to have a grasp of the live political possibilities of organizational democracy.

Proponents of democratic communication sometimes neglect the fact that, in a truly open society, free speech is always tensioned by fearless speech. Everyone should have the right to speak, yes; but that also means that everyone can say whatever they want.[14] At best, these ideals of equal rights and fearless speech have generated a lot of argumentative exchange as democratic citizens argued their way towards truth in the marketplace of ideas. At worst, the tension of equal rights and fearless speech has meant that anybody can utter hateful speech, as American society has witnessed in an era of resurgent White supremacy. As Gershberg and Illing note, "the more open the communication we enjoy, the more endangered democracy finds itself."[15] And just as civic policies and structures struggle to keep up with technological disruption, so organizations also mutate more slowly than media.[16]

A quick example will show what I mean: remember when so many committee meetings used to be interrupted by somebody's cellphone ringer going off? That was a small but obnoxious disruptor of organizational culture. Eventually, organizational culture caught up with technological evolution, reasserting the norms of meetings. These days, it's exceedingly rare to

---

democracy consists of citizens deciding, collectively, what ought to be done, then the manner through which they persuade one another determines nearly everything that follows," Gershberg and Illing note (10).

13. Illing and Gershberg, *Paradox of Democracy*, 1.
14. Illing and Gershberg, *Paradox of Democracy*, 30.
15. Illing and Gershberg, *Paradox of Democracy*, 17.
16. Illing and Gershberg, *Paradox of Democracy*, 4.

hear a phone ringer going off, although it's much more common to hear a text notification creating a vibration in somebody's bag. But of course, the rise of social media, the spread of digital tools, and the ceaseless intrusions of artificial intelligence all mean that organizational cultures are constantly struggling to maintain integrity and keep abreast of change.

Lauren's managers were afraid of the chaotic potential of digital media within their own workplace community. That's why they kept such a tight lid on each social media post. That's why they obsessed on curly quotation marks and scrutinized people's outfits and refused to hear Lauren's reports of mismanagement. Their solution to the paradox Gershberg and Illing have located was to get rid of organizational openness. But you really can't avoid the democratic paradox: you can, of course, clamp down on organizational freedom, but only by putting organizational productivity at risk. The cost of Lauren's managers' choices was that they had to spend a lot of time policing their managerial power, rather than pursuing their organizational mission—or benefiting from the resourcefulness of credentialed and creative communicators like Lauren. And they were surely fighting a losing battle: Gershberg and Illing would point out that because everybody is on multiple platforms, everybody (even control-bound managers) experiences reality as what these authors call "a jarring hybrid of the digital and the physical."[17] This constant state of media disruption in the workplace offers another explanation for why advocacy can be so challenging—even in mission-minded organizations.[18]

Although Deetz would approach the challenges of advocacy within an organization from a different angle than Gershberg and Illing, together these theorists make clear why the rhetorical mode within workplace community is challenging. Engaging this mode forces you to deal with power abuse and media disruption. But I'd like to make the case that the rhetorical mode is indispensable for your workplace community, because, as Wayne Booth would say, we need "the entire range of resources that human beings share for producing effects on one another."[19]

But, look: if you're feeling uneasy about advocacy in your organization, I'm right with you. In fact, it's not been until relatively late in my career that I've started to truly understand why the rhetorical mode matters so much for organizational community.

---

17. Illing and Gershberg, *Paradox of Democracy*, 206.

18. Illing and Gershberg, *Paradox of Democracy*, 207. They add that "the media environment is crucial insofar as it colors not just what we pay attention to but also how we think and orient ourselves to the world" (211).

19. Booth, *Rhetoric of Rhetoric*, xi. Italics removed.

Why I Want to Persuade You to Do More Persuading

I have to confess that, of all the communication approaches discussed in this book, the rhetorical mode makes me feel the most ambivalent. In the middle of writing this book, I left my small college community, where I'd taught and researched for twenty years, and moved to a larger university in another state. The move felt venturesome and fun. But it also deprived me of social capital I had been relying on without knowing it. My course evaluations dipped. My departmental status sank. My reputation on the new campus was—nonexistent. After years of the privilege of being known and understood, I found myself wanting to prove myself to students, colleagues, and administrators. I'm embarrassed to say that the work of self-advocacy felt utterly foreign—so privileged had I been, so comfortably male and White and middle-aged and middle-class, so completely and blandly capable of walking into a room and feeling trusted and respected. In my life before the move to a new job, I could perhaps justify my allergy to advocacy by dismissing self-advocacy as self-interested and egocentric. *At least, I'm not one of those shameless self-promoters!* But now, I had to face the reality that assuming everyone should already know my capabilities and accomplishments was itself an arrogant course of action. Avoiding the rhetorical mode would be telling my colleagues and students, "Trust me, I've got this"—without giving them any reason to do so. To do work that exercised my credentials, I was finding, was not shameless self-advancement. It was the best way to fully belong in my new organizational community.

At the end of the day, I want to persuade you to step out and speak up, because I think the rhetorical mode benefits people like you in conditions of digiwhelm. So, in the second half of this chapter, let's turn to stories from early-to-mid-career professionals in order to encourage persuasion towards managers, team members, clients, and ourselves. Let's think of this as persuasion in four directions: *up, down, out,* and *in*.[20] I'll conclude with a preposition too often ignored in persuasive projects: *among*.

---

20. I use these prepositions as a convenient framework, but the underlying argument of this chapter—that you should engage the rhetorical mode—undercuts these prepositions' hierarchicalism. I speak of communicating up to supervisors or down to teammates, because that's a conventional way of understanding organizational life—not because it's the only or the best way to do so.

Persuading Upward

Rising professionals often need to make arguments to their higher-ups in conditions that seem to forbid such advocacy. Perhaps nothing has made this clearer to me than doing Mode/Switch journalism on sexual harassment—a hellacious, snake-lined rabbit hole of early career life. A few weeks into the fall semester of 2023, my university hosted a book talk by Jennifer VanAntwerp about her recently co-authored book *Sex, Gender, and Engineering*, a thorough discussion of harassment within her own guild. I felt jolted by her talk. How had I been talking with early career professionals for so long without asking about harassment? I went back to my desk and sent out a call to previous research participants, asking if any of them would be willing to share their experiences of harassment at work.[21]

Here are a few of their stories.

One woman told me about being repeatedly hit on by her internship supervisor and finding little support from anyone else—and no one, even in her friend circles, would give her advice. She told me a story about a company party—a blues festival—where the creepy supervisor hovered too close, even inviting her to his back office for a shot of whiskey. He stared at her as she took what she described as the smallest possible sip before exiting as quickly as she politely could. Near the end of her internship, the supervisor upped the ante by telling her that if she didn't go out on a date with him, he'd get himself drunk in his office. This time a bystander rescued her, telling the guy to back off. Later, the rescuer asked the intern, a little reproachfully, why she hadn't fended off the man's approaches. The intern was too gobsmacked to know how to answer. How was she, a vocationally precarious intern, seeking job recommendations and network connections, supposed to fend off the advances of her own supervisor?

Another woman professional described comments she had received that she took to be well-intentioned but nonetheless skeezy. "In a meeting with a distributor after a long presentation, the first comment a guy makes is that it's nice that our company finally hired someone attractive. Meant to be flattering or whatever, but I worked really hard on the presentation. Ya know?"[22] Still another rising professional described a space in the nonprofit sector where she reported being more harassed than ever before. "Looking back, what is interesting in this is that the people who should have been embarrassed weren't . . . I certainly was. Going to my boss to mention it was

---

21. Van Antwerp, quoted in Mattson, "It's Not Just Her Problem."
22. Anonymous, quoted in Mattson, "Workplace Skeeziness."

a bit mortifying, because sometimes it was an accumulation of 'little' things and sometimes it was a little more overt."[23]

Given the pervasiveness of the digital in all physical workspaces today, I shouldn't have been surprised to hear from yet another woman professional—we'll call her Samantha—who told me about a confusing blend of on- and offline harassment. While she was leading a new male employee through training one day, she made a joke, using what she took to be a playful term, "ballsy," saying something like, "This action is kind of against the rules, but if you're feeling ballsy, you could do it anyway." The man later accused her of sexual harassment for using this term. He also initiated a sort of digital and in-person campaign against her, mocking her plus-sized body type.

Each of these stories conveys the challenge and the necessity of self-advocacy in work situations where the advocate simply doesn't have a lot of power. The challenge of such advocacy-upwards in digital environments in particular is that, even beyond your already disempowered status as a rising professional, it can also be difficult to speak with sufficient power and vividness through your webcam. Remote work makes the work of persuasion challenging. My own takeaway from these stories is that some of the most important advocacy upwards happens *on behalf of colleagues*. The bystander plays an indispensable advocative role.

Persuading Downward

Sometimes the persuasion that's needed is towards the people that report to you, as a story from Christian Perry made clear to me. On the day of this story, he was in a hurry. As he angled and nosed his car through the Chicago traffic, he kept glancing at his phone, worrying about the event he'd so carefully prepared for. A Navy man of thirteen years, Christian knew how to plan things with a close eye for detail. He had done the groundwork for this event with extra care in preparation for the governor's arrival, knowing that a lot was on the line. But as a political operative born and bred on Chicago's Southside, he also knew what it was to work with complicated, ego-driven, easily wounded humans. *God doesn't make perfect people*, he liked to say. *God makes good people.* And even working with good people was never a simple proposition. Being a Black man in a predominantly White political campaign had taught him how hard it could be to persuade people to work together for the common good.

---

23. Anonymous, quoted in Mattson, "Workplace Skeeziness."

The stoplights seemed longer than usual that day. As he squinted through his windshield into the Chicago sunlight, he felt the whirlwind of the past few years gathering in his peripheral attention. He took a deep breath, willing himself to be calm. In his experience, when things seemed quiet, that was precisely when—as he likes to say—"God goes crazy." After a stint as a college basketball coach, and the founder of a nonprofit called Grind Grately, he'd begun catching the eye of Springfield, eventually landing a position that doubled his salary. After the murder of George Floyd in May of 2020, he'd organized the largest protest gathering in Chicago's southern Cook County. But he'd also learned to spot cues of mental trouble, even when everyone around him was praising his work. When the Navy had called him up from reserves, and he found himself just about ready to take off for the Horn of Africa, his doctor had said no, he was in no mental condition to go. Not long after, he found himself on the edge of dismissal from a master's program in public administration. But two years of treatment for his major depressive disorder had brought him a measure of healing. Now as the deputy political director for J. B. Pritzker's Illinois gubernatorial reelection, he was advocating downward, trying to persuade the people reporting to him that, even in work that requires hard bargains, you can't forget people's need for grace.

The light changed, and, once more in the swing of traffic, Christian side-eyed his phone. Something was off in that text he'd just read. The chatter sounded wrong. He thought he could detect some anger and swagger in their group messaging. They were acting a little too cocky, perhaps in a way they thought was right for so big a candidate. But now they were starting to swing their weight around at the event trying to dictate to other stakeholders. After all, they worked for the governor. That gave them sway, right? *Wrong, wrong, wrong,* Christian was thinking to himself. He snatched up his phone to do some one-handed texting. He knew what it had cost to persuade local stakeholders to host the event. He knew the good graces Governor Pritzker needed across his party. Christian also knew what a few bad tweets could do to a campaign, what an intercepted text might do if it hit the press, what a stray comment near a live mic could do on the nightly news. What was needed at this minute was not swagger and insolence but humility and grace. He shot a few messages to his team, trying to convey that everybody needed to cool down and stand down. Fortunately, they did more or less exactly that. When Pritzker showed up, all was well, and, to Christian's relief, the event went well. Months later, it was successes like this event that propelled Pritzker to victory in the gubernatorial race.

My takeaways from Christian's story are that persuasion down to people reporting to you requires attention to what the ancients used to call *kairos,* or a sense of what's fitting to say right now. Christian's downward advocacy—in this case, calling for humility towards another campaign—stabilized the situation for his own candidate, too.[24]

Persuasion Outward

Chakena Perry has had to get used to being the youngest professional in a room full of seasoned operatives. When Governor Pritzker (yes, it's the same Pritzker as above, but we're talking about a different Perry!) designated her for the Metropolitan Water Reclamation District of Greater Chicago, Chakena took the role as the youngest commissioner in the history of that organization. Being a politician for her has meant a lot of persuasive work, of course, much of it focused on constituents beyond her organization. It's work she's wanted to do since high school, when she first noticed that politicians were all too often uninterested in helping their own communities. When she expressed a wish to do public service, her friends and loved ones said, "You're too good for politics." Chakena felt sure that was the wrong way to talk about the work of persuasion that politics entailed.

But her first work as a public servant—being a political director for a campaign—gave her a vision for what her friends and loved ones were talking about. To put things mildly, Chakena's boss didn't share her moral commitments. It was a tough job to leave, even so. She knew it could be difficult to find another position. "I prayed about it, you know, every day," she told me, not least because it was a job "that a lot of people will kick a door down for."[25] And she didn't have a lot of financial reserves. She ended up living off credit cards until she landed another position at the Metropolitan Water Reclamation District, where she would eventually serve as a commissioner. Here's what Chakena told me she had learned from doing political work.

Constituents can't be hurried, and political accountability takes a lot of time. She told me people send her emails well after hours and then expect to get a reply back in minutes. "Business hours don't exist in politics," she said. At the same time, she has other accountabilities, as a mom and wife and graduate student (she now holds a University of Chicago MA in public policy). But still she tries to be answerable to her constituents, especially the youthful ones. "I'm still twenty-eight, right? So, I know how it feels to reach out to someone that you look up to . . . Days pass, and you're, like, Did I say the wrong thing? Was my email too long?"[26] She's also felt the imperative to post her political doings on Twitter and Facebook—but

24. Christian Perry, interview by Craig Mattson, February 23, 2022.
25. Chakena Perry, interview by Craig Mattson, February 25, 2022.
26. Chakena Perry, interview by Craig Mattson, February 25, 2022.

sometimes the emailers show up on Facebook and are upset to see her ignoring their emails and posting pictures instead.

Something I noticed about Chakena's persuasive communication is that she knows her stuff but doesn't feel the need to say all the stuff she knows. Her work as commissioner clearly requires deft navigation of systems and information. But the work of persuasive communication for her is not just about spouting talking points; it's also about listening carefully. I was impressed during our interview that she doesn't just perform "listening theater"—she makes eye contact and holds it, attending closely. She's learned to do this from too many meetings where people are just talking past each other. Her wisdom is, "Let's start over. Let's make sure. Let's figure out where we're missing each other."[27]

One story she told me illustrates her favorite wisdom: *say it softly and say it less*. Chicago's not only a windy city; it's a wet city, which makes flood mitigation a central concern for Chakena's constituents. One day, she showed up with another Metropolitan Water Reclamation District commissioner at some water management sites. Chakena took a close look at things, greeting constituents, but let the other commissioner do all the talking. Arriving at the last stormwater site, the other politician was perhaps feeling a little guilty about grabbing all the mic time and asked Chakena if she'd like to speak. Chakena shook her head no. Like any other commissioner, she can discuss the ins and outs of stormwater. But she's also mindful that stormwater doesn't flow better just because you fill the air with talk.

This low-key approach to public communication contrasts with, shall we say, the windy approach of other Chicago politicians. Chakena has learned that sometimes, when things get blustery at the committee table, the best thing might be to table the agenda till everybody's willing to listen to each other. My takeaways from Chakena's engagement with the rhetorical mode is that all too often the sender-receiver model of communication privileges being the sender. Chakena's engagement with the rhetorical mode flips that and prioritizes being the receiver instead.[28]

---

27. Chakena Perry, interview by Craig Mattson, February 25, 2022..

28. Stephen Webb would agree with those political theorists (like Gershberg and Illing) who say "that people have the right to express themselves, no matter what they have to say, and that without such expression there is no freedom." But, he goes on, "Christianity teaches the opposite—that freedom begins in the ear before it reaches the mouth." Webb, *Divine Voice*, 25.

Persuading Inward

I have visited the Drowsy Wolf Studio where Karen Mattson does her pottery work, and I have watched her throw.[29] Seeing her movements, quick, gentle, strong, conveys a kind of spirituality, even in how she uses the wheel. But it has not always been work she could persuade herself to do. Like many millennials, Karen's career path has been winding. In her case, part of the meandering was due to what other people said about work. Their dismissive comments about pottery, for example, made it hard to hear her yearning to make things from clay. She even recalls a television commercial in which a loser guy is shown making bowls instead of doing real work. Whatever else she might manage to do, she didn't want to be that guy.

One day, studying art in college, she was reading outside when a stranger walked by her, tossing a stray remark something like, "You're in the wrong school." She received this as the universe sending a message and moved towards a career in wedding photography. She stayed with it for fourteen years, capturing and editing thousands and thousands of pictures. She now thinks she was in the business about five years too long. But even when she was suffering burnout in the field, she couldn't figure out how to persuade herself to take up with an art form she'd really love—pottery.

She went to school again to become a physical therapy assistant, which she hoped would equip her to serve older citizens. Not only did she admire her aunt who was a nurse, but she hoped that being a PTA would bring ways to serve her parents as they aged. Two years later she was embedded in the field, serving a community of nuns in Adrian, Michigan. The job, at first, seemed remarkably easy to adjust to, especially in comparison with wedding photography. No more editing photos deep into the night; no more shooting weddings on weekends. At the same time, the job proved incredibly stressful, especially mentally. Karen still felt like she was figuring out things out by making vocational mistakes.

She pulled back from physical therapy and did some painting in her house, thinking and dreaming about possible next moves. For some reason, she couldn't stop thinking about a ceramics course she'd taken. But she was still troubled by the sense that other people dismissed pottery as a nonstarter. It was the kind of work that other business owners would describe as *that thing I thought about doing before I found real work to do*. But somehow, in the spring of 2021, Karen persuaded herself to start a company. Her vocational journey has not reached any sort of terminal point. Running a company and doing digital marketing, navigating fulfillment services, and

---

29. Karen is my sister-in-law.

keeping ahead of online buyers—all on top of the work of throwing clay—can be exhausting, especially as demand for her impressive work has picked up. At the same time, at least at the time of our interview, it seemed like she had finally convinced herself to do what she's most equipped to do. Sometimes, she feels apologetic about her work, unwilling to let people know she's working seventy-hour weeks. But Karen also said she'd never done work that was so *satisfying*, so *comfortable*, so *challenging*.

It was a surprising trio of adjectives. But I am struck, as I consider Karen's practice of internal persuasion, that the rhetorical mode entails filtering some voices, keeping others, and listening carefully for your own. Maybe your own voice is most recognizable at the intersection of startlingly unrelated words like *satisfying* and *comfortable* and *challenging*.[30]

Not all stories of persuasion inward, however, entail filtering out other voices so you can hear your own better. Sometimes, advocacy inward simply means changing your own mind.

Joshua Coldagelli told me a story about giving up a career path towards becoming a college basketball coach. His mind change about this lifelong dream job happened during a trip to the Bahamas, while he was employed for the Central Michigan University basketball team. What could be better? You're in a paradisical situation; you're on a path towards a position you've been idealizing all your life. Working for the team had rarely been easy for Josh, but he'd borne with any annoyances on the grounds that doing the lowly work of being a team manager was an essential precursor to the impressive work of being a team coach. But grunt work has a way of concentrating the mind. One night in the Bahamas, Josh was washing team jerseys in the hotel laundry. But because there were only a couple of machines, he ended up staying up all night long, with the jerseys. It turned out to be a thirty-hour shift. The next morning, he schlepped the now clean-smelling and well-folded laundry out to the golf cart and was getting ready to head over to the team when he caught sight of a Caribbean sunrise that made him stop and stare. "I had to just take a moment and stay in the golf cart," he told me. He noted later that "a little bit of peace with that day" also raised questions about his career path. For a while, Josh kept a picture of that sunrise on his laptop screen, as a reminder. That moment of beauty—and the numbing night of work that had preceded it—woke him up and (as he would put it later) *deconstructed his vocational dream*.[31]

The rhetorician Jean Nienkamp has discussed what she calls "internal rhetorics," or ways that people like Karen and Josh argue within themselves

30. Karen Mattson, interview by Craig Mattson, April 25, 2022.
31. Joshua Coldagelli, interview by Craig Mattson, February 24, 2022.

about a course of action. It's hard to hear what your life is saying to you from the inside out, as Karen eventually learned to. But it's just as hard to hear yourself think—and then to change what you think, as both Karen and Josh did. Either way, the rhetorical mode calls us to a careful persuasive labor, even on the quiet platform of our souls.

A Mode Switch Worth Making

As I look across the data I've received from Gen Z and millennial storytellers, I feel grateful for their candor and their courage. Their narratives show how vital it is to practice the rhetorical mode, even in digital settings that make persuasion feel like just another exhausting kind of emotional labor. But one thing I didn't hear people saying was what I think we might call persuasion *among*. I spot this idea from the cluster of wisdom voices we've been listening to throughout this book.

I should say that I haven't always been able to hear these wisdom voices in the rhetorical mode. I grew up in churches in which it seemed like, at the heart of reality was one clear, indisputable voice of authority: the voice of God. Being a human was essentially a project in ignoring every other voice but that one. (This approach to Scripture was subtly reinforced by a typographical practice common in the Bibles of my childhood: printing the words of Jesus in red.) But the longer I've read Scripture, the more it has come to feel like standing in a crowded room listening to clusters of conversation for hints of harmony. It can be confusing. But for those who want to know the God of the Bible, this act of polyphonic listening is indispensable. Even the triune God is a community of voices, after all.

As we've stood among the wisdom voices in each of this book's chapters, I hope you've noticed how their stories and insights require them to take up the work of persuasion.

- Job and his friends remind us that ideas taken for granted as truths across a community can still be wrong. Facing a misconception in his community compels him to engage the rhetorical mode. Because nobody—not his wife, not his friends, not his community—believes what he has to say about his life, he realizes that he must make his case. (Eventually, of course, that case is transformed to something that Job could never have predicted.)

- Or take the philosopher of Ecclesiastes, staring at the sky, tears welling in the morning sun. Qoheleth writes and writhes, looking for words that will speak firmly and vividly in his community. But there's no end to the rhetorical mode. He completes one book only to start another. For him the work of persuasion is never done until the judgment day itself.

- We've also faced a woman with blazing eyes, shouting, "How long are you going to love your simple ways?"[32] Woman Wisdom has built a house and prepared a generous feast—but no one is coming. Just because she builds it doesn't mean they will come. She has to cry aloud to awaken people to their own deepest hungers.

- Then Socrates comes into view, barefoot and bemused as usual. His words are a witness to wisdom beyond the bounds of biblical community. But even as a teacher who prefers conversation above all other modes of communication—there is no rest from the rhetorical mode. Whether he's making speeches or parsing ideas, he's trying to lure Phaedrus into a life of wisdom.

- Just beyond him, we see a gaggle of psalmists, one saying, "Help me!" and another saying, "Give thanks!" and still another saying, "Consider this!" The jangle of voices goes on and on, psalm after psalm, again enacting the relentlessness of rhetorical work never completed in human life and community.

These figures form a small crowd. Listening to what they have to say together shows the importance of the rhetorical mode *among* numerous persuaders. Their standpoints sound remarkably different, and their voices strain at different inflections. But as we stand among them, listening for all we're worth, we can make out a kind of harmonizing principle: living well obliges questions and answers, claims and rejoinders, cries and responses, calls and comebacks.[33]

My sense is that what makes advocacy hard at work is that it feels like it all depends on you, the lonely, indebted professional on the Zoom call. I hope you feel encouraged, simply by standing among the resonant voices of these teachers. They are not speaking in low-voiced ways that suggest they have things under control. They are not stoic and calm. Instead, they speak intensely, disconcertingly loudly, and often at great personal cost. But in every case, the work of advocacy draws them not into that risky isolation we all fear so much, but into a rich *among* in which every speaker and every listener is a giver and a receiver at the same time.

---

32. Proverbs 1:22, NRSV.
33. My teacher on this point is Booth, *My Many Selves*.

CHAPTER 7.5

How to Get People to Do Things

Mode/Switch Workshop

Goal: To spot and evaluate strategies for creating cooperation within your organization.

Synopsis:

IT SOUNDS DICEY TO say this out loud, but sometimes you just need to convince people to do things so you can do your job. Plato called it soul-guidance. Kenneth Burke called it inducing cooperation.[1] But whatever you call it, persuasive communication is an integral part of just about everybody's job. Sometimes when I talk to people about this, they don't see what they're doing as *persuasion*. That feels too much like a manipulative power move, as if you might be curtailing people's free will somehow. Shouldn't you just trust information to do the job, instead of infusing it with extra energy and pushing it? Sometimes, it feels like a failure of authenticity: in order to make an argument, you might have to bend the truth or even compromise your own principles to make your argument convincing.

But the mode of advocacy reminds us that, although we like to think of ourselves as autonomous agents guided by neutral information and impartial conviction, we are actually social creatures whose identities take shape in the talk and argument of the communities that form us. Even sharing seemingly

---

1. Burke, *Rhetoric of Motives*, 41.

neutral information with someone who reports to you (informing them of a policy, for example) is a kind of persuasion: you are saying, "Hey, this matters. It should be important to you, too."[2] But we can put things even more strongly: we have a moral obligation to engage the rhetorical mode with each other. Given the kind of creatures humans are—creatures formed through conversation, argument, listening, performance, dialogue—we have a moral duty to try to use rhetoric as a way to find what we and our coworkers and administrators should be doing. Argument is not about manipulation (at least, it need not be), but about discovery.[3]

The question is not should we engage the mode or not, but how to do it skillfully among all the politics of organizational life.

This workshop aims to help you, as Aristotle would put it, to discern in a given situation the available means of persuasion. Even though he could never have imagined that our given situation might be a webcam lens, he was right to emphasize just how important it is to sit back and look carefully at what's actually available to us in the mode of advocacy. I've invited three early-to-mid-career professionals to walk us through their own situations and to discuss what they've learned to see as available means of persuasion.

You've met all these people before in earlier chapters: Rachel Hennessy works for a software startup as a marketer. Ben Hoekstra does PR in the health industry. And Joe Barrera is a recruiter for EPM Scientific. (I have edited their comments for brevity and clarity.) After a few minutes of conversation, we'll press pause and give you a chance to think through some of the issues related to advocacy that arise for you in your company or church or nonprofit.

> When you advocate things, which do you find most doable—persuading upward to managers, downward to team members, outward to stakeholders, or inward to yourself?

Rachel:

Persuading those who are doing the work with me—it's much easier and it's more collaborative. There's less risk, because at the end of the day, a lot

---

2. Booth, *Rhetoric of Rhetoric*, xii.

3. As Wayne Booth says, human beings as creatures formed in communicative exchange "should make each other, and it is an inescapable value in their lives that it is good to do it well." Booth, *Modern Dogma and the Rhetoric of Assent*, 137.

of us just don't want to get in trouble. We want it to be good. We want the accolades.

Ben:

I come from an upbringing where there was a good amount of hierarchy and respect for authority. And so, for me, persuading upward [feels most doable]—there's a certain amount of "I do my best, and then it's not my responsibility how someone else deals with that." Because of this willingness to kind of work within a hierarchy—and seeing that as not necessarily a negative—I do find myself often in a slightly different position than many other folks in my same generation (being someone on the border of millennial and Gen Z).

Joe:

I think the easier one is persuading others. A huge part of what I've had to do recently is try to connect the people who are on the sales floor and the people who are on senior leadership. That's where the persuasion on both ends has to be.

| Advocacy Reflection: | Think for a moment about what kind of persuasion is easiest for you: up, down, out, or in. What about your job history has made that direction easier for you? |

The rhetorician Walter Fisher said that in order for a story to be persuasive, it has to be coherent and resonant. What do you think makes a story resonant for your supervisor as opposed to one of your fellow team members?

In digital advocacy, what technical and aesthetic details of online interaction (such as lighting or background) have you found most persuasive in other people's remote presentations?

What kind of persuasive labor do you find especially complicated?

Rachel:

Persuading up. A founder has put their whole life into a company. They pour their heart and souls into it every single day. They never get a day off. They have to care so deeply. Otherwise, the whole thing falls apart. It is really hard to persuade someone with that mindset. I don't know if I can point to a single instance of where it's been successful.

A lot of founders will *say*, "I don't know everything," but as soon as their worldview is challenged, all of a sudden, only they know the answer. But they don't actually know the answer.

There's a lot of trust that needs to be built. With these startups, there's not a lot of time to build that trust. A lot of it could be ego. Or it could just be fear, having that sunk cost feeling. *We've already put in so much work for this. It has to work because the investors will be upset.*

It's not like I walk into these jobs and I'm like, *I don't give a rat's ass about your company. I'm just here to make money and take it on the road.* It's not like that. But founders who have put in a lot of their personal money and time—and I mean, they are working constantly—I can never reach the level of passion that they have. So it might be this mismatch of passion or perceived passion.

Ben:

Persuading someone outwardly when you don't entirely agree with the corporate line. It's funny. I'm dealing with some challenges right now with my team. Whenever you inherit a team, you inherit everything that the boss before you did too. And most of the time, that's not a net positive. How do you ensure that you are aligning with what you're asked to do in your job—"Hey, this is what the organization is prioritizing. This is what we need to do"—while still coming across as authentic and not a corporate shill?

Joe:

The hardest one is persuading myself. I honestly struggled with imposter syndrome for a while. When I stepped into management, there was a part of me that felt like, *Am I ready to do this? Am I going to lead my team in the right direction?* If I'm telling myself something, it's hard for me to believe it. But then I go back to read compliments or reassurances from my manager, from my team, and different things that other people have said. I want to try to give myself as much evidence as I can from outside perspectives to reassure myself.

Advocacy Insights:

What do you do when you believe you see something more clearly than your boss, even though they have more passion behind their convictions?

- Don't make light of their commitment. Honor it. Or at least acknowledge that you can't identify with their passion exactly.

- Explain, however, that you want to see the company succeed, so you've done some research that's led to a different conclusion than the boss. Ask them to consider your findings as a thought experiment.

- Make sure to connect your appeals to the interests and needs of the boss. If times are hard, these appeals may be related to the company's survival. If things are going well, these appeals may need to relate to the company's aspirations and the boss's expressed ideals.

- Remember the power of inception: ideas are always more convincing to people if they feel they have come up with them on their own.

What do you do when you need to persuade your team to follow a company policy, even if you don't agree with it yourself?

- If your team is antagonistic, it may be best for you not to disclose your own opinions and instead focus on good reasons that support the controversial policy. Maintain a neutral, moderate tone in such communications. Keep your cards close.

- If your team is supportive of the administration in most cases, you may choose to be more transparent and identify with their frustrations. You can say, "This isn't the policy I would have designed, but the people making it were looking at more factors than just our department. All policies are experimental. Let's go with this for now as best as we can. We can revisit it in a month and talk about how it's going. If it's not working for us, I will be glad to advocate for our department then."

- Remember that you are preparing your team members for future positions of leadership in this or in other organizations. Using artful advocacy helps them think through policy development and execution, which is a valuable part of their own professional formation.

> What should you do when you're having a hard time convincing yourself that you're capable of doing something?
>
> - Engage in a contemplative practice—journaling, going for a quiet walk or run, sitting in silent meditation or prayer. This can help you sort through what the voices in your head are saying, which can be trusted, and which should be disregarded. (This is similar to what Joe was doing in reviewing compliments or reassurances people had given him.)
>
> - Seek the opinion of someone who doesn't generally support you and who looks at the world differently than you do. This will strengthen your informed sense of whether or not you're up for the task.
>
> - Ask trusted friends to play devil's advocate. Hearing opposing arguments from people you trust lets you think through your own capabilities and brings clarity to the situation.

How does the digital disrupt these persuasive efforts?

Rachel:

You have to work so much harder to show your commitment in a digital environment. Currently at this job I've met the founder in person a couple times. The first time I met him—two days prior, he had fired my boss, and so that was a little bit uneasy. I was like, *OK, I don't have a boss. I'm meeting the CEO for the first time. I don't know what's going on. Is my job at risk? Do I have to start thinking about updating my resume?* That was a weird time.

I don't get a lot of face-to-face time, even digitally, with him because he's very busy.

How do I express this through chat? How do I email? How do I write things to be on our website that convey that I'm a trustworthy, worthy source?

Ben:

I think the digital piece is both a plus and a minus. I think digital gives you distance. Let's say, my boss sends me something I don't agree with. I can take a beat and think about how I want to respond. That can be harder on the fly. Maybe you're in a meeting, and it ends in five minutes and it's like, *Do it now or it's not happening* versus an email where I can give thought to a draft of something and then walk away and come back to it.

Distance also means people can hide. If you have to have a hard conversation, it's really easy to just not respond to stuff. People hide behind the excuse that, *It was just an email*. Blame the medium. *I didn't see this. I didn't get to this.* And that might be true. But it's also a mechanism, right? It's also a way people abuse the platform.

Can you tell me about a time when you felt like a persuasion went well?

Joe:

I lead the meetings between me and my team, so it's about five of us. We used to do everything digital, and then recently I've switched that to being a personal meeting where we're all just drinking coffee together on our kitchen island within the office. Being able to see each other in person and joke around—that has allowed a lot more attention between the people in that meeting versus when we work remotely. And it's allowed a lot of people to feel more comfortable to open up about things.

Ben:

A lot of my job is about building relationships with stakeholders. So it's the persuasion for the specific thing in the moment, right? Most of the stakeholders I work with—it's usually not a transactional, one-time relationship. It's a very different thing to get the result you want versus to preserve the relationship long term. The times I've been most successful in doing both are when I've been very clear about the "why" behind things. I try to talk about what's in it for that person. That's a phrase we use often in my world. *I don't need to tell you why this is good for the organization or why I think this is right. I need to tell you why this is good for you and your people.*

I have to be the punching bag sometimes. I've been in many meetings where I just sit there and someone complains about my team for forty-five minutes.

It's surprised me how much a difference that makes. I don't think I thought it would solve a lot of issues—and it does! There are things that I would have thought would still be a huge issue. And I've listened to someone, I've heard them out, and then it just kind of disappears. And that's fascinating to me. Is the persuasion allowing someone to feel empowered and meaningful, because they were heard—even if it didn't change things? I don't know.

Rachel:

You plant an idea, and then you just work on it, you bring it up every now and again, and that's usually how it happens. In order to convince them, they have to think it was their idea. For a woman in tech, they will not hear it unless another man says it. And it is so frustrating. It's a constant messaging of conversations, of materials, of research, of sliding things into their peripheral. But eventually, it comes about.

I wrote out this whole list of webinars that they could do for Women's History Month. It took a full year of bringing that back to say, *You should do a series. We could promote it this way.* But eventually someone said, *What if we did a series of webinars?* And I was like, *Oh, like this? How about all of these things?* Amazing. And so it was like playing a really big game. I don't like to play the game, but I'll play it, I guess. I'm OK with that role for now.

Advocacy Insights:

Based on Rachel's comments:

- Give extra time to remote advocacy. Persuading people of things online will take two or three times the energy and time in advocating as it will in person.

- Seek out in-person meetings before attempting remote advocacy.

- Avoid assuming the worst- or best-case scenario during online interactions. Because remote communication offers fewer social cues, it's easy to exaggerate someone's goodwill or malicious intent.

- Practice indirect persuasion. Don't assume that all advocacy has to be face-to-face. You can be making the case for a good idea of yours via many stakeholders at once. Ideas move at the speed of networks just as much as they move at the speed of powerful individuals.

- Decide when you're willing to "play the game" in order to bring your ideas to fruition. You can't always predict how ideas will take hold or take off.

Based on Ben's comments:

- Make a communication plan for escalating things gradually with a team member or administrator who's ghosting you. It's important to leave yourself another step to take in case this or that communication gets ignored. Don't escalate too quickly.

- Be willing to take some body blows for the good of the project. Letting people complain about you or your team can release pressure. You can always nod and take notes. When you don't know what to say, you can always respond, "I hear what you're saying. I'll talk this over with my team. We're trying to keep a growth mindset just like everybody else."

- Remember that an argument is a relational process. You're making the case for a course of action even when you're simply building their trust in you or getting them to agree to meet with you again. Even the way you respond to their "no" is an act of advocacy, inclining them to agree or disagree with you next time around.

Based on Joe's comments:

- Make the case for periods of shared, focused attention. Digital interaction with those who report to you may require some advocacy about giving attention. It's hard to let go of multitasking, but it can help for you to invite people into a space of single-tasking.

- Persuade yourself to be patient with distracted teammates. When they can't resist checking their devices instead of staring at the webcam, it's not a moral failing on their part; it's also that we find ourselves in a sometimes overwhelming and pressurized environment. Sometimes checking notifications is just irresistible.

- Convince people to meet in person sometimes. Be sure to infuse these meetings with the warm interactions that make the extra effort of in-person meetings worth it.

Afterword

I HAVE BEEN THINKING about you for so many months of writing that it feels to me, as I begin this epilogue, that you should be able to toss this book down, pick up your phone, and text me what you're thinking now. In the Afterword, if anywhere, I crave a mode switch from the broadcast of a book to the dialogue of direct messaging.

But publications don't work that way. And it's a good thing, too.

The *you* I have been imagining and writing towards isn't one person, after all. Sure, I've sometimes fantasized that I know exactly who you are. I've thought I had you in my sights—yes, *there you are*, treading water far, far at sea. You are awash in a changefulness that's been constant since you graduated during one of the many crises of the past twenty years, back when someone shook your hand and handed you a life vest. You turned and smiled at the photographer and leapt off the pier. Perhaps you saw a corporate laker off in the distance, swam towards it, climbed aboard. But it wasn't long before toxins in the work environment made you leap back into the water, headed for a sleek startup. But now, you're back in the waves again—the startup having gone belly up—wondering when a nonprofit pontoon will come chugging by. (Institutions weren't always so undependable in the nineties, were they?) You could swim in one direction or another, but it's hard to see how it matters. It's hard even to see the pier, much less the horizon. The chop of waves is relentless, and you're more tired than a body ever should be.

Other times, the *you* I have envisioned is a person standing rigid against the lighthouse, looking at the waves as they curve massively over the edge of the pier. You look at the enormity of it all and shake your head slowly as kids dive sideways and backwards off the dock. You long for everyone to return to the shore, to take long slow walks, asking questions, discussing ideas. You yearn for a time when people sat on benches, read books, and studied longer horizons. A windsurfer flits by, body bent almost double in the gale. You watch the all the swimmers' heads showing just above whitecaps and, in generous moments, wonder, *People weren't so distractible in the eighties were they?*

Like any author I crave the magic of author-reader connection. I wish to write a book that goes off like a flare, a beacon you can swim towards, a hand you can grasp. So many times over the past months, as I have told people I was writing about digital overwhelm, they have said, "Oh, that's such a *needed book* right now!" And I have looked away, trying to smile reassuringly. But how, I wondered, could my book muster the rescue they imagined?

This will sound callous, but the only way I have found to write these chapters is by not caring too much about who you so weirdly and wondrously are. I know there are realities about your overwhelmed existence that no author's compassion could cure, no writerly wisdom could resolve. Were you to tell me all that's going on in your fraught life, I could only stare at the ground, my lips everting around a feeble silence, a gesture starting and then stopping mid-air. We'd be left looking past each other, smiling a little and nodding.

But I found I could write this book if I kept the writing attentive not to imagined individuals but towards actual craft.

The craft we're sailing in

In many ways, this has been a book of metacognition, trying to develop a feel for the craft we need for the waves we face. Is it the canoe of dialogue, the self and the other facing one another, paddles resting on laps, eyes meeting and then flitting away and meeting again as mutuality slowly forms? Is it the cargo ship of dissemination, a great and powerful engine, scattering the surf in every direction? Is it a raft you'd built for yourself, hacking and carving meaning for vocation with one's hands and tools? Is it a surfboard, on which performative dexterity amazed and delighted all who watched? Or is it the outboard of advocacy, engine roaring, prow cresting, cutting through the opposition?

My caution to readers throughout this book has been not to get stuck in one or two craft you know and trust. The advice recalls Robinson Crusoe building a boat to escape his island. He fells a tree five feet in diameter and spends months with nothing more than his axe, cutting off the roots, hewing away the branches, carving out the hold. It is a massive and impressive vessel, capable of holding some twenty-six people. But when he can finally step back and inspect the craft, he is forced to realize it is too large for him to carry to the water. He looks from the boat to the sea, a hundred yards away, and then back again at the boat. He is astonished at himself: "I never once considered how I should get it off the land: and it was really, in its own nature, more easy for me to guide it over forty-five miles of sea than about forty-five fathoms of land, where it lay, to set it afloat in the water."[1]

This is the mistake we fall into when we fail to match craft to context.

- We write the thousand-word email to the organizational community, fondly thinking that everyone reads everything word for word.
- We hold the two-hour conversation on Teams, sure as our soul that we can cross the divide of any misunderstanding. *This* will be the meeting when the procedure finally becomes clear. But everyone is too busy pretending to listen, nodding vigorously, smiling widely, to hear anything.
- We make a case to the shareholders, confident that the argument is transparently right and good. But they do not hear it, because we do not conform to their idea of a credible source.

This book talked about six modes of communication; there are many more. But when we refuse to switch our modes, we are like Crusoe with his shoulder jammed against the stern of a boat he has built but cannot budge.

The craft we're sailing with

When I speak of craft for steering through the torrent, it is not finally *your skill* alone. The craft of organizational exchange is always a collective capability.

A great part of the craft of writing and speaking and acting and advocating in any company, church, or nonprofit is recognizing just how shared those capabilities are. It feels like you're writing that email alone. It feels like just you having to make the presentation. It feels like you are the only one to hold that critical conversation. But take a look around; your craft depends on the craft of all the others, too. That simple but enormous fact means cultivating patience as people refine their skills for the shared project. It means accepting an offered hand when you topple overboard. It means openness to the idea that you will discover craft with others, mode craft that none of you has right now.

1. Defoe, *Life and Adventures of Robinson Crusoe*, 86.

I began this book by saying that mode craft requires remembering what you already know. But take a final look at what this book has called you to remember and notice that each kind of craft is an emergent and communal achievement.

- *Mutuality*—The dialogic mode is about finding possibilities for slowing down and taking care. It's about remembering that although inboxes and appointments feel like action items, they are spaces for encounter.
- *Cooperation*—The disseminative mode recollects the unlikely goods of one-way communication. We don't have to cable into each other's inner lives to work together. We are too different from one another for that. But letting people emit abrupt broadcasts can be a starting point for cooperation.
- *Coordination*—The semiotic mode recalls us to the work of meaning-making. But all that meaning formation is with and towards others. We will not share the same sense of vocational meaning with each coworker. But we need each other's therapy and skepticism and survivalism to keep coordinating work with them.
- *Attention*—The tacit mode recalls us to the work of attention. But when that most distracting of events occurs—technological breakdown—the crisis is not a solo project but a predicament for the network. We cannot merely sharpen concentration as we engage the tacit mode; we must also share it.
- *Angling*—The performative mode pulls us out of the claustrophobic quarters of the one-on-one and into the complex interactions of an organizational community. On that stage, it is indirectness, nonverbals, irony, small talk, playfulness, inception, and subtext that enable the multilateral communication that working communities rely on.
- *Inducement*—The rhetorical mode draws us into the tug and pull of organizational life. But as we argue with each other, as we persuade upward, downward, outward, inward, we are listening for new, good reasons to take action on shareable projects.

Discussing these achievements has made me wish to ask for more managerial and guru attention for modes of communication in organizational life. Attention to communication modes opens up possibilities for something besides blame for managers or criticism of workers, mockery for millennials or condemnation of Gen Zs. The complexity and the changeability of modes remind us that we are all quarter-lifer deconverts. None of us fits comfortably within our designated generation, and given the evolutions of digital communication, we keep having to begin again. That perpetual genesis makes us skeptical of the bad religion of workism. But out of chaos comes creation and out of deconstruction comes reconstruction of still more navigable craft.

Remembering these things has also narrowed the gap between communication theory and the lived experience of practitioners. I am as an academic all too prone to see the today's workplace challenges as excuses to announce the gospel of high theory. But organizational communicational research and theory can help professionals know where a set of practices comes from, why they make such good sense to so many people, and where they might be headed. Theory helps cultivate a sense of the contingency of popular approaches to current problems. When a TED Talker comes out on stage, it can feel, at least for the brightly lit moment, that they are descending from Sinai. But acquaintance with the conversations of communication theory can cultivate shrewdness about the limitations and hope for the surprising gifts of communication modes scattered across popular consciousness.

"Let your words be few," Qoheleth is growling from the back of the boat. I should wrap this up. But there may be one more thing to say.

As you seek seaworthiness in sundry modes of organizational communication, make sure also to seek communities of wisdom inland from your work—places where you can still hear the surf but where there is quiet space to reflect. I don't just mean listening to more podcasts and scrolling through more reels. The sages of our times are amazing humans, and there are a lot of them. But you and I need more than expertise and insight. We need transformation. The wisdom literatures we have been attending to throughout this book aren't just provocative texts or inspiring voices; they do more than present us with a problem-solution discourse. They introduce us to communities of renewal and change. Within them, you witness such communities taking shape in the interactions of editors and translators and writers and speakers. Around these texts, you can make out gatherings through history, seeking together to cope with pain and overwhelm.

And that is what I hope and seek for us as well: not merely that we make well-judged mode switches to do work better but that we also remain open to questions of spirituality and relationality in the process. What distinguishes Qoheleth, Job, Lady Wisdom, the psalmists, and Plato is their challenge to attend to voices of wisdom from outside our familiar communities. They call us to be open to transformation from directions we have previously closed down. And they beckon us to be made into more generous and more resilient people in the process. These transformations are more than mode switches. But they are what this book's mode craft has been after, all the same.

Acknowledgments

QUALITATIVE RESEARCH WITH THE rising professionals whose stories fill this book prompts me to a mode switch from inquiry to gratitude. It's an easy shift to make. Without your willingness to tell work and life stories—amazing interviewees, I'm looking at you—this book would be impossible. For those who agreed to meet with me for numerous repeat interviews, I bow my head in many directions in sincerest thanks.

What conceptual clarity this book enjoys relies on close conversations with Andrew Holmes, Emma Mattson, and Naaman Wood, each of whom corresponded and video chatted, often on lovingly short notice. Their response to pleas for help were invariably something along the lines of "Well, how about this afternoon? Or now? I'm free now." Andrew has an astonishing gift for bibliography and knows how to critique a framework in a way that makes you feel deeply helped. Naaman buoyed me with his theological learnedness and exuberant conversation. Emma helped with framing the book's ideas; she shaped its tone as well, noting when my prose grew turgid and vocabulary obscure. Her copyediting and manuscript preparation were joyous and expert.

The book's accuracy to the experience of Gen Z and millennial professionals, such as it is, traces to in-depth collaborations with Emily Bosscher, Sarah Hao, Ben Hoekstra, LaShone Manuel, MaKena Mayfield, Andrea Munday, Hannah Sherbrooke, and David Wilstermann, each of whom have been part of the *Mode/Switch* Substack and podcast team.

I wrote this book while moving from one learning community to another. Launching the research at Trinity Christian College, I benefited from a Fusion59 innovation grant awarded by professor Sundeep Vira and was frequently encouraged by collegial support from Bethany Keeley-Jonker, Lenore Knight Johnson, Mackenzi Huyser, and Aaron Kuecker. I completed the book after taking a position at Calvin University, where I have benefited from generous conversation with Matt Lundberg, Sam Smartt, Michael Wildschut, and Jane Zwart. My thanks, too, for the donors who support the Arther H. DeKruyter Chair in Faith and Communication, which has afforded me needed research time and funding. Academic communities like these are shelters for long work.

I write this book not only with gratitude to millennial and Gen Z professionals but also in hope for their wisdom, resilience, and generosity.

Bibliography

Abercrombie, Nick, and Brian Longhurst. *Audiences: A Sociological Theory of Performance and Imagination*. London: SAGE, 1998.
Allen, David. *Getting Things Done*. New York: Penguin, 2001.
Anderson, Rob. "Anonymity, Presence, and the Dialogic Self in a Technological Culture." In *The Reach of Dialogue: Confirmation, Voice, and Community*, edited by Rob Anderson, Kenneth N. Cissna, and Ronald C. Arnett, 11. New Jersey: Hampton, 1994.
Angel Aid. "Passion with a Purpose." https://www.angelaidcares.org/purpose.
———. "Relief for Raregivers Who Need It Most." https://www.angelaidcares.org/.
Anonymous. Interview with Craig Mattson, February 18, 2022.
———. Interview with Craig Mattson, January 3, 2022.
———. Interview with Craig Mattson, May 2, 2022.
Aristotle. *On Rhetoric: A Theory of Civic Discourse*. 2nd ed. Translated by George A. Kennedy. Oxford: Oxford University Press, 2006.
Arnett, Ronald C. *Dialogic Education: Conversation about Ideas and Between Persons*. Carbondale: Southern Illinois University Press, 1992.
Austin, J. L. *How to Do Things with Words*. Oxford: Oxford University Press, 1962.
Bailenson, Jeremy. "Nonverbal Overload: A Theoretical Argument for the Causes of Zoom Fatigue." *Technology, Mind, and Behavior* 2, no. 1 (February 23, 2021). https://tmb.apaopen.org/pub/nonverbal-overload/release/2
Barbaro, Michael. "The Online Search Wars Got Scary. Fast." *The Daily*. Podcast audio. February 15, 2023. https://www.nytimes.com/2023/02/15/podcasts/the-daily/chat-gpt-microsoft-bing-artificial-intelligence.html.
Barclay, John M.G. *Paul and the Gift*. Grand Rapids: Eerdmans, 2017.
Barthes, Roland. *Mythologies*. Translated by Richard Howard and Annette Lavers. New York: Hill and Wang, 2012.
Berbaum, Jon. "Household Economics at Highland Solutions—Jon Berbaum." Interview by Craig Mattson. *Spiritual Capital* S1, ep. 40. Podcast audio. https://podcasts.apple.com/us/podcast/household-economics-at-highland-solutions-jon-berbaum/id1510610001?i=1000502104669.
Berger, Arthur Asa. *Signs in Contemporary Culture: An Introduction to Semiotics*. 2nd ed. Sheffield: Sheffield, 1999.

Berlant, Lauren. *Cruel Optimism*. Durham, NC: Duke University Press, 2011.
———. *The Queen of America Goes to Washington City*. Durham, NC: Duke University Press, 1997.
Black, Joycee. Interview by Craig Mattson. March 4, 2022.
Booth, Wayne. *Modern Dogma and the Rhetoric of Assent*. Chicago: University of Chicago Press, 1974.
———. *My Many Selves: The Quest for a Plausible Harmony*. Logan, UT: Utah State University Press, 2006.
———. *The Rhetoric of Rhetoric: The Quest for Effective Communication*. Malden, MA: Blackwell, 2004.
Brueggemann, Walter. *Materiality as Resistance: Five Elements for Moral Action in the Real World*. Louisville: Westminster John Knox, 2020.
———. *Praying the Psalms: Engaging Scripture and the Life of the Spirit*. 2nd ed. Eugene, OR: Cascade, 2007.
Brueggemann, Walter, and William H. Bellinger Jr. *Psalms*. New Cambridge Bible Commentary. Cambridge: Cambridge University Press, 2014.
Buber, Martin. *Between Man and Man*. New York: Routledge & Kegan Paul, 1947.
———. *I and Thou*. Translated by Ronald Gregor Smith. New York: Charles Scribner's Sons, 1937.
Burke, Kenneth. *Language as Symbolic Action*. Berkeley: University of California Press, 1966.
———. *A Rhetoric of Motives*. Berkeley: University of California Press, 1969.
Burton, Tara Isabella. *Strange Rites: New Religions for a Godless World*. New York: PublicAffairs, 2020.
Butler, Judith. *Excitable Speech: A Politics of the Performative*. Abingdon: Routledge, 1997.
Byock, Satya Doyle. *Quarterlife: The Search for Self in Early Adulthood*. New York: Random House, 2022.
Canlis, Julie. *Calvin's Ladder: A Spiritual Theology of Ascent and Ascension*. Grand Rapids: Eerdmans, 2010.
Carey, James. *Communication as Culture: Essays on Media and Society*. New York: Routledge, 1992.
Carter, Jackson. *Do Your Job: The Leadership Principles that Bill Belichick and the New England Patriots Have Used to Become the Best Dynasty in the NFL*. N.p.: Lessons in Leadership Institute, 2018.
Chen, Carolyn. *Work Pray Code: When Work Becomes Religion in Silicon Valley*. Princeton: Princeton University Press, 2022.
Christiano, Paul. "Where I Agree and Disagree with Eliezer." *Less Wrong*, June 19, 2022. https://www.lesswrong.com/posts/CoZhXrhpQxpy9xw9y/where-i-agree-and-disagree-with-eliezer.
Coldagelli, Joshua. Interview by Craig Mattson. February 24, 2022.
Condit, Celeste. *How Should We Study the Symbolizing Animal?* London: Pearson Education, 2004.
Crary, Jonathan. *Suspensions of Perception: Attention, Spectacle, and Modern Culture*. Cambridge, MA: The MIT Press, 2000.
Crenshaw, James. *The Psalms: An Introduction*. Grand Rapids: Eerdmans, 2001.
Crouch, Andy. *The Life We're Looking For*. New York: Convergent, 2022.

Das, Avinash Chandra, Greg Phalin, Ishwar Lal Patidar, et al. "The next frontier of customer engagement: AI-enabled customer service." *McKinsey and Company*, March 27, 2023. https://www.mckinsey.com/capabilities/operations/our-insights/the-next-frontier-of-customer-engagement-ai-enabled-customer-service.

Daugherty, Paul R., and H. James Wilson. *Human + Machine: Reimagining Work in the Age of AI*. Cambridge, MA: Harvard Business Review, 2018.

Davis, Ellen. *Getting Involved with God: Rediscovering the Old Testament*. Lanham, MD: Cowley, 2001.

———. *Proverbs, Ecclesiastes, The Song of Songs*. Louisville: Westminster John Knox, 2000.

Deetz, Stanley A. "Corporate Governance, Communication, and Getting Social Values into the Decisional Chain." *Management Communication Quarterly* 16, no. 4 (May 2003) 606–11.

———. *Democracy in an Age of Corporate Colonization: Developments in Communication and the Politics of Everyday Life*. Albany, NY: State University of New York Press, 1992.

———. *Transforming Communication, Transforming Business: Building Responsive and Responsible Workplaces*. Cresskill, NJ: Hampton, 1994.

Defoe, Daniel. *The Life and Adventures of Robinson Crusoe as Related by Himself*. Google Books. https://shorturl.at/gvAGQ.

"Email Statistics Report, 2018–2022." The Radicati Group, Inc., March 2018. https://www.radicati.com/wp/wp-content/uploads/2018/01/Email_Statistics_Report,_2018-2022_Executive_Summary.pdf.

Emanuel, Natalia, Emma Harrington, and Amanda Pallais. "The Power of Proximity to Coworkers: Training for Tomorrow or Productivity Today?" April 24, 2023. https://nataliaemanuel.github.io/ne_website/EHP_Power_of_Proximity.pdf.

Enns, Peter. *Ecclesiastes: The Two Horizons Old Testament Commentary*. Grand Rapids: Eerdmans, 2011.

Folkertsma, Kelly. Interview by Craig Mattson. February 4, 2022.

Ford, David. *Christian Wisdom*. Cambridge Studies in Christian Doctrine. Edited by Daniel W. Hardy. Cambridge: Cambridge University Press, 2007.

———. *The Shape of Living: Spiritual Directions for Everyday Life*. Norwich: Canterbury, 2012.

Frankenfeld, Adam. Interview by Craig Mattson. January 3, 2022.

Frankfurt, Harry. *On Bullshit*. Princeton: Princeton University Press, 2005.

Frey, Carl Benedikt, and Giorgio Presidente. "Disrupting science: How remote collaboration impacts innovation." *Vox EU*, May 6, 2022. https://voxeu.org/article/how-remote-collaboration-impacts-innovation.

Giridharadas, Anand. *Winners Take All*. New York: Knopf, 2018.

Gitlin, Todd. *Media Unlimited: How the Torrent of Images and Sounds Overwhelms Our Lives*. New York: Metropolitan, 2001.

Gladstone, Brooke. "The Fraught Promise of Salvation Through Technology." *On the Media*. Podcast audio. October 15, 2021. https://www.wnycstudios.org/podcasts/otm/segments/promise-salvation-through-technology-on-the-media.

Godin, Seth. *Purple Cow: Transform Your Business by Being Remarkable*. New York: Penguin, 2004.

———. *This Is Marketing*. New York: Portfolio, 2018.

Goffman, Erving. *The Presentation of Self in Everyday Life*. New York: Anchor, 1959.

Graebner, David. *Bullshit Jobs: A Theory*. New York: Simon and Schuster, 2019.
Gray, Michael. "Paterson Thinking Wavelength Process." *Plan Your Purpose*. https://planyourpurpose.com/paterson-thinking-wavelength-process/.
Griffin, Em, Andrew Ledbetter, and Glenn Sparks. *A First Look at Communication Theory*. 10th ed. New York: McGraw Hill, 2018.
Habermas, Jurgen. *An Awareness of What Is Missing: Faith and Reason in a Post-Secular Age*. Translated by Ciarin Cronin. Cambridge: Polity, 2010.
Harris, Malcolm. *Kids These Days: Human Capital and the Making of Millennials*. New York: Back Bay, 2017.
Hawkins, Jim, and Tiffany C. Penner. "Advertising Injustices: Marketing Race and Credit America." *Emory Law Journal* 70, no. 7 (2021). https://scholarlycommons.law.emory.edu/elj/vol70/iss7/7/.
Hoekstra, Ben. Personal email to Craig Mattson. May 8, 2023.
Holmes, Andrew. Interview by Craig Mattson. March 31, 2022.
Horgan, Amelia. *Lost in Work: Escaping Capitalism*. London: Pluto, 2021.
Hughes, Lauren. Interview by Craig Mattson. March 31, 2022.
Hwang, Tim. *Subprime Attention Crisis: Advertising and the Time Bomb at the Heart of the Internet*. New York: FSG Originals x Logic, 2020.
Illing, Sean, and Zac Gershberg. *The Paradox of Democracy: Free Speech, Open Media, and Perilous Persuasion*. Chicago: University of Chicago Press, 2022.
Jaffe, Sarah. *Work Won't Love You Back: How Devotion to Our Jobs Keeps Us Exploited, Exhausted, and Alone*. New York: Bold Type, 2022.
Jenkins, Eric. "The Modes of Visual Rhetoric: Circulating Memes as Expressions." *Quarterly Journal of Speech* 100, no. 4 (November 2014) 442–66.
———. *Special Affects: Cinema, Animation and the Translation of Consumer Culture*. Edinburgh: Edinburgh University Press, 2014.
———. *Surfing the Anthropocene: The Big Tension & Digital Affect*. New York: Peter Lang, 2020.
Kahneman, Daniel. *Thinking Fast and Slow*. New York: Farrar, Straus and Giroux, 2011.
Kearney, Richard. *Modern Movements in European Philosophy: Phenomenology, Critical Theory, Structuralism*. 2nd ed. Manchester, UK: Manchester University Press, 1993.
Keeley-Jonker, Bethany, and Craig Mattson. "Stop Talking That Way: An Affective Approach to Uncanny Speech in the Christian College Classroom." *Christian Scholar's Review* 45, no. 2 (2016) 143–58.
Klein, Ezra. "This Changes Everything." *The New York Times*, March 12, 2023. https://www.nytimes.com/2023/03/12/opinion/chatbots-artificial-intelligence-future-weirdness.html.
Lanham, Richard. *The Economics of Attention: Style and Substance in the Age of Information*. Chicago: University of Chicago Press, 2006.
Lanier, Jaron. *Ten Arguments for Deleting Your Social Media Right Now*. New York: Henry Holt and Co., 2018.
Liming, Sheila. "The 'Quiet Catastrophe' Brewing in Our Social Lives." Interview by Ezra Klein. *The Ezra Klein Show*. Podcast audio. April 18, 2023. https://www.nytimes.com/2023/04/18/opinion/ezra-klein-podcast-sheila-liming.html.
Lindbergh, Anne Morrow. *Gift from the Sea*. New York: Pantheon, 1955.

Lutgen-Sandvik, Pamela, and Beverly Davenport Sypher, eds. *Destructive Organizational Communication: Processes, Consequences, and Constructive Ways of Organizing.* New York: Routledge, 2009.

Massumi, Brian. *Parables for the Virtual: Movement, Affect, Sensation.* Durham, NC: Duke University Press, 2002.

Mattson, Craig. "Barefoot Burnout." *The Mode/Switch,* June 25, 2022. https://themodeswitch.substack.com/p/barefoot-and-burned-out.

———. "How to Get Unstuck: Headspace for 'Technical Difficulties'." *The Mode/Switch,* November 19, 2022. https://themodeswitch.substack.com/p/how-to-get-unstuck.

———. "Is There a Hack for Awkwardness?" *The Mode/Switch,* October 8, 2022. https://themodeswitch.substack.com/p/is-there-a-hack-for-awkwardness.

———. "It's Not Just Her Problem." *The Mode/Switch,* September 17, 2022. https://themodeswitch.substack.com/p/its-not-just-her-problem.

———. "On the Art of Being Good People." *The Mode/Switch,* October 1, 2022. https://themodeswitch.substack.com/p/on-the-art-of-being-good-people.

———. "Question: Why Do Clients Require Overcommunication?" *The Mode/Switch,* January 29, 2022. https://themodeswitch.substack.com/p/question-why-do-clients-always-require.

———. "The Solution to Loneliness at Work." *The Mode/Switch,* September 10, 2022. https://themodeswitch.substack.com/p/the-solution-to-loneliness-at-work.

———. "When Clients Dispute and Colleagues Disparage,: Bring Your Whole Self to Work Anyway." *The Mode/Switch,* February 12, 2022. https://themodeswitch.substack.com/p/when-clients-dispute-and-colleagues.

———. "When It's Your Job to Fire Your Coworker." *The Mode/Switch,* March 12, 2022. https://themodeswitch.substack.com/p/when-its-your-job-to-fire-your-coworker.

———. *Why Spiritual Capital Matters: Activating Latent Resources in Your Organizational Community.* Eugene, OR: Wipf and Stock, 2021.

———. "Workplace Skeeziness: Rising Professionals and Sexual Harassment." *The Mode/Switch,* November 5, 2022. https://themodeswitch.substack.com/p/workplace-skeeziness.

———. "You Can Always Google It, Right?" *The Mode/Switch,* December 3, 2022. https://themodeswitch.substack.com/p/you-can-always-google-it-right.

Mattson, Emma. Personal correspondence with Craig Mattson. November 10, 2022.

Mattson, Karen. Interview by Craig Mattson. April 25, 2022.

McCann, Elysia. "Can ChatGPT-4 Elevate Your Customer Service?" *eLearning Industry,* April 28, 2023. https://elearningindustry.com/can-chatgpt-4-elevate-your-customer-service.

McLuhan, Marshall. "Media and Cultural Change." In *Essential McLuhan,* edited by Eric McLuhan and Frank Zingrone, 89–96. New York: Basic Books, 1995.

McKune, Kara. "Don't Be Sucked in by Netflix and Performative Activism." *The Independent,* March 30, 2021. https://www.independent.co.uk/dont-be-sucked-in-by-netflix-and-performative-activism/.

Melling, Dyvon. "I Can Be Too Transparent." Interview by Craig Mattson. *The Mode/Switch,* April 30, 2022. https://themodeswitch.substack.com/p/i-can-be-too-transparent.

Miller, Donald. *Building a Storybrand: Clarify Your Message So Customers Will Listen.* New York: HarperCollins Leadership, 2017.

Minnesma, Brittany. Interview by Craig Mattson. February 9, 2022.
Munday, Andrea. Interview by Craig Mattson. March 14, 2022.
Newport, Cal. *Deep Work: Rules for Focused Success in a Distracted World*. New York: Grand Central, 2016.
———. *Digital Minimalism: Choosing a Focused Life in a Noisy World*. New York: Penguin, 2019.
———. *A World without Email: Reimagining Work in an Age of Communication Overload*. New York: Penguin Random House, 2021.
Nubu Snacks. "Rita—The Inspired Artist—Presented by Nubu." YouTube video. January 25, 2022. https://www.youtube.com/@NubuSnacks.
Nyquist, Kaleb. Interview by Craig Mattson. July 20, 2022.
O'Gieblyn, Meghan. *God Human Animal Machine*. New York: Doubleday, 2021.
O'Loughlin, Cristol Barrett. "Caring for the Caregivers: 3 Tools for Self-Care." TEDxTalks. www.youtube.com/watch?v=fJNLIlkrwTw.
Odak, Stipe. "The Technical Book of Job: Reading Job from a Transhumanist Perspective." *Disputatio Philosophica* 13, no. 1 (2011) 91–101. https://philpapers.org/rec/ODATTB.
Ong, Walter J. *Orality and Literacy: On the Technologizing of the Word*. London: Methuen & Co, 1982.
———. *Ramus, Method, and the Decline of Dialogue*. Chicago: University of Chicago Press, 2005.
Orendorff, Em. Interview by Craig Mattson. May 2, 2022.
Pearce, Barnett, and Vernon Cronen. *Making Social Worlds: A Communication Perspective*. Malden, MA: Blackwell, 2008.
Peters, John Durham. *The Marvelous Clouds: Toward a Philosophy of Elemental Media*. Chicago: University of Chicago Press, 2015.
———. *Speaking into the Air*. Chicago: University of Chicago Press, 1999.
Petersen, Anne Helen. *Can't Even: How Millennials Became the Burnout Generation*. Boston: Mariner, 2021.
———. "How Email Took Over the World w. Anne Helen Petersen." Interview by Sarah Marshall. *You're Wrong About*. Podcast audio. April 11, 2022. https://www.buzzsprout.com/1112270/10413675-how-email-took-over-the-world-with-anne-helen-petersen.
Petersen, Anne Helen, and Charlie Warzel. *Out of Office: The Big Problem and Bigger Promise of Working from Home*. New York: Alfred A. Knopf, 2021.
Pirsig, Robert. *Zen and the Art of Motorcycle Maintenance*. New York: William Morrow & Co., 1974.
Plato. *Phaedrus*. Translated by Alexander Nehamas and Paul Woodruff. London: Hackett, 1995.
Polanyi, Michael. *Personal Knowledge: Towards a Post-Critical Philosophy*. Chicago: University of Chicago Press, 1974.
———. *The Tacit Dimension*. Chicago: University of Chicago Press, 1966.
Postman, Neil. *Amusing Ourselves to Death: Public Discourse in the Age of Show Business*. New York: Penguin, 2005.
Princen, Thomas. *The Logic of Sufficiency*. Boston: MIT Press, 2005.
Rafalski, Kacper. "Instant Assistance: How AI Chatbots Are Improving Customer Service." Netguru, April 19, 2023. https://www.netguru.com/blog/ai-chatbots-improving-customer-service.

Reppmann, Aron. *The Truth of Love and the Love of Truth: The Philosophical Relevance of Eros and Philia in Plato's Lysis and Phaedrus.* PhD diss., Loyola University of Chicago, 2006.
Rice, Jennifer. *Distant Publics: Development Rhetoric and the Subject of Crisis.* Pittsburgh: University of Pittsburgh Press, 2012.
Rickert, Thomas J. *Ambient Rhetoric: The Attunements of Rhetorical Being.* Pittsburgh: University of Pittsburgh Press, 2013.
Rogers, Everett M. *A History of Communication Study: A Biographical Approach.* New York: Free Press, 1994.
Rogers, Paige. Interview by Craig Mattson. January 3, 2022.
Rorty, Richard. *Philosophy and the Mirror of Nature.* Princeton: Princeton University Press, 1979.
Rose, Nikolas. *Governing the Soul.* London: Free Association, 1999.
Rowe, C. Kavin. *World Upside Down: Reading Acts in the Graeco-Roman Age.* Oxford: Oxford University Press, 2010.
Sacasas, L. M. *The Convivial Society.* https://theconvivialsociety.substack.com/.
Seerveld, Cal. *God Picks Up the Pieces.* Sioux Center, IA: Dordt, 2023.
Shannon, Claude E. *The Mathematical Theory of Communication.* Urbana: University of Illinois Press, 1971.
Sinek, Simon. *Find Your Why.* New York: Portfolio, 2017.
———. *The Infinite Game.* New York: Portfolio, 2019.
———. *Start with Why.* New York: Portfolio, 2011.
Song, Felicia Wu. *Restless Devices: Recovering Personhood, Presence, and Place in the Digital Age.* Downers Grove, IL: IVP Academic, 2021.
Spade, Dean. *Mutual Aid: Building Solidarity During This Crisis (and the Next).* New York: Verso, 2020.
Srnicek, Nick. *Inventing the Future: Postcapitalism and a World Without Work.* New York: Verso, 2016.
Stanovich, Keith. "On the Distinction Between Rationality and Intelligence." In *The Oxford Handbook of Thinking and Reasoning*, edited by Keith J. Holyoak and Robert G. Morrison, 433–55. Oxford: Oxford University Press, 2012.
Taylor, Charles. *A Secular Age.* Cambridge: The Belknap Press of Harvard University Press, 2018.
Thompson, Derek. "The AI Disaster Scenario." *The Atlantic*, February 27, 2023. https://www.theatlantic.com/newsletters/archive/2023/02/ai-chatgpt-microsoft-bing-chatbot-questions/673202/.
———. "The Biggest Problem With Remote Work." *The Atlantic*, July 2022. https://www.theatlantic.com/newsletters/archive/2022/07/remote-work-wfh-debate-management/670482.
———. "Why Americans Care About Work So Much." *The Atlantic*, March 31, 2023. https://www.theatlantic.com/ideas/archive/2023/03/work-revolution-ai-wfh-new-book/673572/.
———. "Workism Is Making Americans Miserable." *The Atlantic*, February 24, 2019. https://www.theatlantic.com/ideas/archive/2019/02/religion-workism-making-americans-miserable/583441/.
Thoreau, Henry David. *Walden.* N.p.: Google Books, 1854. https://books.google.com/books/about/Walden.html?id=yiQ3AAAAIAAJ.
Thrift, Nigel. *Knowing Capitalism.* London: Sage, 2005.

Trivedi, Mayank. "10 Ways Artificial Intelligence Can Improve Customer Service. *TA Digital*, n.d. www.tadigital.com/insights/perspectives/10-ways-artificial-intelligence-can-improve-customer-service.

Turkle, Sherry. *Alone Together: Why We Expect More from Technology and Less from Each Other*. New York: Basic, 2012.

———. *Reclaiming Conversation: The Power of Talk in a Digital Age*. New York: Penguin, 2016.

———. *The Second Self: Computers and the Human Spirit*. New York: Simon and Schuster, 1985.

Twist, Lynn. *The Soul of Money: Transforming Your Relationship with Money and Life*. New York: W. W. Norton and Co., 2017.

VanderWeele, Michael. "Marilynne Robinson's Gilead and the Difficult Gift of Human Exchange." *Christianity & Literature* 59, no. 2 (2010) 217–39.

Veitkus, Donna. Interview by Craig Mattson. May 18, 2022.

Webb, Stephen. *The Divine Voice: Christian Proclamation and the Theology of Sound*. Eugene, OR: Wipf and Stock, 2012.

———. *The Gifting God: A Trinitarian Ethics of Excess*. Oxford: Oxford University Press, 1996.

Weissbourd, Richard, Milena Batanova, Virginia Lovison, and Eric Torres. "Loneliness in America." *Harvard Graduate School of Education*, February 2021. https://mcc.gse.harvard.edu/reports/loneliness-in-america.

Wieland, Stacy, Bauer, and Stanley Deetz. "Role of Entrepreneurialism in Colonizing Identities." In *Destructive Organizational Communication: Processes, Consequences, and Constructive Ways of Organizing*, edited by Pamela Lutgen-Sandvik and Beverly Davenport, 99–120. Sypher, NY: Routledge, 2009.

Wiener, Nobert. *God and Golem, Inc.: A Comment on Certain Points where Cybernetics Impinges on Religion*. Cambridge: MIT Press, 1966.

Williams, James. *Stand Out of Our Light: Freedom and Resistance in the Attention Economy*. Cambridge: Cambridge University Press, 2018.

Williams, Latifah. Interview by Craig Mattson. February 4, 2022.

Williams, Raymond. *Culture and Society 1780–1950*. New York: Columbia University Press, 1958.

Wilner, Abbie. *Quarterlife Crisis: The Unique Challenges of Life in Your Twenties*. New York: TarcherPerigee, 2001.

Wilson, Lindsay. *Job: The Two Horizons Old Testament Commentary*. Grand Rapids: Eerdmans, 2015.

Winkowitsch, Olivia. Interview by Craig Mattson. January 28, 2022.

Wynia, Ryan. Interview by Craig Mattson. March 3, 2022.

Zengotita, Thomas de. *Mediated: How the Media Shapes Your World and the Way You Live in It*. New York: Bloomsbury, 2005.

Index

Abercrombie, Nicholas, 139–40, 155, 156n7
affect, xx, xxii, 1, 4, 10, 12, 21, 27, 29–30, 34, 40, 46, 57, 69, 77, 84, 124, 135, 151, 160, 198, 199
algorithms, algorithmic, xv n10, 2, 6–7, 134
Allen, David, 20–21, 195
Anderson, Ron, 17–18, 195
Aristotle, 8n17, 69, 177,195
Arnett, Ron, 17–18n11, 195
artificial intelligence, xi, xix-xx, 48–49, 103, 126, 133, 165, 195, 198, 202
attention, x, xii, xiv, xxii, xxiv, 4, 8, 10–11, 16, 18, 21, 25, 29, 35, 37–38, 61, 72, 75, 79, 82–83, 85, 95, 106–8, 110, 112–15, 118, 120, 122, 127, 150–52, 155, 157, 160–61, 165, 169, 183, 186, 190, 196, 198, 202
attention economy, x, xxii, xxv, 35, 82–83, 85, 88, 202
Austin, J. L., 141–49

Barbaro, Michael, xix n3, 195
Bailenson, Jeremy N., 153–56
baptism, xviii, 64
Berbaum, Jon, 9
Berlant, Lauren, 4n7, 67, 91, 196
Black, Joycee, 55–58, 63, 148, 153
Boomer, xv

broadcast, xviii, xxiii, 52, 54–56, 59–61, 63–65, 67–71, 111, 187, 190
Buber, Martin, 23, 26, 196
Buechner, Frederick, 86
Burke, Kenneth, 16, 91, 97, 106, 116, 176, 196
Burton, Tara Isabella, x n4, 88, 196
Butler, Judith, 141–42, 147–50
Byock, Satra, ix n2, 196

Canlis, Julie, 96n63, 196
Carey, James, 15, 196
Chen, Carolyn, x 114, 78, 87–88, 196
Christiano, Paul, xix n4, 196
chronemic, chronemics, chronemically, 41–42
conversation, xi, xiii, 1–2, 7, 9, 14–19, 23, 26–30, 32, 46, 49–52, 54–62, 64, 67–70, 72–75, 77, 80, 84, 90, 93, 98,100, 111–12, 124, 133–35, 140, 142, 150, 154–56, 160–61, 174–75, 177, 183, 189, 193–95
COVID-19, xii, 23, 48, 50, 53, 89, 144
Crouch, Andy, ix n1, 196
cybernetic(s), 15, 17–18, 22, 29, 31–32, 51, 107, 122, 202

Davis, Ellen, 25–26n30,32, 30n40, 58–59, 197
Deetz, Stanley, 52n16, 161–63, 165

dialogue, dialogic, xiiii, 4, 9, 14–15, 17–18, 22–24, 27, 29–32, 47, 50–53, 56–62, 64–65, 68–71, 73, 79, 80, 110–11, 113, 136, 177, 187–88, 190, 195, 200
digital overwhelm, ix, xvi, xx–xxii, xxiv, xxvi, 1, 11–12, 14, 27, 46–47, 49, 51, 68, 77, 84, 107, 110, 133, 142, 144, 146, 188
Dieleman, Kyle, 28n36
digiwhelm, xi, xxi, xvii, xxv, xxvii, 1–2, 9–12, 16, 18–19, 31, 47, 51–52, 58, 123, 157, 166
digital minimalism, ix, 17, 22, 31, 200
disseminate, dissemination, 2, 4, 15n5, 45, 51–65, 67–69, 73, 79–80, 107, 188, 190
Donaldson, Mallory, 54–56

Ecclesiastes, xv, xxvi, 27, 59, 78–79, 80n11–13, 82, 86n32, 95, 174, 197
email, 14–22
existential, existentialism, existentialist, xv n10, 17, 23, 95, 101

feeling(s), xvii, xx, 4, 8, 10–11, 18, 20, 27–29, 56, 69–70, 72, 89, 93, 95, 101, 107–8, 117, 119, 124, 126, 129, 148, 158, 165–66, 168, 171, 180
Ford, David, xiv n9, xxvi n12, 63, 197
Franklin, Cecilia, 137–40, 148–50

Gershberg, Zac, ix n1, 163–65
gift(s), gifting, xxiv, 27, 29–31, 40, 43–44, 58, 61–62, 64, 70, 72, 95–96, 107, 110, 112, 122, 140–41, 149, 191, 193, 195, 198, 202
Gen X, xv
Gen Z, x, xv, xix, xx, xxv, 2, 4, 6, 14, 27, 79, 85, 89, 122, 153, 160–61, 174, 178, 193–94
generation, x n2, xix, 22, 109, 153, 178, 190
Gitlin, Todd, xv n10, 83, 197
Gladstone, Brooke, xv n10, 197
Godin, Seth, x, 82

Griffin, Em, 22n20, 88, 92, 163, 198

Hwang, Tim, x n5, 198

Illing, Sean, ix n1, 163–65

Jenkins, Eric, 3–4n5–8, 198
Job (biblical figure and book of), xxiii n9, xxiv, xxvi, 23–27, 29–30, 32, 61, 66–67, 174

Kahneman, Daniel, 6n9, 198
Klein, Ezra, xix–xx n5-n6, 73, 198

Lady Wisdom, 59–60, 62, 191
Lanham, Richard, x n5, 118, 152, 157, 198
Lanier, Jaron, xviii n1, 198
Lasswell, Harold, xxiv, 138–40
LGBTQ, 27, 28
Lindbergh, Anne Morrow, 26–27n34, 198
Longhurst, Brian, 139–40, 155, 156n7

Marshall, Sarah, 43
Massumi, Brian, xx n7, 199
May-Gruthusen, Tyler, 124, 126, 132–33
McLuhan, Marshall, 15, 199
Miller, Donald, x, 85
millennial, millennials, ix n2, x, xv, xix, xx, xxv, 2, 4–5, 27, 78–79, 85, 115, 122, 153, 160–61, 172, 174, 178, 190, 193–94
mode, definition, xi, 3
mode craft, 5, 8–9, 32, 65, 69, 103, 151–52, 154, 157, 189–90
mode(s) of communication, 4, 6, 17, 22, 24, 47, 135, 149, 151, 191
mode-switch(ing), 2, 3, 5–6, 8–9, 15, 17, 68–69, 150
model(s) of communication, 47, 51, 141
mutuality, xxiv, 14, 24–25, 27, 29–30, 33–34, 36, 39–40, 43, 56, 59, 61–62, 67, 142, 188, 190

neuroscience, 6
neuropsychology, xi, 6

Newport, Cal, ix n, 15–17, 21–22, 26, 31, 79, 111, 200

O'Gieblyn, Meghan, xv n10, xxiv n11, 15n3, 200
Odak, Stipe, xv n10, 200
Ong, Walter, 15, 200
opacity (in technology), xx
Orendorff, Em, 50n12, 118–20
organizational communication, x, xviii, xx–xxi, xxiv, xxvi, 51–52, 54–57, 140, 150–51, 160–61, 163, 191, 199, 202

Perry, Chakena, 97–98, 100, 104, 170–71
Perry, Christian, 168–70
performative, performativity, 50, 114, 134–53, 156, 188, 190
Peters, John Durham, xviii n2, xxvi n12–13, 8n18, 23n22, 29, 31n41, 47n1, 47n2, 49, 57–60, 110, 135, 139, 141, 200
Petersen, Anne Helen, 14n1, 43n1, 63, 87, 200
Pirsig, Robert, 123–24, 128, 129
Plato, xxiii n10, xxiv, 110–13, 124, 176, 191, 200–201
podcast, vii, xii, xxi, 9, 27, 43, 65–75, 94, 191, 193, 195, 197–98, 200
Polanyi, Michael, 6n9, 110, 113–14, 116–19, 124, 200
Princen, Thomas, 15n3
Proverbs, xv, xxvi–xxvii, 25n29, 59–63, 175n32
Psalms, xv, xxvii, 135–36, 150–51, 175, 191

quarterlife, ix, x, xii, xiv, 122, 196, 202
Qoheleth (from Ecclesiastes), xxvi, 79–80, 86, 95–96, 174, 191

race, racism, racist, 52, 56, 102, 160
Rice, Jenny Edbauer, 4n7
Rickert, Thomas, 51, 64
rhetoric, rhetorical, 4, 8n17, 19, 21, 36, 69–70, 158–75, 177, 190
Roose, Kevin, xix

Sacasas, L. M., ix n1, 201
Saussure, Ferdinand, 80–81
semiotic, 4, 76–96, 190
Sinek, Simon, x, 78, 85, 201
Socrates, xxiii, xxvi, 59, 109–113, 175
Song, Felecia Wu, ix n1, 201
spirituality, xxv, 20, 28, 54, 58, 86, 88, 172, 191
Stanovich, Keith, 6–8n10–16, 201
surface currents, xxi–xxii, xxiv
Synerges, Jessie, 146, 150

tacit, tacitness, 4, 6, 8, 43, 106–122, 124, 133, 190
talk, xii–xiii, xv, xviii, 1–2, 9, 18–19, 23–24, 27–28, 33, 39, 40, 43–44, 49, 53, 56, 58, 61, 67–69, 73, 75, 77–78, 82, 85–86, 107, 109–110, 113, 121, 132, 145, 147, 167, 170–71, 176, 181, 183, 185, 190
technological
  breakdown, xviii, 106–7, 110, 112, 120–22, 133, 190
  density, 10, 77
  development, xx, xxiv–xxv
  disruption, xx, xxiii, 27, 164
  error, 113
  excess, 11
  experience, 29
  environments, 16
  innovation, 12
  perspectives, 51, 161
Thompson, Derek, x n3, xix n4, 87–88, 121–22, 201
Thoreau, Henry David, 49–50
TikTok, xviii, 89, 109
Turkle, Sherry, xx n8, 49–51, 111, 202

unilateral communication, 51–52, 57, 65, 137
upwelling, upwelling currents, xxi–xxii

voice, xvi, xxvi, 8, 12, 15, 19, 22, 24–26, 32–34, 37, 39, 43, 47, 53, 59–60, 63, 67, 71–73, 77–79, 87, 89, 106, 109, 117, 135–36, 143–44, 155, 158–59, 163, 171, 173–75, 182, 191, 195, 202

Warzel, Charlie, 14n1
Webb, Stephen, 31, 44, 171, 202
Weiner, Norbert, xxiv n10, 15
Williams, Alex, 91
Williams, James, x n5, 202
Williams, Raymond, 4n7, 202
Wilner, Abby, ix n2, 202
Wilson, Lindsay, 25–26n29,33, 202
windy ridge (of dialogue), 26–27, 51

wisdom literature, xvi, 136, 191
Woman Wisdom, xxvi, 59, 61–63, 66–67, 175
workism, x, 87, 89, 191, 201

Zechariah, 28
Zengotita, Thomas de, xv n10, 202
Zoom, 27, 53–55, 57, 117, 119, 122, 140, 152–57, 175, 195

www.ingramcontent.com/pod-product-compliance
Lightning Source LLC
Chambersburg PA
CBHW031355230426
43670CB00006B/553